Published by PEN American Center,
an affiliate of International PEN,
the worldwide association of writers
working to advance literature
and defend free expression.

PEN America: A Journal for Writers and Readers
Issue 7

PEN American Center
588 Broadway, Suite 303
New York, NY 10012

This issue is made possible in part by the generous funding of The Lillian Goldman
Charitable Trust and The Kaplen Foundation.

Printed in the United States of America by McNaughton & Gunn.

Postmaster: Send address changes to PEN AMERICA, c/o PEN American Center, 588 Broadway,
Suite 303, New York, NY 10012.

ISBN: 0-934638-25-x

ISSN: 1536-0261

Because of limited resources, at present we are unable to review unsolicited submissions
of writing except from members of PEN American Center. We do, however, seek color
photographs for the cover and black-and-white images (single photos as well as photo essays)
for the inside. We do not accept submissions via e-mail; these will be deleted unopened.
For more information, visit *www.pen.org/journal*.

7 | World Voices

EDITOR
M Mark

MANAGING EDITOR
Emily Gordon

ASSISTANT EDITORS
Molly Antopol, Jenny Brown, Sara Crosby, Nikki D'Errico, Anna Kushner,
Laura McGinley, Jay Baron Nicorvo, Seamus O'Malley, Lily Saint,
Sara Jane Stoner

INTERNS
Willa Cmiel, Alexander Cuadros, India Donaldson, Jonathan Garcia,
Kate Harvey, Jesse Hudnutt, Tommy Rudnick, Lindsey Schwoeri

LAYOUT/ART EDITOR
Justin Goldberg

ADVISORY BOARD
Patricia Bosworth, Thulani Davis, Lynn Goldberg, Amy P. Goldman,
Neil Gordon, Jessica Hagedorn, Robert Kelly, Ann Lauterbach, Phillip Lopate,
Albert Mobilio, Honor Moore, Laurie Muchnick, Geoffrey O'Brien, Grace Paley,
Ann Patty, Robert Polito, Elaine Showalter

CONTENTS

PEN World Voices
THE NEW YORK FESTIVAL OF INTERNATIONAL LITERATURE

EVENTS

International Noir

Literature and Power

CONVERSATIONS

Postcolonial Passages

Enormous Changes

Reinventing Home

In Search of the Sensual

Continental Divides

Power Struggles

A History of Trauma

POETRY

ART

Photography by Beowulf Sheehan

Sculpture by Yukinori Yamamura

Cover and page 8: "Form +" (2003)
Resin, one thousand pieces of gold leaf affixed by the audience
The National Gallery, Bangkok, Thailand
Sponsored by Watchara Prayoonkam, Plernpattana School

See page 206 for writer and artist biographies.

EDITOR'S NOTE

The first annual PEN World Voices festival brought together 125 writers from around the globe for a week of intense conversation about language, culture, crime, catastrophe, death, sex, religion—the facts of life, political and personal, that goad those who make literature in a time of turmoil. "Tyrants fear the truth of books because it's a truth that's in hock to nobody," PEN president Salman Rushdie observed during one discussion. "It's a single artist's unfettered vision of the world." The mix and clash of individual visions at that first gathering was such a heady success that we're at it again, with the 2006 World Voices festival, April 25–30. In the meantime, thanks to heroic efforts by this journal's volunteer transcribers, proofreaders, fact-checkers, and copy editors, we bring you words from the 2005 festival. Here's a preview.

Svetlana Alexievich: "After Chernobyl, they buried milk, they buried meat, they buried bread. . . . They sliced off the top layer of the soil, which had been contaminated, and they buried it. They took ground and they buried it in the ground. And everyone involved turned into a philosopher." François Bizot: "I think we should maybe have the courage to identify ourselves with and humanize the torturer." Carolin Emcke: "Victims of violence . . . lose their ability to give an account, to give a narrative of what happened to them, because they lose trust that anybody will care." Philip Gourevitch: "There are three words that probably most motivate my reporting on the aftermath of political violence: unimaginable, unspeakable, and unthinkable. . . . They are the words by which the press gives you permission to forget and ignore." Francine Prose: "I've been reading books about Hitler, books about Stalin. . . . I've been reading them the way a hypochondriac reads health newsletters, looking for the warning signs."

Lyonel Trouillot: "I reflect violence in my work because one writes with one's gaze. But it would be a mistake for a New York or a Parisian reader to view this violence as a new exoticism. Violence is one aspect of the reality of my country—a country where one lives, one makes love, one drinks, one sings." Elif Shafak: "In the Middle East, sexuality is also about delight, pleasure, and yes, sexual perversion and the delight you derive from that." Hanif Kureishi: "Our religions—not only Islam, but also, obviously, Christianity—think and talk about sexuality all the time. Watching this chap Ratzinger and one of his cardinals on the TV, I heard a word . . . which made my blood go cold: the 're-evangelization' of Europe." Shashi Tharoor: "My novels speak to an India of multiple realities, and of multiple interpretations of reality. . . . If we had to do an Indian version of E pluribus unum, it would be E pluribus pluribum." Michael Ondaatje: "You can have a real person in the real world who is simply too unbelievable for fiction. . . . A woman working in human rights told me she was driving in Colombo, and the American ambassador's car came by with the flag, and in the backseat was a clown." Zakes Mda: "This is a love story, you know, the eternal triangle: man, woman, whale."

—M Mark

THE POWER OF THE PEN
Does Writing Change Anything?

SALMAN RUSHDIE: A butterfly flaps its wings in India and we feel the breeze on our cheeks in New York. A throat is cleared somewhere in Africa and in California there's an answering cough. Everything that happens affects something else, so to answer "yes" to the question before us is not to make a large claim. Books come into the world, and the world is not what it was before those books came into it. The same can be said of babies or diseases. Books, since we are speaking of books, come into the world and change the lives of their authors, for good or ill, and sometimes change the lives of their readers too. This change in the reader is a rare event. Mostly we read books and set them aside, or hurl them from us with great force, and pass on. Yet sometimes there is a small residue that has an effect. The reason for this is the always unexpected and unpredictable intervention of that rare and sneaky phenomenon: love.

One may read and like, or admire, or respect a book and yet remain entirely unchanged by its contents. But love gets under your guard and shakes things up. Such is its sneaky nature. When a reader falls in love with a book, it leaves its essence inside him like radioactive fallout in an arable field. And after that there are certain crops that will no longer grow in him, while other stranger, more fantastic growths may occasionally be produced. We love relatively few books in our lives, and those books become part of the way we see our lives. We read our lives through them, and their descriptions of the inner and outer worlds become mixed up with ours; they become ours. Love does this. Hate does not. To hate a book is only to confirm to oneself what one already knows or thinks one knows. But the power of books to inspire both love and hate is an indication of their ability to make alterations in the fabric of what is.

Writing names the world, and the power of description should not be underestimated. Literature remembers its religious origins in some of those first stories. Stories of sky gods and sea gods not only became the source of an ocean of stories that flowed from them but also served as the foundations of the world into which they, the myths, were born. There would have been little blood sacrifice in Latin America or ancient Greece if it had not been for the gods. Iphigenia would have lived and Clytemnestra would have had no need to murder Agamemnon and the entire story of the House of Atreus would have been different. This would have been bad for the history of the theater, no doubt, but good in many ways for the family concerned. Writing invented the gods and was a game the gods themselves played, and the consequences of that writing, holy writ, are still working themselves out today, which just shows that the demonstrable fictionality of fiction does nothing to lessen its power, especially if you call it the truth. But writing broke away from the gods and in that rupture much of its power was lost. Prophecy is no longer the game, except for futurologists, but then futurology is fiction too. It can be defined as the art of being wrong about the future. For the rest of us, the proper study of mankind is man. We have no priests, we can appeal to no ultimate arbiter, though there are critics among us who would claim such a role for themselves.

In spite of this, fiction does retain the occasional surprising ability to initiate social change. Here is the fugitive slave Eliza, running from Simon Legree. Here is Oliver Twist asking for more. Here is a boy wizard with a lightning scar on his forehead bringing books back into the lives of a generation that was forgetting how to read. *Uncle Tom's Cabin* changed attitudes towards slavery, and Charles Dickens's portraits of child poverty inspired legal reforms, and J. K. Rowling changed the culture of childhood, making millions of boys and girls look forward to 800-page novels, and probably popularizing vibrating toy broomsticks at boarding schools. On the opening night of *Death of a Salesman*, the head of Gimbels department store rushed from the theater vowing never to fire his own aging Willy Loman.

In this age of information, in this age of information overkill, literature can still bring the human news, the heart's and mind's news. The poetry of Milosz and Herbert and Szymborska has done much to create the consciousness, to say nothing of the conscience, of these great poets' time and place. The same may be said of Derek Walcott. Nuruddin Farah, so long in exile from Somalia, has carried Somalia in his heart these many years, and written it into being, brought into the world's sight that Somalia to which the world might otherwise have remained blind. From China, from Japan, from Cuba, from Iran, literature brings information, the base metal of information, transmuted into the gold of art. And our knowledge of the world is forever altered by such transformation or alchemy.

This week, we honor the memory of Susan Sontag and Arthur Miller, great writers, intellectuals and truth tellers. The old idea of the intellectual as the one who speaks truth to power is still worth holding on to. Tyrants fear the truth of books because it's a truth that's in hock to nobody. It's a single artist's unfettered vision of the world. They fear it even more because it's incomplete, because the act of reading completes it, so that the book's truth is slightly different in each reader's inner world. These are the true revolutions of literature, these invisible, intimate communions of strangers, these tiny revolutions inside each reader's imagination. And the enemies of the imagination, all the different goon squads of gods and power, want to shut these revolutions down and can't. Not even the author of a book can know exactly what effect his book will have. But good books do have effects and some of these effects are powerful and all of them, thank goodness, are impossible to predict in advance. Literature is a loose cannon. This is a very good thing.

MARGARET ATWOOD: Does writing change anything? I took this question literally, and I'm reading two pieces. One is about our feeling as writers—probably not, we think sometimes. And the second is the opposite answer. The first piece is called "The Tent."

> You're in a tent. It's vast and cold outside; very vast, very cold. It's a howling wilderness. There are rocks in it, and sand, and deep boggy pits you can sink into without a trace. There are ruins as well, many ruins. In and around the ruins there are broken musical instruments, old bathtubs, bones of extinct land mammals, shoes minus their feet, auto parts. There are thorny shrubs, gnarled trees, high winds, but you have a small candle in your tent. You can keep warm. Many things are howling out there, in the howling wilderness. Many people are howling, some howling grief because those they love have died or been killed. Others howl in triumph because they have caused the loved ones of their enemies to die or be killed. Some howl to summon help, some howl for revenge, others howl for blood. The noise is deafening. It's also frightening. Some of the howling is coming close to you, in your tent, where you crouch in silence hoping you won't be seen. You're frightened for yourself, but especially for those you love. You want to protect them. You want to gather them inside your tent for protection.
>
> The trouble is your tent is made of paper. Paper won't keep anything out. You know you must write on the walls, on the paper walls on the inside of your tent. You must write upside down and backwards. You must cover every available space on the paper with writing. Some of the writing has to describe the howling that's going on outside, night and day among the sand dunes and the ice chunks and the

ruins and bones and so forth. It has to tell the truth about the howling. But this is difficult to do because you can't see through the paper walls, and so you can't be exact about the truth, and you don't want to go out there, into the howling wilderness, to see exactly for yourself.

Some of the writing has to be about your loved ones, and the need you feel to protect them. And this is difficult as well because not all of them can hear the howling in the same way you do. Some of them think it sounds like a picnic out there in the wilderness, like a big band, like a hot beach party. They resent being cooped up in such a cramped space with you and your small candle and your fearfulness and your annoying obsession with calligraphy, an obsession that makes no sense to them. And they keep trying to scramble out under the walls of the tent. This doesn't stop you from your writing. You write as if your life depended on it. Your life and theirs. You inscribe in shorthand their natures, their features, their habits, their histories. You change the names of course because you don't want to create evidence. You don't want to attract the wrong sort of attention to these loved ones of yours, some of whom, you're now discovering, are not people at all, but cities and landscapes, towns and lakes, and clothing you used to wear, and neighborhood cafés and long-lost dogs.

You don't want to attract the howlers, but they're attracted anyway, as if by a scent. The walls of the paper tent are so thin, but they can see the light of your candle. They can see your outline, and naturally they're curious because you might be prey. You might be something they can kill, and then howl over in celebration, and then eat one way or another. You're too conspicuous. You've made yourself conspicuous. You've given yourself away. They're coming closer, gathering together. They're taking time off from their howling to peer, to sniff around. Why do you think this writing of yours, this graphomania in a flimsy cave, this scribbling back and forth and up and down over the walls of what is beginning to seem like a prison, is capable of protecting anyone at all, yourself included? It's an illusion—the belief that your doodling is a kind of armor, a kind of charm—because no one knows better than you do how fragile your tent really is. Already there's a clomping of leather-covered feet, there's a scratching, there's a scrabbling, there's a sound of rasping breath. Wind comes in. Your candle tips over and flares up and a loose tent flap catches fire, and through the widening black-edged gap, you can see the eyes of the howlers, red and shining, and the light from your burning paper shelter. But you keep writing anyway, because what else can you do?

When we say "Does writing change anything?" we usually speak from the writer's point of view. But if you take the question a couple of levels back and realize that a lot of people in the world can't write at all, just the ability to change from being somebody who can't write to being somebody who can makes a huge difference in that person's life, in the life of their family and their community. This poem is called "A Poor Woman Learns to Write."

She squats, bare feet
splayed out, not
graceful; skirt tucked around ankles.

Her face is lined and cracked.
She looks old,
older than anything.

She's probably thirty.
Her hands also are lined and cracked
and awkward. Her hair concealed.

She prints with a stick, laboriously
in the wet grey dirt,
frowning with anxiety.

Great big letters.
There. It's finished.
Her first word so far.

She never thought she could do this,
Not her.
This was for others.

She looks up, smiles
as if apologizing,
but she's not. Not this time. She did it right.

What does the mud say?
Her name. We can't read it.
But we can guess. Look at her face:

Joyful Flower? A Radiant One? Sun On Water?

NURUDDIN FARAH: On my first day at school, a teacher, a man who was teaching me and who knew my name, asked me what my name was. And I said I couldn't remember. And I was struck hard time and time again, but I insisted I didn't know, and the reason is that I have never liked direct questions. And if somebody comes to me and says, "What is your name?" I never remember. And therefore when I received the question that said, "Does writing change anything?" I thought, Let me read this passage from *Maps* and then ask the audience if writing changes anything.

The man who was brought to circumcise me, when my turn came, made me sit alone, insisting that I read a few Koranic verses of my choice—and that I wait for him as he honed the knife he was going to use against a sharp stone he had come along with. I was overcome by fear—fear of pain, fear of being lonely, fear of being separated forever from Misra. (She wasn't there anyway; she wasn't allowed to come. In her place, there came a man, one of my many uncles.) The sticky saliva in my mouth, the drumming of fright beating in my ears, the numbness of my body wherever I touched, felt: my legs, my hands, my thighs, my sex, what pain!

Then the man asked me to look up at the heavens and to concentrate on anything my eyes fell on. There was an aperture in the clouds and there was a bird which I spotted, a bird flying high and in haste towards the opening in the heavens. I concentrated on the bird's movements, concentrated on it until it became a dot in the heavenly distance. To mask my fear, I invested all my energy in the look, and the bird's flight reminded me of similar flights of my own fantasies. When I looked again, I couldn't see the bird. I could only see a tapestry of clouds which was woven in order to provide the bird with a hiding-place. The world, I told myself, was in my eyes and the bird had flown away with it, carrying it in its beak, light as a straw, small as an atom. Now that I had lost sight of the bird (I wasn't sure if it was an eagle or if it wasn't!), there was nothing but sunlight for a long while, and the sun was in my eye and it blinded me to the rest of the cosmos. Until the bird re-emerged out of the sun's brightness, beautiful, feminine, playful, and it became again the center of my world and I was inside it, in flight, light as are children's fantasies, impervious to the realities surrounding me, and then, sudden as bushfire, ZAK!

It is such a horrid territory, the territory of pain. And I crossed it alone—no thought of Misra, no amount of consolatory remarks made by the uncle who had come with me, and no verse of the

Koran could've reduced the pain or even eliminated it altogether. Do I remember when the pain lodged in my body which it lived in for almost a month thereafter? It entered my groin first. Or rather, that is what I seem to remember. I recall thinking that I had seen the bird's apparition and that the rest of the world had been small as a speck in the sky—then the man pulled at the foreskin of my manhood, producing, first in my groin, then in the remaining parts of my body, a pain so acute my ears were set ablaze with dolorous flames. These flames spread gradually—then my feet felt frozen, my eyes warm with tears, my cheeks moist with crying and my throat dry as the desert. It was only then that I looked and I saw blood—a pool of blood in whose waters I swam and which helped me cross to the other side so I would be a man—once and for all.

I saw the man break an egg. I couldn't tell why he did so. Perhaps the idea was to reduce the pain or help stop my losing any more blood. I thought that the white and yellow of the egg mixed well with my own blood and the colors which I saw, the beauty of what I saw, took the pain away, for at least a few decisive seconds. My bare thighs were spotted with cold sprouts of pained hair and I rubbed them, smoothing the hair-erections so the blood would return. I was helped to stand, I don't remember by whom, and was led away from the spot I had been sitting on. Possibly, the eggshell was the hat my manhood wore, possibly not; possibly, once the skin was pushed back, I was bandaged with cotton or other similar material, although I cannot remember anything save the pain, which made me faint. I awoke. Alone. On a bed.

JONATHAN FRANZEN: To the extent that the written word is a word of political utterance, it obviously can change something. Probably at least 50 percent of the time for the worse. For every *Germinal* there's a *Protocols of the Elders of Zion*, for every *Silent Spring* there's a tract by Rush Limbaugh, if not several. For every Communist Manifesto there's the same Communist Manifesto put to a different use. For me, tonight's question is interesting only as it pertains to really good books, to writers like Jane Austen and Leo Tolstoy, to writing that's too multifaceted or ambivalent or delightful to be socially effective. The question then becomes, Can the kind of writing that can't change anything change something? And here I think at best we're talking about very personal and subtle interior changes. I definitely feel as if I've been changed by Austen and Tolstoy, and yet the more closely I look at the relationship between the self and the words on the page, the more mysterious and tricky things get. I'm going to read a pair of little stories on the subject of this trickiness by the American fiction writer Lydia Davis. The first one is called "Almost No Memory":

A certain woman had a very sharp consciousness but almost no memory. She remembered enough to get by from day to day. She remembered enough to work, and she worked hard. She did good work, and was paid for it, and earned enough to get by, but she did not remember her work, so that she could not answer questions about it, when people asked, as they did ask, since the work she did was interesting.

She remembered enough to get by, and to do her work, but she did not learn from what she did, or heard, or read. For she did read, she loved to read, and she took good notes on what she read, on the ideas that came to her from what she read, since she did have some ideas of her own, and even on her ideas about these ideas. Some of her ideas were even very good ideas, since she had a very sharp consciousness. And so she kept good notebooks and added to them year by year, and because many years passed this way, she had a long shelf of these notebooks, in which her handwriting became smaller and smaller.

Sometimes, when she was tired of reading a book, or when she was moved by a sudden curiosity she did not altogether understand, she would take an earlier notebook from the shelf and read a little of it, and she would be interested in what she read. She would be interested in the notes she had once taken on a book she was reading or on her own ideas. It would seem all new to her, and indeed most of it would be new to her. Sometimes she would only read and think, and sometimes she would make a note in her current notebook of what she was reading in a notebook from an earlier time, or she would make a note of an idea that came to her from what she was reading. Other times she would want to make a note but choose not to, since she did not think it quite right to make a note of what was already a note, though she did not fully understand what was not right about it. She wanted to make a note of a note she was reading, because this was her way of understanding what she read, though she was not assimilating what she read into her mind, or not for long, but only into another notebook. Or she wanted to make a note because to make a note was her way of thinking this thought.

Although most of what she read was new to her, sometimes she immediately recognized what she read and had no doubt that she herself had written it, and thought it. It seemed perfectly familiar to her, as though she had just thought it that very day, though in fact she had not thought it for some years, unless reading it again was the same as thinking it again, or the same as thinking it for the first time, and though she might never have thought it again, if she had not happened to read it in her notebook. And so she knew by this that these notebooks truly had a great deal to do with her, though it was hard for her to understand, and troubled her to try to understand, just how they had to do with her, how much they were of her and how much they were outside her and not of her, as they sat there on the shelf, being what she knew but did not know, being what she had read but did not remember reading, being what she had thought but did not now think, or remember thinking, or if she remembered, then did not know whether she was thinking it now or whether she had only once thought it, or understand why she had had a thought once and then years later the same thought, or a thought once and then never that same thought again.

A second story. Slightly sunnier, and as with Margaret, the sunnier thought is shorter. This story is called "Happiest Moment."

If you ask her what is a favorite story she has written, she will hesitate for a long time and then say it may be this story that she read in a book once: An English-language teacher in China asked his Chinese student to say what was the happiest moment in his life. The student hesitated for a long time. At last he smiled with embarrassment and said his wife had gone to Beijing and had eaten duck there, and she often told him about it, and he would have to say the happiest moment of his life was her trip, and the eating of the duck.

ANTONIO MUÑOZ MOLINA: Right in front of me, on a crowded subway train, a woman is reading Marcel Proust. I have never seen her before, and most likely I will never see her again after one or the other of us gets off the train. Yet I have the feeling of having met a silent accomplice, someone with whom I share a secret, a hidden treasure. She smiles faintly as she reads, unaware of my looking at her and remote from the clanking noises of the train, pleasantly alone in spite of the crowd that surrounds her. I recognize the smile on her face, and would like to make out which of the volumes of *In Search of Lost Time* she is reading at the moment. But I don't want to seem obtrusive, even creepy, as I am not in a Latin country, and I have learned that in the United States, you should not stare at people the same way you could in Spain or Italy.

What exactly is prompting her to smile? I can't help wondering. Who, among the many memorable characters invented by Proust, is she reading about? What faraway place has she been transported to? As the number 6 train rushes downtown, so absorbed in the words written by someone a century ago, she won't even raise her head when the train screeches to a halt at 59th Street. This is the subtle power of the pen—one of them at least. The image of someone reading a novel on the train is more or less commonplace these days. Yet, when you come to think of it, it is a kind of miracle as well.

At the moment the woman opened the book and plunged into her reading, some sort of cosmic yet invisible shift took place. She is no longer on the train on this workday morning. She has fled, at least partially, to a different country. She is surrounded not by solemn, sleepy New York subway riders, but perhaps by the haughty guests at an elegant Parisian dinner. She is living in this present moment, between 8:50 and 8:55 A.M., and at the same time in the half-imagined, half-remembered evening Marcel Proust wrote about, and also in the actual time during which Proust—asthmatic, insomniac—was writing, when day was undistinguishable from night because the thick curtains were always drawn. A dying man trying to put off the end so that he could finish the same novel this lady in front of me reads so effortlessly. Even with a smile on her face. Maybe she's finding out some truth about herself. Maybe Proust is influencing her ideas on love or jealousy, is modifying the way she perceives the passing of time or the nature of memory. Had I not read Proust myself, would I be able to notice smells and flavors and sounds the same way I do?

Does writing change anything? It is easy to generalize when all these big questions are raised, but as a writer of fiction, I'm not personally fond of general ideas and solid statements. I see this woman in front of me and I know how profoundly her actual life is being transformed by the pages of a novel. Like radio waves, the ripples of writing expand invisibly and constantly in all directions and they are even more powerful because they reach us at our innermost self. You cannot fully read a book without being alone. But through this very solitude you become intimately involved with people whom you might never have met otherwise, either because they have been dead for centuries or because they spoke languages you cannot understand. And nonetheless, they have become your closest friends, your wisest advisors, the wizards that hypnotize you, the lovers you have always dreamed of.

When I was twelve, a white-haired novelist who had written in French and who had died at the beginning of the twentieth century changed my life forever. Reading Jules Verne's novels, I fell under the spell of an imaginary world, adventure stories and cartoons far beyond the actual experiences of my life, yet more exciting and full of promises than anything my own life could offer me at that time. The world was wider than the small and backwards Spanish province I was born in, and the lives I came across in those novels appealed to me far more powerfully than any personal expectation I could figure out for myself. There was something more for me to learn in those books—the very fact that someone had imagined and written them, this man with a white beard who very soon became a kind of father figure for me, a hero to model my own future after. I would never be a farmer like my father and my grandparents. I would not work as a clerk in a store or an office. What this man did, I would do. Come what may, I would write books.

For the last thirty-seven years I have been trying to fulfill that childish whim, and I don't know whether something I have written has brought about a small, enduring change in the life of my readers. Judging from my own experience as a reader, I always try to follow this maxim: Be careful what you write and how you write, because you never know who might read your words, how and where they are going to resonate. In the late '30s, Cyril Connolly was painfully aware that by writing a couple of lines in an article he might send a young man to die in the Spanish Civil War. Very often, writers complain bitterly about the futility of their solitary endeavor, but our contemporary world, for better or for worse, was created by the writing of at least two self-absorbed graphomaniacs: Jean-Jacques Rousseau and Karl Marx.

The train has come to a bumpy stop and at last the lady in front of me raises her eyes from Proust as if awaking from a pleasant sleep. Now she looks at me and there is a flash of curiosity and then recognition in her face as she stealthily takes in the title of the book I am reading, which happens to be Aharon Appelfeld's *The Story of a Life*. For a second, our eyes meet before I get up and leave the train at 51st Street—two fellow Freemasons exchanging a secret signal in an unfriendly environment, both of us temporary exiles, seeking shelter in other people's memories or fictions.

HISTORY OF MY FACE

My lips came with a caravan of slaves
That belonged to the Grand Sanussi.
In Al-Jaghbub he freed them.
They still live in the poor section of Benghazi
Near the hospital where I was born.

They never meant to settle
In Tokara those Greeks
Whose eyebrows I wear
—then they smelled the wild sage
And declared my country their birthplace.

The Knights of St. John invaded Tripoli.
The residents of the city
Sought help from Istanbul. In 1531
The Turks brought along my nose.

My hair stretches back
To a concubine of Septimus Severus.
She made his breakfast,
Bore four of his sons.

Uqba took my city
In the name of God.
We sit by his grave
And I sing to you:
    Sweet lashes, arrow-sharp,
    Is that my face I see
    Reflected in your eyes?

—*Khaled Mattawa*

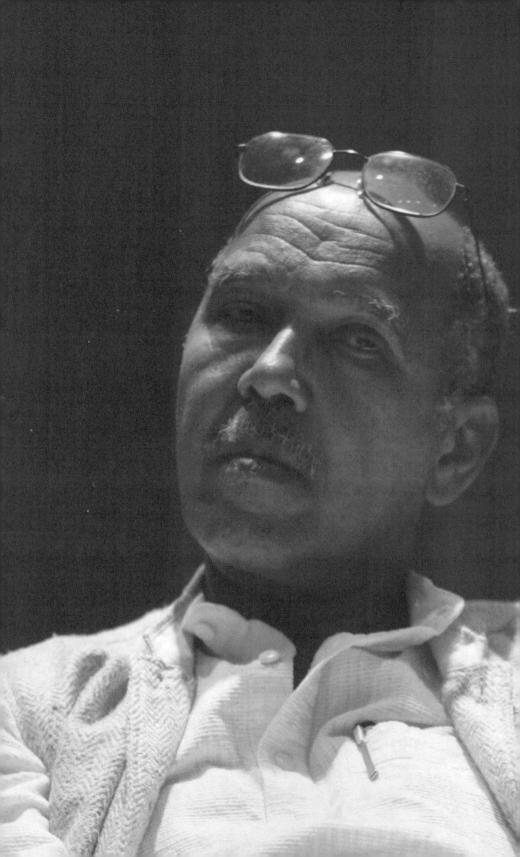

NURUDDIN FARAH

CROSSOVER ARTISTS

Writing in Another Language

ELIF SHAFAK: I want to talk about how I made the journey from the Turkish to the English language. Before doing that, I would like to draw a historical framework—how literature and language have developed in Turkey—so I can give a better sense of where I come from. I will start with a small example from the world of art: Maurice Ravel's *Boléro*. As you all remember, *Boléro* was unusual at the time it was composed because it's based on the technique of deliberate repetition. It's an eighteen-minute-long piece in which the same musical pattern is repeated again, again, and again—seventeen times.

Now please think of a Turkish citizen in the year 1928 or 1930 in Istanbul. You are traveling from one coast to the other. You take the ferryboat. The journey lasts forty minutes, maybe an hour. As you sit there, on a bench, you start hearing the *Boléro* play again and again, until you reach the other coast. The whole idea was part of the state's project to build another culture out of the ashes of the Ottoman Empire by modernizing, Westernizing, and secularizing the society from above.

I chose this example because I think it shows us how art is sometimes used by nation-states, by nationalist ideologies, by patriarchal structures. Perhaps no form has served nationalist causes or the building of nation-states more than literature itself. In Turkey, the novel especially served this end because it was a new genre. It was the voice of Westernization when the Turkish reformers were trying to accelerate the process of Westernization. It was brought as the voice of the bourgeoisie when there was no Muslim bourgeoisie. The Turkish reformers tried to create a Muslim bourgeoisie by transferring the property of the minorities into the hands of the Muslims. The genre of the novel was introduced to Turkish society at a crucial time, a turning point in history.

Early Turkish novelists, right from the beginning, were men. Almost all of them came from very wealthy families; they were educated either in Western universities or colleges or by private Western teachers. They knew the philosophy and the language of Western societies. Many of them were state employees, which gives us an idea of their limits. People wanted to serve the state, and they were more occupied with the state than with society. Modernization in Turkey occurred from above, not from below. Language and literature were essential to this.

In time, especially as novelists were actually given the cultural mission to revive society, the image of the Father Novelist emerged in Turkey. There was an expectation that the novelist would be like a paternal gaze, leading the society via his work of art. The novelist had to be above his characters, his book, his language, and his readers. That is the traditional Father Novelist that I refuse to accept.

In 1923 the Turkish Republic was established, and in 1925 the Reformist regime changed the alphabet in a day. People who were literate woke up illiterate the next morning. They couldn't read the newspapers anymore. Everyone in the nation, old and young, middle-aged, women, men—like children—had to learn the alphabet again. Today in Turkey we have generations of people who cannot read their family's tombstones, let alone archival documents. You walk by a tombstone in Istanbul and you have no idea who that dead person is because you cannot read the inscription. There was a huge rupture between the Ottoman time and the new regime. The reformists deliberately wanted this, because the more you distance yourself from the past, the more future you have to modernize and Westernize a society.

The Turkish language has been cleansed, Turkified—the reformists got rid of Persian words, Arabic words, Sufi expressions. The language has been disenchanted. This is not a problem, perhaps, in the genre of poetry because it is a very old tradition; it has its own rules and rhythm. However, when you come to the novel, language isn't as important as what you're saying. I try to go back to the Sufi tradition that has been purged—the old words that have been purged—and I return them to the language. Not only have the words been lost and the vocabulary shrunk, but the curiosity for the past has been lost. Information and knowledge cannot flow from one generation to another, which creates a big cultural gap.

Because of my passion for language, I refuse to take that gap for granted. I think it has something to do with my childhood; I had to live in different countries—France and Spain, Jordan and Amman, Germany. Every time I came back to Turkey, I realized not that I had forgotten my Turkish but that I had lost contact with expressions—the subtleties of the language, the slang—which made me realize you can lose your native tongue. You cannot take it for granted. It made me realize that maybe I have to pay more attention to it. So I started to study my own language as if it were a foreign language. In the short run, I felt bad; in the long run, it helped to enrich my language. It's ironic that today in Turkey, literary critics praise the richness of my Turkish. It's precisely because I lost contact with my language, and because I felt like an outsider when I came back to that language, that I pay more attention and maybe value the language more than other Turkish novelists.

That said, when I moved into the English language it was, in a way, such a relief. You have an amazing vocabulary in the English language. I truly love it when I hear the word "chutzpah" from a person who's not Jewish. The word "chutzpah" has traveled like the Nomads from one community to another, and nobody says, "Okay, this word comes from a Jewish origin. Let's get rid of it." Nobody's saying, "This word has comes from an Irish origin. It's four hundred years old. Let's get rid of it." What the Turkish reformists failed to see was that we do not have a power over language; language has a power over us. When you try to limit language, you limit your own imagination. In that sense, I very much enjoyed, despite the challenge I had to face, writing in English.

The second thing I experienced was humor. My writing has a lot of humor, and I found it difficult to deal with that desire for humor in Turkish because the language is so disenchanted; it leaves no room for irony. There's a solid tradition of humor in Turkey, but it is very direct humor. You have to know what you are criticizing. It's political humor, but not irony. In English, I found more gates for that humor, additional doors. I found a more masculine voice, which I enjoyed also. But I do not see this as an either/or choice, and that is part of the dilemma I experienced in Turkey when my most recent novel came out.

Unlike the previous four novels, this one was written in English—*The Saint of Incipient Insanities*—and when the book was translated into Turkish and came out in Turkey, many people in Turkey didn't know what to do with it. Just the fact that it was written in English became something to criticize. Turkish nationalists—these are not necessarily people calling themselves nationalists—were very much upset because they saw writing in another language as a cultural betrayal, as if I were abandoning my mother tongue. It's always an either/or framework. When you do something there it means you have abandoned the other side. I do not believe in that. I think it's possible to be multicultural, multilingual, and even multifaith.

MINAE MIZUMURA: There is a general rule when you are bilingual: If you have a choice between two languages or three languages, the language you choose to write in is generally the dominant language. I think that's the case with most writers. You can think of someone like Kafka, who as a child was Czech, and Nabokov, who switched from Russian to English. Many writers who come from the English and French empires switch from the minor language to the major language. But there are always exceptions to the rule.

I wish I could tell you that I'm perfectly happy with the choice I made, but I can't quite say that, especially when I know that 99 percent of you have not read my work because it's written in Japanese. If I were speaking in Japan in front of a Japanese audience and if I wrote books in English, they would surely have been translated into Japanese. The most nonsensical, stupid stuff will be translated into Japanese because so many Japanese people want to read American things.

I can't really say that I'm 100 percent happy with this asymmetrical situation. I wrote an autobiographical novel about ten years ago—*Shishosetsu: From Left to Right*. As you can see, *shishosetsu* is a Japanese word that means "I-novel," autobiographical novel. "From left to right" is an English expression. The title is bilingual, and the book itself is, in a way, bilingual. But it's not really bilingual because it's written in Japanese with many English expressions thrown in. It's written horizontally, whereas 99.9 percent of Japanese texts are written vertically. I had to write it horizontally because there are so many English expressions.

I know that some Spanish Americans are doing this with the Spanish language—throwing Spanish words into English texts—but the effect is very much different in Japanese because we don't just use a phonetic alphabet. We use Chinese characters that came from China, and we have two kinds of phonetic alphabets. It's very pictorial. We have the English sentences thrown in, so the visual impact or the clash of the two totally different languages is much more striking.

From Left to Right reflects my cultural upbringing and tells the story of how I became a writer. Ever since Marcel Proust's *À la recherche du temps perdu*, how-I-became-a-writer stories have flourished. You can say that *Shishosetsu: From Left to Right* is a variant of such stories. You may even detect in my novel the sort of complacent, congratulatory tone characteristic of such stories. Yet my novel is also darker. My story does not suggest a how-I-became-a-writer story; it's a how-I-became-a-Japanese-writer story. That story necessarily runs parallel to a sad tale of how I failed to become an American writer or a writer of the English language.

I was born in Japan and came to the States with my family when I was twelve. My father had been stationed in New York by a Japanese company. That was back in the 1960s, when Japanese products such as transistor radios, cameras, and tape reorders began selling overseas. Accordingly, the Japanese companies started sending their men overseas with their families. Little did my family know when we arrived that we would be spending the next twenty years in the States. Little did I know that I would grow up entirely in the States. Moreover, little did any of us expect that the girl who came to America at the age of twelve—a girl who was not particularly stupid—would twenty years later still find herself uncomfortable with the English language. But that's what happened.

As I look back on my life, I cannot help thinking that I would have been writing in English now if some crucial conditions had been different. If I were a white girl, I would not have felt so alienated from the American society, though I may have rejected English at first. If my parents had come to the States like so many Japanese before the war, then America would have become my country and English my principal language. I would be writing in English. But my parents considered themselves long-term visitors; they always thought we would eventually go back, and my sisters and I would find nice Japanese husbands.

Maybe if I were not Japanese and were not so nationalistic, I might have abandoned my Japanese more easily. And if I had known at the time the linguistic power structure of the world—that you could have infinitely more advantages as a writer of English than of Japanese—if I had known that, I might have chosen English. I'm often described as a writer who chose to write in Japanese rather than in English, who chose a local and singular language over the universal language. I am portrayed as someone who has made a sort of ideological choice. I wish that were the case, but it isn't. I did not know I had a choice.

It depends on what kind of writing you want to do as a novelist. If I'd wanted to write a fantastic novel, for example, or if I were more interested in abstract, avant-garde-ish novels, my own English might have sufficed. But I'm an orthodox, nineteenth-century-realism kind of writer, and I want every detail to carry cultural weight. I want everything to be completely, verbally, historically sound. As the kind of novelist I am, I don't think I have a choice to write in English.

I did everything in my power during those twenty years to avoid writing in the English language. The main thing I did, which I think is the stupidest thing I did, was to learn French. I went to graduate school at Yale. I wrote paper after paper in French. I received honors in French. I lived in France. If you look at the past linguistic politics, French was the only language in which you could say, "I don't know English, but that's okay because I know French." Politics played into my psyche but twenty years later, with all due respect to people who write in French and to French culture, what is it to have spent my youth learning French instead of learning English in America? I think it was a very frivolous thing.

However, at the bottom of all these evil conditions is the worthy existence of Japanese literature, modern Japanese literature, which may need some explanation. You think it's natural that there is such a thing as Japanese literature, but when you consider all the non-Western countries at the turn of the century, it's very rare to have a national literature. Most countries have been colonized; their principal language has become the language of the colonizer. The well-educated have been schooled in the colonizer's language—in French, sometimes in Dutch. Japan, because it escaped being colonized—it colonized its neighbors—was able to develop the language to such a high level politically, scientifically, mathematically, and literally. But within twenty to thirty years, between 1867 and 1890, the Japanese language borrowed so much from Chinese tradition and from the southern tradition that it transformed into a wonderfully rich language. My parents brought with them a whole collection of Japanese novels that were published before 1925. Japanese literature is the only non-Western literature that would have a full collection of modern novels by the year 1925. Until recently, I never realized that if I had been brought up Korean, I would not have kept the Korean language because Korea was occupied by Japan and did not develop a national literature until much later. The same thing even with Chinese, which had a very excellent classical tradition but was unable to develop a modern Chinese literature because of all the political upheavals, and because of Japanese literature.

Japan did have this very early, established national literature that played a major role in my choices. I would go to high school and my body would be there but not my soul. My heart wasn't there. I'd come home from school and start reading all those collected volumes that came from my grandparents' basement. I read and read and read. By the time I grew up, my Japanese was archaic. People speaking to me would think they were speaking to an old lady.

That is why my first work was a continuation of a novel left unfinished seventy years ago by Natsume Soseki. He is the founder of modern Japanese literature. He had a stomach ulcer and when he was serializing the novel—it was a cliffhanger—he was about to write his ending but he died. That was his last work and it was supposed to represent his last thought on modern Japan. Nobody wanted to touch it. There were so many conjectures about how he would have finished it, but nobody dared to touch it. It was easy for me to do because I was so used to his kind of language, which was now archaic. I was able to start my career finishing that work, which created a rather big sensation in Japan. It was a lucky start for me.

SHAN SA: I apologize, first of all, for my accent. It's a really horrible, Chinese-French accent because I'm Chinese and I'm living in Paris now and I'm writing in French. I want to share with you my experience on that literary emigration from East to West. I have to first confess that when I was a teenager, I really despised Western culture. My parents went to France, and my father was a professor in a Paris university. He told us about the splendor of Paris and how great French literature is. I was a teenager; I rebelled against that idea. I despised Balzac and Zola and how boring they were. I focused all my free time after school on classical literature, which is so beautiful, so powerful—that is, the literature of China that has gathered from five thousand years like a treasure. It was like a huge ocean that I spent all my time swimming in. It was a very important time for me because when I left China, I had read all the classical novels and I knew the famous Tao Dynasty poems by heart. But now I've forgotten them because I have all this language mixed in my mind. Even though I didn't understand it totally, I really was deeply in love with my Chinese culture.

I left China when I was almost eighteen, and decided to begin a new life in the Western world after Tiananmen in 1989. I arrived in Paris without knowing about French culture because I had refused to see it when I was a child. I didn't speak French at all. I spoke English, which helped me learn French very quickly. I will always remember my first lesson in French philosophy. My teacher said, "Descartes said, '*Je pense, donc je suis,*'" I think, so I am. For Chinese people, and for Asian culture, the human being is a part of the universe. The thinking machine is the universe; the cosmos is not a human being. We're only a small part of it. Why is it such a hopeful pretension to say that the world is inside our minds, and that because we think, there is the world?

While I made progress in my French, I studied philosophy, but it took a very long time for me to understand "I think, so I am." When I started writing French, four years after my arrival in France, I very fortunately met the French painter Balthus and stayed at his place for two years, working as his secretary. I wrote my first novel in French in the afternoon. His place was a very peaceful chalet in the mountains, and I really had time to read, to visit the beautiful, rich French literature. I fell in love with Flaubert, Maupassant, Madame de Lafayette, and I discovered the difference between Chinese literature and European literature.

The difference is like in painting: In the traditional Chinese way, painters draw the contour, the line. The landscape comes from the few colors but with the simplicity of the lines. Chinese poetry is a work of the imagination. In the traditional European way, painting is laying a base of colors; you use more colors, you get the contour; you can make a portrait, a landscape. It's a totally different direction of expression.

Asian poetry is about suggestion. We never describe inner voice and consciousness because consciousness doesn't exist in our tradition. We believe that there is a life after life; we believe in reincarnation. But there is not this kind of space inside the individual. All is about cosmos and collectivity. As a Chinese poet, I won't say "I hate" or "I love" or "I'm angry." I will say, "I look at the cloud passing in the heavens. I look at the tree and the seasons are changing." Those natural landscapes, the feeling that a tree, a flower, the daylight can give me, expresses my emotion. That is the Chinese way to express the individual. The European way is more direct.

When I started to write, I had to find my French, which was an invented language, and I was aware that I was walking on a path where nobody had been. No one could tell me, "That word is good" or "That word is bad," because when I use a French word, I have my Chinese literariness and I have my Chinese judgment of this world. I wrote my novel. People loved that first version because it was Chinese, not French. Then I corrected it. I think I rewrote it twenty times. I think that is the only way I could learn French—by writing, by touching the words, and then by judging them myself. Now with my fifth novel out in Paris I can say that I really know about every word, like so many individuals whose faces I know—I know how they smell, their perfume, how to put them together.

I think writing is a gesture; it's inventing another language. Every writer has his own language. Writing is quite complex work; it's work like a composer's. It's the music of the voice, different voices. A very powerful novel is one that has very powerful music. It's like the work of a painter. With a painting, you have to choose the frame and you have to choose the beginning and end. That is the painter's work and his genius. A writer has to choose pace and a time when the novel starts and when it will be finished. A film director has complex talents because he has to mix music, colors, actions, and stories together. The writer is a strange animal who has to think about everything and do everything. Writing in another language is just the path but not the place where we want to go, and the place where we want to go is the place of our dreams, the place that everybody wants to go: a place of passion and truth and life and death.

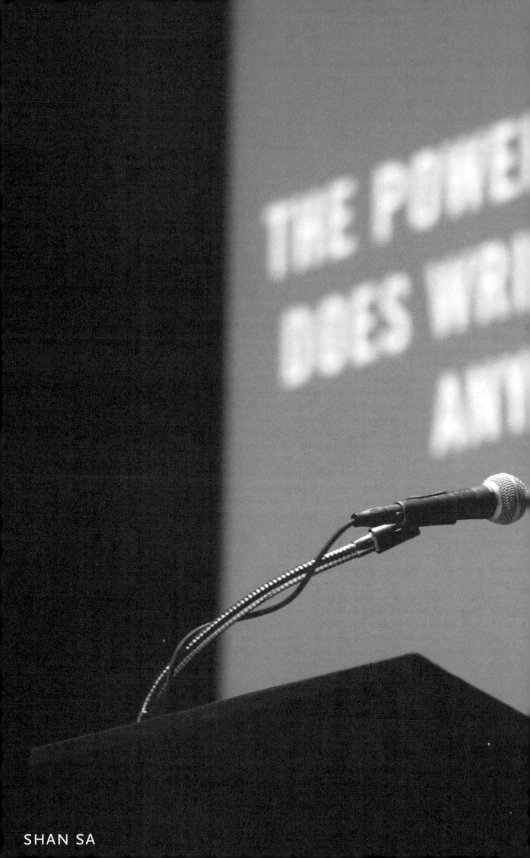

SHAN SA

POSTCOLONIAL PASSAGES

Assia Djebar and Lyonel Trouillot

ASSIA DJEBAR: Lyonel Trouillot's last novel, *Bicentenaire*, has not been translated, but it's a great pleasure for me as an Algerian writer to engage in dialogue with Lyonel. His book describes the celebrations that go awry on the eve of the third centennial of Haiti's independence. This could have happened in Algeria, not two hundred years after independence—the country isn't that old—but it could have well taken place in the 1990s, thirty years after independence. And the demonstrations could have ended up the same way.

Of course, we're not here to discuss political history. We're writers, fiction writers, and I think our comments will have to do with how we write about violence—with urgency—both as it's taking place and after it has taken place. One of the things that brings us together is the fact that we both use the language of the former colonial entity. However, the violence that occurs on the street afterward has nothing to do with the colonial power.

LYONEL TROUILLOT: For me, language is a secondary issue, whether I write in Creole or in French. Language is the heritage of colonization. We got it in a less than desirable fashion, but it remains with us. Unfortunately, few benefit from and enjoy the wealth that bilingualism between Creole and French could entail. I would like there to be free expression in both Creole and French, so that Creole could be a language of prestige and of writing, which is not the case today. On the other hand, I would like my countrymen to be able to freely express themselves in French and not have the current situation, in which only a hundred thousand people in a population of eight million are capable of using French.

It's the text that chooses the language. I've decided to write a text in French, and the text decides to be written in Creole, and vice versa.

DJEBAR: For me, language is not a question of minor import. I do write in French and I only write in French. I speak an Arabic dialect and I have a memory of Berber, but I don't speak it. My ancestors spoke it but it was lost. Now there is a renaissance of Berber, and my mother tongue is Arabic, and I have a great deal of affection for Arabic. But I studied in French because I lived in Algeria under the French colonization. At the time, France was a secular country, but I was always referred to as the Muslim Frenchwoman, and that's what appeared on my identity card. I did learn to write in Arabic, but only sections of the Koran.

I do believe that language is extremely important and I wish, as Lyonel says, that many people in Algeria could be bilingual and even trilingual. But my experience is that people in Algeria who express themselves in French do so without taboo, and when they discuss questions about love or sex, they do so without any internal barriers. On the other hand, those who write in Arabic are affected by the religious shadow, not to mention that most of the books have a religious connection. The level of teaching Arabic in my country is not the same as the level of French. Ten years ago in my country writers were murdered not so much because of the content of their work but because they were Francophone.

TROUILLOT: I still think it's important to distinguish between the social situation inside a society, and literature and writing and the function of a language inside a society. Today I would have to say that the language and the texts written in Creole are much more capricious, with a much greater thematic variety, and the poetry written in Creole has much more fantasy than what is written in French. This has to do with the historical age of the society.

I would also like to talk about fetishism in a language. This is not a question of the language itself. The fact that there's more thematic liberty, more freedom for subjects in French among Algerian writers, doesn't have to do with the wealth of the French language or the poverty of Arabic. But rather it has to do with a question of historical development. Language is a tool and domain for the writer, but if we look at Haiti, for example, thirty years ago, we could see that many of the Creole writers were addressing political issues. Why? Because Duvalier was using French as the language of exclusion, so it was logical that they would pick Creole as a language of opposition. It was a historic need. That is not the case anymore. Now Creole language writers have a much wider selection of themes.

DJEBAR: When I started to write novels and fiction in French, I found that French allowed me to follow the female body from the outside, something that the Arabic language didn't permit me to do. This was not a question of it being twentieth-century French or French from Marie de France; that's how it worked for me. I found that the female body moved with French. Ten years ago, when violence broke out over a period of two or three years, I had a lot of good friends who were killed because of the French language—French teachers who were murdered. The only way I could achieve a balance was by using the French language in memory of the victims of intolerance, and I would agree that French, as Lyonel said, is a domain. Right now I could say that I've established a dialogue with many of the great Arabic writers. For example, I'm working on Ibn Hazm's book *The Ring of the Dove*, which was written in the eleventh century. I can say that I'm tapping the richness of Arabic to continue my trajectory in French.

TROUILLOT: One of the sources of happiness in Haiti—Haiti is a country with a lot of unhappiness, but it does have some flickering moments of happiness—is that the writer in Haiti today is really free to pick his language, unlike in the French Antilles, where Creole writers are pushed into a corner. Haitian writers who live and write in Haiti today write in French and Creole, going back and forth. We have assumed bilingualism without any trauma, and I think that's very positive.

We can compare the island of Manhattan to the island of Haiti: We both think we're the center of the world, but a writer in Haiti is content to write for two thousand readers.

DJEBAR: That's enough. We don't have that in Algeria.

TROUILLOT: That's why I find the situation of my confreres in Guadeloupe and Martinique so interesting: If they have a literary dispute, it has to be dealt with by the publishing companies in Paris, whereas if we have a literary dispute we can handle it in Port-au-Prince. That gives us a certain degree of specificity. Our literature is not aimed at other people's market. That gives us a certain degree of solitude, but it also gives us authenticity.

DJEBAR: In Algeria, we have a population of thirty million, which is substantially more than Haiti. Twenty million of those are French speakers, and nevertheless, despite that, we don't have an authentic publishing industry for people who are writing in Algeria in French. Young writers who write in French in Algeria are writing for someone else, for another market. And whenever your motivation is to write for another market, you fall prey to a certain exoticism. For example, right now, if a Muslim woman in France is writing for Gallimard or any other publishing house, they want her to discuss why a Muslim woman would or wouldn't wear the veil. The question is how you feel as an individual, and if you have two thousand readers who feel the same way you do, that's enough to continue your literary path.

TROUILLOT: It's true that when you come from countries like Algeria or Haiti that were victims of colonization and are currently searching for themselves and developing a being, there is a tendency to try to reduce the reality of those countries to a reality of violence. I reflect violence in my work because one writes with one's gaze. But it would be a mistake for a New York or a Parisian reader to view this violence as a sort of new exoticism. Violence is one aspect of the reality of my country—a country where one lives, one makes love, one drinks, one sings. I say this both to you as the reader and to me as the writer, so that I will not replace cocoa trees with cadavers.

from **WOMEN OF ALGIERS IN THEIR APARTMENT**

The only free women in the city go out in single white files before dawn, to do three or four hours of cleaning in the glass offices of low-, middle-, and high-level civil servants who will arrive later on. They burst out laughing in the stairwells, clean up the clutter, with their heads still held high, slowly lifting their headdresses, and all the while they exchange ironic comments on the respective floor managers, those who protectively ask them about their children's studies, and those who don't talk because one doesn't speak to women.

—*Assia Djebar* (translated by Marjolijn de Jager)

ENORMOUS CHANGES

Ha Jin and Eliot Weinberger

ELIOT WEINBERGER: Your life has had such an amazing trajectory from semiliterate Chinese soldier to distinguished American novelist in such a short amount of time. You joined the army when you were fourteen, I believe.

HA JIN: Yes, toward the end of 1969. Almost fourteen—not fourteen yet, but I lied because the requirement was sixteen. My father was an officer and since most of my schoolmates had fathers who were officers, they were going into the army.

WEINBERGER: That seemed the only thing to do, your only possible career?

JIN: I think it was a better choice at the time. The other choice would have been to go to the countryside to work in the fields. That would have been more tedious, and the food would have been worse.

WEINBERGER: Whenever I read your books, even when there are poor people just having a little piece of rice, it always makes me incredibly hungry.

JIN: In the first book, particularly during the first two months, in the middle of the winter, two companies in the regiment were really starving to some extent. All the young soldiers were boys from the countryside—they ate a lot because the weather was very cold.

WEINBERGER: You were up on the North Korea border?

JIN: Yes, off the coast of Russia, as well. That's kind of Siberia. There were no vegetables. There were turnips and cabbages, but they were all frozen. That's the only way to preserve the vegetables. The older companies would dig cellars during the fall. They knew how to prepare and save food and vegetables for the winter. But the recruit companies didn't do anything like that. That's why during the first two months, most of us starved. Perhaps that caused the descriptions of food.

WEINBERGER: What did you do in the army?

JIN: The first half year, I was a regular artillery man. They have a first artillery man, a second artillery man. I was the fourth one. Basically my job was just to carry the shells. But half a year later, I was picked to be trained as a radio man and to learn how to send out and receive telegrams. It took a long time to finish the training, almost a year.

WEINBERGER: It's good training for a writer—you learned compression, right?

JIN: In fact, it was quite a headache because you listen to the signals all the time. Some of my fellow soldiers lost their hair—they couldn't get used to that kind of electric signal and stimulation of that kind. I had to be very concentrated to follow the signals and write down the messages.

WEINBERGER: I gather you barely knew how to read. With most writers, one asks "When did you begin to write?" But in your case, it's "When did you begin to read?"

JIN: I would say toward the end of the second year. Before then, books were not available. In the summer of 1971, China began to republish some classics. At the time, reading was very hard for me. I remember the first page of *The Chronicle of the Three Kingdoms* took me four hours to figure out. So I had to put it aside. I began to read a dictionary. It was very small, but once I went through it, I knew more words than before. I began to read whatever I could lay my hands on.

WEINBERGER: Was there any one book that started you off?

JIN: No particular book. At the time, there were a lot of propaganda novels that were not well written at all, but we couldn't read anything else. So whatever I could get hold of. My parents managed to buy a sack of textbooks from an old scholar who had been banished to the frontier of China to teach middle school there. Then he retired, returned to Shanghai, and sold his books. So my parents and brother sat with him among those books. There were a few high school textbooks, old ones, published before the Cultural Revolution. Those books had some ancient poems in them, and I think they were the best literature I could read at the time.

WEINBERGER: You were in the army for six years and then you became a telegraph person?

JIN: Five and a half. It took such a long time to train as a telegrapher, and so they tried to keep me as a kind of junior officer. Most of my comrades, the telegraphers, automatically became junior officers. But I was determined to go to college. I wouldn't stay in the army. That's why I left. The schools at the time were still closed, so I worked for another three years in a little company again as a telegrapher. I think I quite enjoyed it. I had my own room. I could read whatever I could get a hold of, and from the second year on, I began to follow the English learner's program in China. That's how I began to learn English.

WEINBERGER: You were learning on your own.

JIN: Yes.

WEINBERGER: Did you know anyone who spoke English?

JIN: No; before I went to college I didn't know anybody.

WEINBERGER: You were just imagining how all these words were pronounced?

JIN: The radio station broadcast the program for a half hour a day from 5:30 to 6:00, seven days a week. It was very simple. This is a glass; that is a chair. It always began and ended with a slogan and in the middle you had some basic sentences. But it was a very slow process—just a half hour a day.

WEINBERGER: So it was "Long live the chair of Chairman Mao; long live the glass of Chairman Mao"?

JIN: Yes, "Here comes the Party," and those kinds of slogans. We were made to read books by Marx and Engels and other revolutionary authors. At the time, I knew that Friedrich Engels had written a book in English, *The Condition of the Working Class in England*. I thought that some day I might read that book. I haven't read it yet, though I did buy a copy. Somehow, I'm superstitious about it.

WEINBERGER: Your life will be over when you finally read it.

JIN: Yes.

WEINBERGER: Is there any literature you read when you were working as a telegrapher that's particularly important to you? Did you have any idea of heading toward literature in your life at this point?

JIN: No. Honestly, I never thought I would study literature or write anything literary. I thought I would be an engineer, just have a college education. I think I followed my own instinct. When I went into the army, it was rumored that there would be a war and after a year, the border came down, so I was confused.

WEINBERGER: A war with whom?

JIN: With the Russians. Then the border came down. As a result, I really felt lost because suddenly I didn't know. The question would be, "What should I do in peace?" I was semiliterate, and so I thought I had to get some kind of education in order to be a useful person living in peace.

WEINBERGER: You went to the university to study engineering?

JIN: No, I couldn't because that would have required different kinds of tests. To study science, I would have had to take examinations in chemistry and physics. Chemistry would be impossible to study on your own, whereas for examinees in the humanities and social sciences, you just took math and some others like politics and language. So that's why I decided I didn't have a choice: I had to go into the social sciences and humanities. My first choice was philosophy, then classics, then world history, then library science. Each person was given five choices at the time. I didn't have a fifth choice—I put English there. But since I put English as a choice, I had to take the exam.

WEINBERGER: They made you become an English major?

JIN: Yes, I passed the exam barely. I got sixty-two points for the written part. It happened that there were not many examinees who would take English as a choice. The city had about a quarter of a million people living in it, but there were sixteen people who put down English as a choice. As a result, sixteen students were put in a huge classroom for an exam. Half of them didn't know a word of English. There were not many people who would pick English, so that's how they assigned me to major in it.

WEINBERGER: That's amazing. Were you studying mainly English literature? Or just English?

JIN: In fact, English literature was not offered in that school. We were trained just for the language—to speak and listen. Most of us would be translators and teachers eventually. But toward the end of 1980, American literature suddenly became very popular. Professors in the Chinese literature department specialized in foreign literatures, so they talked a lot about American literature. The English majors or Russian majors or Japanese majors all went to their lectures and listened to them speak about Hemingway and Faulkner and a lot of Jewish writers—Malamud was popular. But very few of the professors had read the books. They didn't have the answers. They learned about American authors from critical articles written by somebody else, in Beijing or somewhere, and then they talked about them.

WEINBERGER: Were you actually reading any of these American writers?

JIN: Not when I was an undergrad. But that's how I became interested in American literature. Some of the students in my year were twenty years older than others. Some were very advanced in English, and one didn't go to any classes. He just read Charles Dickens in his bedroom all the time. He was far ahead of the rest of us. People like me didn't think of English as a choice; we didn't know anything. So on the first day, we were given a test, a dictation, and we couldn't write down any words. As a result, we were put in the slow classes. For the rest of college, the four years, we stayed in the same class. Even among the slow classes, there are two levels—I think I was at the bottom. That was humiliating; that's why I never liked English at all. I just followed whatever I could do and then—because I suddenly became interested in American literature—I knew that I would have to pass the English test, which would be quite rigorous, in order to continue studying American literature. That's why toward the end of the third year, I began to work very hard on the language.

WEINBERGER: And you passed?

JIN: Yes, fortunately I passed. I had to teach myself American literature because that course was not offered. So I had to read whatever I could find.

WEINBERGER: Were you reading translations or histories?

JIN: Some translations, but literary histories written by Chinese scholars. Very often they were biased, because they didn't have full access to American literary works. So, as a result, my job was to know what this book is about. What is the story and structure of the book? But I couldn't have the book in my hands.

WEINBERGER: How did you get to the United States?

JIN: Once I became a graduate student, I began to work with American professors—Fulbright professors. I began to study literature seriously. The professors were very generous. They bought books out of their own pockets and brought them back to China. They gave us books by Faulkner and Flannery O'Connor. That's when I began to read real books and later, when I finished my graduate work for the master's degree, my American professors recommended me to study American literature in the States. It was almost assumed that this was part of the training and that if I could continue, I should.

WEINBERGER: This was what year?

JIN: 1985.

WEINBERGER: The idea was you would go to the United States for a few years, then go back to China?

JIN: Yes, that's why it was smooth—because I came to study literature and nobody assumed I would stay. I thought I would go back too. It was quite easy for me to get out at the time. Although I got a scholarship from Brandeis University, I came out on a J visa, which means that the government officially sent me, although I didn't spend the government's money.

WEINBERGER: You were at Brandeis in graduate school. What was that like in terms of a first discovery of the United States?

JIN: I knew by then something about American literature and culture, but my first impression was how different the landscape was from the Chinese landscape. In Chinese landscapes, everywhere you go, you see outcrops, all barren, gray and yellow—the land is not tillable. But here, there is grass everywhere. I went to the Charles River because the graduate student dormitory was nearby.

I saw people fishing and they caught big bass and carp that they wouldn't keep—they'd dump the fish right in the water. That was an eye-opener. I wrote to my friend and said, "Nature has been very generous to America. This land is so abundant."

WEINBERGER: I gather that's where you started writing, when you were at Brandeis?

JIN: No, not that year. Frank Bidart used to teach at Brandeis as poet in residence, but since I was a graduate student, I was not allowed to take his class for credit. So I sat in on his class but my graduate seminar interfered with the workshop, so I couldn't go every week. Still, as an auditor, I had to turn in my work. One day I wrote a poem called "The Dead Soldier's Talk," and he liked it very much. It was later published in *The Paris Review*.

WEINBERGER: The first poem you ever wrote was in English, and it was published in *The Paris Review*?

JIN: Yes, that was how it started. He told me, "You should continue to write." Then, a year later, when I was working as a janitor/night watchman in a factory in Watertown, Massachusetts, I wrote the poems in *Between Silences*. That was 1990. I didn't know what to do with them, but I just felt I'd reached a point—I had to write something.

   The next year, Alan Shapiro, who was poetry editor at the University of Chicago Press, visited Brandeis as a lecturer and read the manuscript. He liked it and accepted it for that press. At the time, I didn't know the value of it—it's a good press—and for a first book of poems, it should be a good beginning. I just didn't care; I was absent-minded. I thought this was an excursion and I would return to China.

WEINBERGER: Return to China and do what?

JIN: To teach.

WEINBERGER: To teach? And not be a writer at all?

JIN: No, to teach. That's why I really didn't take the first book seriously. I didn't know I was supposed to give readings or promote the book. In writers' terms, you should continue to carry on the momentum for the next book. I didn't know anything about that.

WEINBERGER: At what point did you switch to fiction?

JIN: After I was done with the first book. I began to write stories, very slowly. But my major work was to finish my dissertation.

WEINBERGER: Which was on?

JIN: Pound and Yeats and Auden, with reference to the Chinese material.

WEINBERGER: Then Tiananmen happened, and you realized you couldn't go back.

JIN: True. For a long time, I was in shock because everything for me was turned upside down. I had served in the People's Liberation Army. We were funded by the people to serve people, to protect people; that's why we were called the People's Army. I couldn't serve a state like that. At the time, all the schools were owned by the state. So any jobs would have been like a state appointment. I had this kind of strong anger. Also, my son finally came. For years, we'd tried to bring him to the U.S., but his papers couldn't get through and he couldn't get a passport, not to mention a visa. But in the chaos of the Tiananmen massacre, everything went rapidly; people just didn't care. He got all the papers.

WEINBERGER: How old was he?

JIN: He was almost six. But the problem was that neither my wife nor I could go back to get him, so he had to come by himself. That was a risk, but we didn't have a choice. So we let him fly on his own, but he was not allowed to switch planes. My wife and I went to San Francisco to collect him from the airport. When he landed there, I remember clearly that the first thought I had was that he must be American. That was very clear to me—he must be American. I didn't want him to be trapped in a cycle of violence and suffering. I didn't know what to do about my life and what would be the next step. But for him, I would stay here for some years. That's why I went to B.U., to do critical writing as a way to buy time.

WEINBERGER: You became a student at B.U. so you could stay on in the United States?

JIN: Yes, because the United States gave an extended visa and medical insurance to all Chinese students and scholars. I had a child here and I had to be a graduate student otherwise I couldn't find health insurance for the family. That was part of it. It was also to learn how to write fiction. Fortunately, before I finished the degree, Emory University hired me. I think that was a turning point because writing became a matter of survival. If I didn't continue to publish, I couldn't keep the job, obviously.

WEINBERGER: You were working to expand from telegrapher to poet to short-story writer to a writer of short novels—and later to a much longer novel. In this time, what other writers interested you the most? Were there other writers whom you felt in context with or in the company of?

JIN: I was a beginner in poetry. At Emory, I taught poetry writing and poetry courses most of the time. I learned a lot from Frank Bidart. I love poetry and some American poets like Louise Glück and many other contemporary poets. But as I shifted to fiction writing, I began to read more Russian authors—contemporary translations of classical Russian fiction. I was nourished by it. This started even at B.U. We were introduced to Dostoevsky, Chekhov. Chekhov was a big part of it.

WEINBERGER: Gogol also?

JIN: Gogol, yes. So I still carry that kind of education with me.

WEINBERGER: Many people compared *Waiting* to Jane Austen, and *Waiting* reminded me of Henry James in the sense that nothing happens but it's a total page-turner. Were you reading any of these people?

JIN: I'd read their work for my graduate seminars, but I wasn't aware of the influence. But that might be because Turgenev was really like James's teacher almost—they were very close. In fact, Turgenev was a key figure in Western fiction, even in the English language—the sentiment, the sensibility is there. So I did learn a lot from his work.

WEINBERGER: How did you get to *War Trash*—the idea of a big historical novel re-creating that moment in history during the Korean War? And why the Korean War?

JIN: Again, it was out of necessity. I had a contract for *The Bridegroom*, but I hadn't finished the stories yet. My publisher had five or six stories—that's all I had at the time—but they wanted to go ahead and publish the book. I couldn't dissuade them. My wife suggested, "Why don't you write something short but complete to replace it?" At the time, I had been reading books on the Korean War. I didn't have a clear idea about what I was going to do, but I knew quite a bit about that. I'd often told my wife about some episodes and details, and she suggested that I write a book based on the material I had collected. I began to work and thought it would be a hundred and fifty pages long. But it dragged on and on and the first draft was a little over four hundred pages. That rarely happened; most of the time, I wrote the first draft and it was a very skinny thing. During the process of editing and revision, it got thicker and richer, so I always added things.

WEINBERGER: So you're a writer who adds instead of cutting out?

JIN: Yes, I think because I wrote poetry. So I always wrote too condensed; I couldn't expand it much. But this happened in the reverse and I was surprised by it. When I was in the army, we stayed on the border between Russia, China, and Korea and we assumed there was going to be a war. If it happened, few of us would have been able to go back to China. I think most of us feared we'd be captured by the enemy. Once you were caught, either you died or you killed yourself. But if you came back alive, you'd be a disgrace to your family—you would be, in fact, the dregs of society. I think I had seen some form of abuse in China. Soldiers were treated very badly. Suddenly the fear was released in the writing and that drove me to continue.

WEINBERGER: I'm curious that *War Trash* is the memoirs of an old man. I couldn't decide whether I liked that. Whether I wanted to know that he survived all of this, since you know from the first page that it's a memoir. Was that a hard decision to make?

JIN: In a way, yes. But it's also a kind of challenge—giving the outcome of the story away and then suspending the interest of the reader. Also in this form of memoir, the protagonist is supposed to survive. I decided on memoir because, by nature, a memoir is episodic. Whatever is interesting and related to the narrator's life can be included. This really left a lot of space for my research. I think I made the right choice. I read memoirs by the former POWs, Chinese and Americans, that are short, small articles, and the memories are fragmentary. In some cases, the victims wouldn't like to remember. Mostly, they had to please the authorities. There was a strong sense of censorship behind the writing. As a result, it's impossible to find the one person among them who has a complete story. Usually, a POW is captured and put in jail and that's it—his fifty yards of vision is very limited. He doesn't know what's going on outside. That's why I had to create a character who could move around, who could interact with his captors and other factions.

WEINBERGER: He is a kind of unofficial interpreter.

JIN: Yes—that's why I decided on a junior officer able to speak English, needed by different sides. At the same time, he is an outsider. Most of the memoirs I read were very patriotic; they were Commies. They all emphasized their loyalty to the party and they were revolutionaries. The memoirs of the POWs who went to Taiwan always emphasized that they were loyal to the free world. They condemned the Commies and praised the U.S. armies. So I had to have a person who is neutral.

WEINBERGER: That's why you put him in America? So he's writing his memoir from America?

JIN: Yes, but he's supposed to return to China. He's again inside and outside at the same time.

WEINBERGER: I read somewhere that your next book is set in America.

JIN: Yes. It's a very difficult book.

WEINBERGER: I was a little shocked because all of your books after all are based on memory and imagination—a re-creation of China, though you haven't been in China for a long time. It must be very difficult to write about the reality that you're seeing outside the door.

JIN: You're right, I haven't returned to China for twenty years. I'm unfamiliar with the current situation. Also, as I continue, I don't feel I'm that attached to China as a subject anymore. When I started, I was quite naïve. I went to the Harvard library, where, in the basement, they stored all the old journals and magazines and newspapers. Very few people would use them. They were just piled there. I remember I saw them, the piles, and I was moved. I thought my job would be simple: to translate history into literature. Writing about China book after book, I thought my life would be spent that way. But, as I continued, it was not the case. I think there was a deep alienation. I think the English language played some role in this because I'm writing about China in English. All the setting and subjects are Chinese. This put me in limbo—trapped between two languages and two cultures. That's one of the reasons I wanted to liberate myself.

There's another reason. The American immigrant experience is closer to me, to my heart, as a subject. But of course there are consequences; it's a huge hurdle for me to jump. That means I have to resolve a lot of the things I already worked out for a novel or story set in China. Even the language has to be changed to some extent.

WEINBERGER: What's your status in China? Are your books published in China?

JIN: Only *Waiting* is published there. I don't think the others can be published. Some books, maybe, but books like *The Crazed* and *War Trash* would be absolutely impossible.

WEINBERGER: And you haven't been back?

JIN: In the first ten years, I tried and I couldn't have my passport renewed. Then I became a citizen; I wasn't eager anymore.

WEINBERGER: You have no desire to go back?

JIN: Sure, but I don't feel comfortable to go back. For me, it's personal. I would like to see the Chinese government apologize for the Tiananmen massacre and before that happens, it would be very hard for me to go. That event really shaped my life, changed my life. For me, it's personal, not public trauma.

WEINBERGER: I'm sure you'll never see the moment when the Chinese government apologizes for Tiananmen.

JIN: I don't know. I think it's possible. It's hard. You can't depend on a government like that. It is very capricious; you don't know what would happen next. As a result, it's better to hold on to my own principle, my own work, and live my own life.

TSITSI DANGAREMBGA

INAPPROPRIATE APPROPRIATION

A Believer *Event*

RICK MOODY: I think the pressing question of the PEN World Voices Festival is "Why, exactly, are we bothering?" The United States of America has become a culture that exports and no longer imports. If I were to project up here a graph of literature in translation published in the United States, you would see, over the last twenty-five years, a steep decline in the number of titles published in this country in translation. It's now hovering near the 5 percent mark of the twenty thousand–odd books published annually in this country, and that includes engineering manuals and the like. So in terms of literature, the art of what we do in language, an infinitesimal number of books are being published in English. Personally, I think that's political. I think it has a lot to do with a general trend in the culture away from intellectual investigation and toward a kind of recoiling from the rest of the world.

That's what I'm going to try to address with these panelists tonight. *The Believer* came up with a great topic for the discussion: the rules of cross-cultural appropriation. The late '70s and early '80s, when I was first writing, was a period when identity politics was as forceful as it ever got. And there was a real unwritten law that certain kinds of cultural appropriation were not to be done. In other words, a man writing first person from a woman's point of view was considered faintly distasteful and inadvisable; a white writer trying to write from a black point of view was considered inadvisable; a first-world writer writing about the third world—same kind of thing. That has loosened up a bit, I think, these days. Imagination is given a slightly freer rein, but in a cultural context, literature is taken less seriously and translation barely happens in this country at all.

Chimamanda, do you think that there are rules of cross-cultural appropriation or rules for composition in fiction at all? Your novel *Purple Hibiscus* was written in English and seems, even though it's about post-colonial Nigeria, influenced in some ways by Western novel writing, and I'm curious if you thought about that while you were writing it.

CHIMAMANDA NGOZI ADICHIE: First of all, I'm ambivalent about the idea of rules when it comes to literature because I think that fiction, and literature in general, should be magical and you should let yourself be free. But going back to your examples of cross-cultural appropriation—men writing from the point of view of women and white people writing from the point of view of black people not being seen as good—I think it's important to keep things in context. I come from a place that for a long time has been grossly misrepresented by people who have written about it. When I read a book about Africa by a non-African, I'm very careful and oftentimes resentful because I think that people go into Africa and bend the reality of Africa to fit their preconceived notions. I think the same could be said for writing about women when you're a man, writing about blackness when you're white, and while I think such writing should be done, it requires sensitivity. It's easy to say that we should do whatever we want because we're writing fiction, but it's also important to remember context and to be circumspect.

MOODY: Chimamanda, can you give us examples of works where you feel the representation issue is particularly troubling?

ADICHIE: *The Shadow of the Sun* by Ryszard Kapuściński has a little blurb on the cover that describes it as the greatest intelligence to bear on Africa since Conrad. And I really was insulted by that, because it isn't the greatest intelligence to bear on Africa, and I didn't think, by the way, that Conrad was particularly writing Africa as Africa was. What's troubling is that this claim sets the norm for how we see Africa: If you're going to walk in Africa, you're told to read that book to understand Africa. But this is really not what Africa is, at least not from the point of view of Africans in Africa, which I think is an important point of view. These books distort reality—there are many examples. Maybe I shouldn't name names because it's less about the specific people and more about the larger phenomenon of writing without an open mind.

MOODY: So there are some rules in some cases, or at least sensitivities that we have to think about in these moments when we try to write about other cultures.

PATRICK ROTH: I feel we have to judge case by case. I mean, there is a novel, *Amerika*, by Franz Kafka, and you're not going to tell me that he wasn't allowed to write about America. A couple of years ago, I read about a German writer who supposedly wrote a novel that took place in the former East German Republic and I thought that was wonderful. When I read it, I thought, That's a great idea, because we all had fantasies about the East German Republic at the time. Why wouldn't it be legit for us to broach that subject? Why not write a novel from the point of view of a woman, using the female part in yourself as a man—I mean, why not? Who would want to put a limit on that? It would be literary suicide to limit yourself in that case.

MOODY: Isn't it true that Kafka had never been to America when he wrote *Amerika*?

ROTH: That's the whole point. Exactly.

MOODY: So it's all about imagination.

TSITSI DANGAREMBGA: I'm not sure whether it's all about imagination because imagination is informed. How is general imagination about Africa informed in this part of the world? I agree with Chimamanda that there must be some limits. A young lady in my part of the world, in South Africa, wrote a short story about a maid on her Sunday off. This young lady was a white South African. She went to one of the best schools, which meant she must have been one of the top 10 percent in terms of earning power—upper class—and she chooses to have, as her character, a lower-class African maid. What could she possibly know about this person? The writer was so young, she obviously hadn't had the chance to think about the implications of what she was doing, but it seemed to her like the kind of story that would win her acclaim, which it did: She got a prize in a short-story competition. But the way she represented this character was so completely false.

I had the same experience some years ago when a writer from this country wrote about a girl in my part of the world. She named this girl Nhamo, a word that means negative things in many contexts, but especially in the sense of grief. The title of this book about Nhamo was *A Girl Named Disaster*. Now, grief and trouble: There are similarities, but the essence—the nuances—are quite different.

Interestingly enough, this book was translated into German and the German translators had some qualms, so they asked me to read the book and write a foreword, which I did. I gave my opinion that actually the translation of this word that was the girl's name, Nhamo, was not adequate in the title. Of course they had to go back to the writer to ask her to endorse my foreword and she refused. As a Zimbabwean who understands what the German people were trying to do, and the English, I had said, "Well, let's put a preface to this that would give it a different context," and the writer refused. I think that kind of cross-cultural appropriation is really illegitimate, but there is no way to stop it. There are no rules to cross-cultural appropriation.

ADICHIE: I want to respond to Patrick. I'm not at all advocating limiting anybody or anything—not at all. As I said, I really don't believe in rules. A writer like John Gregory Brown, who is somebody I really admire, has written a book from the point of view of a woman, which I believed as a woman. But at the same time, I do think that it's too easy to simply say, "Why not? Why not use the imagination? Why not let the imagination run free?" I think there is something to be said for authenticity, that if you're going to write about a particular experience in specifics, then the least you can do is to learn about it.

MINAE MIZUMURA: Can I just shift the topic? Right now, people are using the word "appropriation" and supposing that the people who appropriate are the dominant people—white people appropriating black discourse or African discourse or men appropriating women's discourse, et cetera. The verb "appropriate" has a force that makes you believe it's the dominant subject who is doing it. Yet if you look at the history of humanity from two or three thousand years back, it's the *dominated* cultures that do the appropriating. I'm thinking of Japanese literature: Twenty years after major restorations, we appropriated Western literature, and that became our literature, and we transformed ourselves through the literature. That sort of asymmetrical process still continues and, one hundred years later, we continue to appropriate American culture.

Now, when a Japanese writer is writing in Japanese, she might use a certain alphabet for Japanese characters that was once used only for Western names, because it sounds more modern, more American, more global, more international. The ironic fact is that this literature that appropriates American literature but doesn't really speak truth about Japan is what gets reappropriated into America, because it's the easiest to translate. What I think is the best of Japanese literature hardly ever gets translated. It's the easiest and the already appropriated Japanese literature that gets reappropriated.

DANGAREMBGA: I would argue also that in the term "appropriation," there is a notion of force. If a person is assimilating a literature—for example, Francophone Africans were assimilated into the French culture—can we then say that they have appropriated the culture? I think being assimilated and having your culture appropriated are two different things.

In Zimbabwe now we have two opposed parties: one very nationalist and one more, according to Western norms, liberal. I was talking to some younger people in this liberal party and I said to them, "Do you know what you're taking on? We are veterans; we've been through the whole colonial rigmarole. Do you know what we are taking on?" And I quoted to them this limerick: "There was a young lady of Niger / Who rode on the back of a tiger / They came back from the ride with the lady inside / And a smile on the face of the tiger." They said, "Yes, Tsitsi, we know the West is a tiger, but we think we're strong enough—we can tame the tiger." This is in the same sense of not understanding the difference between appropriation and assimilation. Perhaps we think we are appropriating, but we are actually being assimilated. This is problematic—we need to know where we stand so that we can have authentic voices. It's a kind of alienation if you think you're appropriating and actually you're being assimilated; your voice cannot be authentic.

KATJA LANGE-MÜLLER: I can understand this only indirectly. The question seems backward. The question for me as a writer is not "May I do this?" but "Can I do this?" Whether I manage to portray a man is not my decision. This is what the reader decides. If I practice a self-censorship, which says, "May I do this at all?" I might as well stop writing.

DANGAREMBGA: I agree entirely. The audience decides. But between you, the creator, and the audience, there is a third party. This third party is the people who have the power, the money, the distribution resources—they physically get your work out there. If you present your work to these people and they say, "This is no good," simply because they feel that a woman should not be writing it, how are you going to get your work out there? Look at nineteenth-century British writers like George Eliot. They did not even dare to appear physically in front of their publishers because they knew they wouldn't get published.

Maybe in Germany, the situation is better, but for those people in the world who are still being appropriated, that situation still pertains. For example, a Zimbabwean writer like Chenjerai Hove, who made his name with a novel called *Bones* about a woman spirit medium, was only celebrated because people said, "Wow! He's writing in a woman's voice!" at a time when there were not so many women writers. But how many women writers like that novel, or even women readers? Very few. We have to understand the interval between creative work and the fact of that creative work getting out there. Many cultural and economic decisions prevent voices from being heard.

MOODY: I agree with that. That's how we find ourselves in this country with a paucity of translated literature.

LANGE-MÜLLER: I started writing in a country where what was published and what was not published was really a political decision because it was the GDR. Writers who were suspect wondered while writing whether they would be published or not. One can say that one does compromise because one does think about the readers, but in reality, those compromises were not convincing as literature.

MOODY: I want to move to a hidden subtext in this. Globalization and the economic climate in which we find ourselves suppress local culture in favor of a strange corporate über-culture. I want to address myself to Yoko, who is Japanese and has lived in Japan and yet writes in Germany, and has written in German as well. I'm interested in your own experience of cross-cultural thinking and if you function now in a global context or if you still think of yourself as a local writer.

YOKO TAWADA: I don't think that at this point it is possible to even talk about Japanese literature or culture because that culture has already absorbed so many others, like the Chinese or Western cultures. The same is true for American culture, which has absorbed other cultures from all over the world. All cultures at this point are pluralist, and we who live in these cultures don't belong to just one culture but to many. This does not mean that everything is the same; there are many differences. But you cannot pin them down nationally. One can only take the differences between, say, German culture and American culture as a way to differentiate between these literatures. Kafka could write the book *Amerika* because America itself is a fiction.

MIZUMURA: I still think that's idealistic. I understand what Yoko means: Every culture is an amalgam of others. But, for example, I have a grandmother who was a geisha. Now, this is a very good topic for a writer to exploit. She eloped with a man twenty-five years younger because she couldn't stand her life. I have this topic and still haven't done anything with it, but I want to write about it. I have a choice between whether to write it realistically and interestingly for myself, using all the historical context and proper names that people outside Japan would never understand and all the contours of the Japanese society, which only Japanese readers would understand, or whether to come up with something like *Memoirs of a Geisha*, which became a best-seller a few years ago. If you want your book to be translated, which I think a lot of authors do, you face these concrete problems: whether you make it more accessible to the global audience, or you don't care, you just want it to be your own thing.

DANGAREMBGA: If I could say something to Minae personally: People who care would like the version that you care about. At the end of the day, it's a question of money: Do you want your money now or do you want a legacy that remains for years?

I want to come back to the idea of appropriation and Kafka daring to write a novel called *Amerika*—there you are. But let's say *I* decided to write a novel called *Amerika*—who would publish it? I'm not just talking off the top of my head here because I've had this experience. *Nervous Conditions* is now recognized as a good novel, but what did it take to get it published? All Zimbabwean publishing houses, which were run by men at that time, turned me down, and it took a women's organization with a South African woman at the head to pick up that novel.

Between the time of writing the novel and continuing with my life, I did other things, and now I find I'm in the same situation with filmmaking. I turned to filmmaking because I thought writing wasn't working, not knowing that actually it was working, and I have the same problem with film. I've just made a film and people turned it down—Sundance eventually picked it up, but the National Arts Merits Awards in Zimbabwe said it was confused and substandard. We use certain criteria when it comes to judging on a public scale, which really do not always have to do with the merit of the work.

ROTH: This is a way of looking at things that's foreign to me. You write your stuff; you're alone with your psyche, which does not give a damn about whether your book is going to get published, does not give a damn about whether it's going to make money. If you get caught in these questions, you're not going to be able to write—or your writing is not going to be worth anything. It's not a question of whether I should, whether I may, whether I can, artistically speaking, it's whether I *must*, whether I'm actually compelled to. The writing process, as far as I'm concerned, is about pushing myself to the point where I can only do this one thing, and I absolutely have to do this one thing—otherwise life would not proceed for me. I could not care less at that point about who's going to publish it, is anyone going to like it, is so-and-so going to understand this or that. That is of absolutely no concern to me. I think it is pure poison.

ADICHIE: I find it particularly curious that here in the United States, there's such a thing as a black section of the bookstore—that it's really about what you look like. If I wrote a book about Poland, for example, I would still end up in the black section of the bookstores. There are still categories.

When I was trying to get an agent for *Purple Hibiscus*, I got a really nice response from a woman who said she liked the book very much but she didn't know how to sell me. She said, "You're black, but you're not African American, so I can't sell you as African American, and I can't sell you as ethnic, because right now in the United States, ethnic is Indian." So I considered becoming Indian for a short while.

MOODY: One of the effects of globalization is massive vertical integration of American publishing companies. Twenty years ago, there were two or three times as many publishers as there are now.

In line with this vertical integration comes unwillingness to take risks in terms of what gets published, and this is concurrent with a refining and dumbing down of the critical vocabulary in the country. Globalization selects for a certain kind of aesthetic. In American fiction, we're generally selecting for naturalism against an experimental impulse. We're left with a narrow bandwidth. Is there a similar process happening globally?

DANGAREMBGA: I think it's definitely happening globally. If you look at Zimbabwe, the culture that travels is the culture that people here know, and that culture is not being subsidized by Zimbabweans. The Zimbabwean government hasn't got that much money, so it subsidizes culture that's locally consumed. The culture that travels is generally subsidized by bodies from outside the country that very definitely have an agenda. We see that narrowing process.

As Americans, you don't have to think you're the baddest people in the world. I know that Germans used to think they were, but now maybe Americans think they take that position. But no. Just the fact that there's a gathering like this means that there are still sensitivities out there that we can put to good use. We just need to keep linking up in this kind of forum.

MIZUMURA: You're constantly reminded of the fact that just because what you're writing is different, so remote from what the global market wants, it's not going to be translated. My first book is a continuation of a Japanese classic and I knew from the start that it would never be translated. To have the feeling and write it is sad, because I read in English all the time and I love reading in English. I love Jane Austen, for example, and the people who enjoy Jane Austen would, I'm sure, enjoy my work if they could read in Japanese, but it's not going to get translated.

DANGAREMBGA: But then isn't the problem, "Who are you writing for?" I've had that problem in the reverse in that I have been so pressed to write things that I know European audiences would like, and I'm very capable at that. I kept on having to say, "No, I'm not going to write it until my authentic voice comes back."

MIZUMURA: I think our problem is a little different because you're writing in English.

ROTH: These are just opinions, like a filmmaker talking about his camera when he would really like to show you the film.

DANGAREMBGA: I disagree. I'm having a wonderful time here, and for me, these are issues of life and death.

I've taken to you, Patrick, so I didn't want to say this when you began to speak, but the very fact that you have the luxury to say "I'm not going to write anything unless I write my authentic voice" is something that most people in my country cannot afford to do. We have the British coming in, saying "Write this, write that, go on television, say this, say that, tell people how you've been tortured." People do it because they are hungry. Why are they hungry? It is not because the land has been taken over. It is because in the aftermath of the land being taken over, all aid was frozen. There was an embargo. That's why people are hungry. If we had fertilizer, if we had money for seed, people would not be hungry. We haven't got the luxury of that, we really have not got it. We have to fiddle to the master's tune and some of us are trying not to do that, and we take advantage of audiences like this to harangue people and say, "Please, think differently."

REINVENTING HOME

Michael Ondaatje and Chimamanda Ngozi Adichie

MICHAEL ONDAATJE: In *Purple Hibiscus*, on the acknowledgments page at the end, there's a wonderful sense of community—I almost want you to read that because it feels like part of the book. Can you talk about the community that helped you with this book? Was it in Nigeria or in the United States or both?

CHIMAMANDA NGOZI ADICHIE: It was both. My family, of course. I have a younger brother who read the drafts and who was there when I was very depressed after I got rejections. I have friends who are readers, who would read my work, and I have parents who think that everything I write is wonderful—a huge lie, of course. I think I'm very lucky to have people who are supportive and a large family network and friends and cousins and friends of cousins. They all see my success as something collective. After I was shortlisted for the Orange, for example, when I went back home, people said, "*We* will win next time."

Actually, I read your acknowledgments as well in *The English Patient*, which I think I might copy for my next book.

ONDAATJE: They get longer and longer, my acknowledgments. I've started to put in books I've never even read. How long did the novel take to write?

ADICHIE: It took about a year and a half to do the draft.

ONDAATJE: That's too short. No, no—it's perfect.

ADICHIE: Well, to do the first draft, and then of course I had to do edits and rewrites and that sort of thing.

ONDAATJE: Were you in the U.S. when you were writing that book?

ADICHIE: I was. I was in my senior year of college and very homesick, very nostalgic. I really wanted to sort of reinvent Nigeria in this book, which I think I did. If I'd written the book in Nigeria, it would have been very different.

ONDAATJE: Do you feel you could have written it in Nigeria?

ADICHIE: Not this book, no. It would have been different. I drew a lot of the mood of the book from my sense of being homesick and nostalgic. When I'm homesick, I'm given to idealizing things and suddenly the rains smell like perfume and that sort of thing.

ONDAATJE: That part is idealized, but certainly none of the politics or the family life or the family drama.

ADICHIE: Before I wrote *Purple Hibiscus*, I'd written a book that just wasn't working and wasn't very good. It was about the United States, about Nigerians who were here and the immigrant experience—I'd wanted to write a Nigerian book. I wanted to deal with Nigerian issues. I think it's impossible to write a contemporary novel about Nigeria without having to deal with politics. Everything's political. And religion is huge in Nigeria. As the economy gets worse, people turn to religion and it becomes increasingly unreasonable, and I wanted to write about that as well.

ONDAATJE: You were telling me you've written some essays on religion in Nigeria today.

ADICHIE: We have a wave of very materialistic fundamentalist Christianity in Nigeria. It's the sort of Christianity in which you have pastors who are sleek and rich who tell you that God wants you to have a Mercedes-Benz—that's God's plan for you. Of course this works because life is difficult and the economy is getting worse. This Christianity also gets conservative in strange ways: People talk about prohibiting women from wearing short skirts in public because God finds it offensive. In my opinion, this just deflects attention from the issues we really should be talking about.

I wrote an essay once about how I feel that this Christianity is anti-woman and anti-truth because we're not dealing with what we should deal with. What's interesting is that when you talk about things like that in Nigeria, you're seen as devilish—"The devil is using you!" Very little debate is going on. People say, "God will save Nigeria!" Nobody's really doing anything to save Nigeria because God is supposed to descend and save us. It's getting worse, which I find worrying. I wrote another piece just before I left Nigeria, which hasn't been published but will be in one of the newspapers, about how we need to stop talking God and start acting God. Very few people are happy about it, of course. People say, "She has been corrupted by the West!"

ONDAATJE: So when did you first come to North America? Some of your family are living here now?

ADICHIE: I have a sister who lives here. I used to visit when I was much younger because my father would teach one semester in universities here, mostly in California at San Diego State. I spent summers with him and then I'd go back to Nigeria. I actually came here to live and go to school when I was about nineteen and that was different. I was older and there was more culture shock.

ONDAATJE: Do you think this double vision has been helpful to you? Having a perspective from the United States as well as from Nigeria?

ADICHIE: Absolutely. I think I would be an entirely different person if I hadn't come here. Things that I question now, I sometimes wonder if I would question if I hadn't left home. Things I celebrate and enjoy, I wonder if I would do so with the same passion if I hadn't left home. I came to the United States and suddenly I'm interested in things like identity that I never thought about when I was back in Nigeria.

ONDAATJE: *Purple Hibiscus* is about the process of the narrator, the young girl who tells the story, learning to ask questions. There's almost a running line where she says, "I wish I had said that," when her brother says something or accuses somebody of something. She says, "I wish I had said that" or "I wish I had done that," and gradually, by the last part of the book, she's actually doing it. That is a question that evolves in the book.

ADICHIE: Yes, although the narrator is nothing like me, so I worry when I get questions of this sort.

ONDAATJE: Let me put it another way: It's traditional to accuse the first novel of being autobiographical, and you have in this book an amazing patri-arch, a father who is devastating and complex and a mother who is essentially controlled by him for most of the book. Your father was a teacher and your mother was in administration at the university. So there's a distinction there.

Anything else you would say about that?

ADICHIE: I'm very aware that when you're relatively young and you write a novel, it's immediately assumed to be your story, and I didn't want that to happen. My life is fairly boring, so I couldn't possibly write about it anyway. I wanted to write about a family that was different from mine, about a narrator who was so different from me that I would then be in a position to free her. I think having a narrator who is very much like you sometimes leads to censorship. I have tried to write about somebody like me and I can't just let the character go. I think, No, I can't let her do that because I have to protect myself. Kambili is unlike me in that she's voiceless and shy and almost self-hating. There's a self-hating element to the dynamics of the family also, which just doesn't exist in my family. My family is, unfortunately, very normal. It's not colorful and interesting like yours in *Running in the Family*.

ONDAATJE: That's all invented too, actually.

ADICHIE: It's invented?

ONDAATJE: You think this is autobiographical, the kind of stuff I write?

ADICHIE: No, no, no. I thought *Running in the Family* was based on your family. Wasn't it?

ONDAATJE: It was my family exaggerated, I think.

ADICHIE: But at least the kernels existed. I couldn't possibly do that with my family because we're boring and normal and ordinary.

ONDAATJE: Well, I just don't believe that.

ADICHIE: When I was told that I was going to do this conversation with you, of course I was terribly excited, and I was worried that I would pass out in a faint. In case I do, please understand it's because I'm very much in awe of your work. I think particularly of the beauty of your language. When I read as a writer, I try to imagine how it's done. How did he come up with this? It's the effortlessness of your prose. It's almost as if it just flows out. I wanted to know how you do it. I wanted to know if you work in drafts. Do you, for example, write the story first and then go back to turn it into art, so to speak?

ONDAATJE: First of all, there's nothing effortless. I find that my first drafts are deadly. I write a first draft without any kind of plan at all. If I'm working on a novel, I don't have a sense of what the novel is about. I'm not sure who all the characters will be. I'm not sure what's going to happen. I begin with the germ of an incident perhaps.

ADICHIE: What was the germ in *Anil's Ghost*?

ONDAATJE: That was a tough one because I wanted to write about the situation in Sri Lanka and I knew that everyone I talked to had a different point of view. In the end, I decided I had to write it as a double-barreled narration, so I had to have Anil and Sarath joined at the hip and arguing as they went through the whole novel. It was the idea of two people in a car traveling and not fully agreeing with each other. It was like a road movie in some ways. Gradually, more and more people entered the book. I also thought that if Anil had been brought up in Sri Lanka and educated in the West and then gone back there on a political mission of sorts, she would discover that she didn't really know the country she was from—that idea of the insider who had become an outsider because of living in the West. But that was less of a germ than a usual thing, which is an image of somebody talking to somebody else at night, as in *The English Patient*: a patient in a bed talking to a nurse.

ADICHIE: So that was the germ for *The English Patient*?

ONDAATJE: That was one of the germs—germs anyway, not gems. But what happens for me is I go back and rewrite many, many times. As I rewrite, everything gets honed down and seems casual as well as not being repetitive. It's not a very easy thing for me to write at a leisurely pace.

ADICHIE: So the rewritings then are sort of general? You don't have rewritings where you focus on the language?

ONDAATJE: No, I don't think about the language at all. I worry more about what's going to happen next. When I'm actually writing the scene, I let the language take care of itself. I'm more interested in discovering what's occurring in the two or three characters I'm writing about. The main energy for me when I'm writing is to discover character as opposed to writing well. When I'm editing, I cut out all the repetitions and so forth.

When you were growing up, did you read a lot of books from the West?

ADICHIE: I grew up reading a lot of British children's books.

ONDAATJE: Enid Blyton?

ADICHIE: She was my favorite for a long time. I think it has a lot to do with the British colonial exercise that we all had Enid Blyton. I just adored her work, and when I started to write as a child, I was writing the sorts of stories that I was reading. There were white people eating apples and playing in the snow, although I had never seen snow at the time. There weren't many books by African writers at the time, and I didn't read any until I was about ten.

ONDAATJE: That's not bad—a lot of people don't read books by people in their own country until they're about thirty.

ADICHIE: I was lucky. I lived on a university campus so I had access to books. The writer who has ended up being most important to me, Chinua Achebe, happened to live on the university campus as well. Generally, I would have been a bit older before I got to read books that had people like me in them.

ONDAATJE: I've noticed when I go back to Sri Lanka that I'm really from an oral tradition as opposed to a written tradition. Do you find that?

ADICHIE: Absolutely. I'm often struck by a sense of loss, really, because our traditions are oral and because I think the advent of colonialism and Westernization was a break. The oral traditions are almost dying and we don't have a bridge between the two. People are writing now, but the oral traditions aren't being recorded. Sometimes I try to write stories that have that oral flavor to them and I don't know if I get it right. There's something sad about it for me.

ONDAATJE: I know you're working on a novel right now. When you are researching or writing, are you talking to people, listening to people about a certain period of time?

ADICHIE: The novel in progress is relatively historical; it's set in the '60s during a very difficult time in Nigerian history—in Biafra just before and during the war. People who lived through it—my parents and their friends and my uncles and cousins particularly—have incredible stories about what they went through, about really tiny things that I find so moving. I can't help but think about how these stories will be lost because I can't use all of them. I'm overwhelmed by the things I've discovered. There's something humbling about it. So yes, I am talking to lots of people and struck by how we have a tradition of passing stories down that's dying because it's not being used.

ONDAATJE: When I was researching *Running in the Family*, I tried to find books about the '30s and '40s, and there was nothing. I think I found one diary; one uncle had a diary—he was the only one who'd put pen to paper. The real tradition of storytelling came at dinner. That was when people talked and lied and lied more strongly.

A quote of yours: "Nigeria is truly crumbling and I don't know if it will come back together." Do you remember saying this?

ADICHIE: No, but I think it's true. Nigeria is crumbling. I worry about the future of Nigeria because we haven't quite decided on what basis we are a country. There's talk about a national conference so that people from all sorts of ethnic groups and religions will sit down and talk. It's not happening, and ethnic nationalism is on the rise. For example, I see myself first as an Igbo woman rather than a Nigerian. Many people who are Yoruba see themselves first as Yoruba. There are cracks, and I hope that the country won't implode. I worry about Nigeria's future.

ONDAATJE: *Purple Hibiscus* focuses mostly on a family and is narrated by the daughter, and yet the story is told in a very distinct political time and the family's drama is mirrored by the political drama outside, even though in no way is the book heavily symbolic or metaphorical. Can you talk a little about the political situation of that specific time of the novel?

ADICHIE: What I did was merge two of the regimes. It's set in the early '90s, but I've also merged the regime that was there in the late '80s. In the late '80s, we had Babangida, then later we had Abacha. For many Nigerians, this was a time of silence, when you couldn't speak out; you had to be very careful what you said. I used a number of things that actually did happen in *Purple Hibiscus*: the newspaper editor who is killed—that happened in '85. Newspapers were shut down; people were afraid.

In the small university town where I grew up, lecturers would come together to talk and they were fiercely pro-freedom, anti-military, but it was all said in a hush-hush way: "Nothing should go past this room because we don't want to be arrested." It was an unpleasant time in our history. I wanted to write about it because there is fictional potential in that kind of setting, but also because I think it's central to what Nigeria is. The fact that we have had a series of military regimes is central to the way we are today. Now we have, ostensibly, a democracy, but our president used to be head of state in the '70s and we still have a military way of thinking. We haven't quite understood that we are the ones who own Nigeria. We still think our president owns Nigeria and that he gets to decide for us. We've been brainwashed by having so many military regimes. I was very keen to give a sense of what it was like.

ONDAATJE: I think it would be great if you read a section from the book.

ADICHIE: I'll just read from the beginning, though it doesn't do much for the politics:

> Things started to fall apart at home when my brother, Jaja, did not go to communion and Papa flung his heavy missal and broke the figurines on the *étagère*. We had just returned from church. Mama placed the fresh palm fronds, which were wet with holy water, on the dining table and then went upstairs to change. Later, she would knot the palm fronds into sagging cross shapes and hang them on the wall beside our gold-framed family photo. They would stay there until next Ash Wednesday, when we would take the fronds to church, to have them burned for ash. Papa, wearing a long, gray robe like the rest of the oblates, helped distribute ash every year. His line moved the slowest because he pressed hard on each forehead to make a perfect cross with his ash-covered thumb and slowly, meaningfully enunciated every word of "dust and unto dust you shall return."
>
> Papa always sat in the front pew for Mass, at the end beside the middle aisle, with Mama, Jaja, and me sitting next to him. He was first to receive communion. Most people did not kneel to receive communion at the marble altar, with the blond life-size Virgin Mary mounted nearby, but Papa did. He would hold his eyes shut so hard that his face tightened into a grimace, and then he would stick his tongue out as far as it could go. Afterward, he sat back on his seat and watched the rest of the congregation troop to the altar, palms pressed together and extended, like a saucer held sideways, just as Father Benedict had taught them to do. Even though Father Benedict had been at St. Agnes for seven years, people still referred to him as "our new priest." Perhaps they would not have if he had not been white. He still looked new. The colors of his face, the colors of condensed milk and a cut-open soursop, had not tanned at all in the fierce heat of seven Nigerian harmattans. And his British nose was still as pinched

and as narrow as it always was, the same nose that had had me worried that he did not get enough air when he first came to Enugu. Father Benedict had changed things in the parish, such as insisting that the Credo and Kyrie be recited only in Latin; Igbo was not acceptable. Also, hand clapping was to be kept at a minimum, lest the solemnity of Mass be compromised. But he allowed offertory songs in Igbo; he called them native songs, and when he said "native" his straight-line lips turned down at the corners to form an inverted U. During his sermons, Father Benedict usually referred to the pope, Papa, and Jesus—in that order. He used Papa to illustrate the gospels. "When we let our light shine before men, we are reflecting Christ's Triumphant Entry," he said that Palm Sunday. "Look at Brother Eugene. He could have chosen to be like other Big Men in this country; he could have decided to sit at home and do nothing after the coup, to make sure the government did not threaten his businesses. But no, he used the *Standard* to speak the truth even though it meant the paper lost advertising. Brother Eugene spoke out for freedom. How many of us have stood up for the truth? How many of us have reflected the Triumphant Entry?"

The congregation said "Yes" or "God bless him" or "Amen," but not too loudly so they would not sound like the mushroom Pentecostal churches; then they listened intently, quietly. Even the babies stopped crying, as if they, too, were listening. On some Sundays, the congregation listened closely even when Father Benedict talked about things everybody already knew, about Papa making the biggest donations to Peter's pence and St. Vincent de Paul. Or about Papa paying for the cartons of communion wine, for the new ovens at the convent where the Reverend Sisters baked the host, for the new wing to St. Agnes Hospital where Father Benedict gave extreme unction. And I would sit with my knees pressed together, next to Jaja, trying hard to keep my face blank, to keep the pride from showing, because Papa said modesty was very important.

ONDAATJE: Thank you. There's a wonderful portrait of that rich society, too. There's a bit when they're going away: "Papa stood by the hibiscuses, giving directions, one hand sunk in the pocket of his white tunic, while the others pointed from item to car. 'The suitcases go in the Mercedes, and those vegetables also. The yams will go in the Peugeot 505, with the cases of Remy-Martin and cartons of juice. See if the stacks of *okporoko* will fit in, too. The bags of rice and *garri* and beans and plantains go in the Volvo.'" So this was a family trip.

ADICHIE: It's very much what it's like when people go back to their ancestral villages to spend Christmas. It's an incredible movement of food and people. When you're on the highway and you're driving, the cars are zipping past you and they're so heavy that they're low because they're just stacked with yams.

I was reading something about you and one of the images in *Anil's Ghost*—the Buddhist image of being unearthed, of being buried and being found. I read somewhere that you said this was a metaphor for human life.

ONDAATJE: I think I was talking about a book of poems I wrote called *Handwriting*. When I first started to write about what was happening in Sri Lanka, it came out in poems. I was with a close friend, an archaeologist, when there was the unearthing of Buddhist statues. Suddenly, that became metaphorical for the violence and burials of humans that had been happening.

ADICHIE: So are you aware of metaphor and intended metaphor as you write? Were you aware of this as a metaphor as you wrote or is it something that you realize as you look back?

ONDAATJE: I'm not very conscious of the metaphor. There are always accidental metaphors, and in fact, those are the best, I think—accidental similes and metaphors and parallels. When you are in the process of editing, you start going through your work and seeing where the metaphor is too heavy-handed or maybe insufficiently depicted. One of the editorial things you do is disguise a lot of things, if you can, and not say so much. You pull back so the book will be suggestive rather than blatant.

ADICHIE: I think your work is beautifully suggestive. One of the powerful things about *Anil's Ghost*, and also *The English Patient*, is how much is left unsaid. I sometimes wished I could reach into the book and pull out more information. Will you read from *Anil's Ghost*?

ONDAATJE:

It was 1 A.M. when Sarath and Anil arrived in the center of Colombo, having driven through the city's empty grey streets. As they got to the Emergency Services, she said, "Is it okay? Us moving him like this?"

"It's okay. We're taking him to my brother. With luck he'll be somewhere there in Emergency."

"You have a brother here?"

Sarath parked and was still for a moment. "God, I'm exhausted."

"Do you want to stay here and sleep? I can take him in."

"It's okay. I'd better talk to my brother anyway. If he's there."

Gunesena was asleep and they woke him and walked him between them into the building. Sarath spoke to someone at the desk and the three of them sat down to wait, Gunesena's hands on his lap like a boxer's. There was a daylight sense of work going on around Admissions, though everyone moved in slow motion and quietly. A man in a striped shirt came towards them and chatted with Sarath.

"This is Anil."

The man in the striped shirt nodded at her.

"My brother, Gamini."

"Right," she said, flatly.

"He's my younger brother—he's our doctor."

There had been no touching between him and Sarath, not a handshake.

"Come—" Gamini helped Gunesena to his feet and they all followed him into a small room. Gamini unstoppered a bottle and began swabbing the man's palms. She noticed he wasn't wearing gloves, not even a lab coat. It looked as if he had just come from an interrupted card game. He injected the anesthetic into the man's hands.

"I didn't know he had a brother," she said, breaking the silence.

"Oh we don't see much of each other. I don't speak of him either, you know. We go our own way."

"He knew you were here, though, and what shift you were on."

"I suppose so."

They were both intentionally excluding Sarath from their conversation.

"How long have you been working with him?" Gamini now asked.

She said, "Three weeks."

"Your hands—they are steady," Sarath said. "Have you recovered?"

"Yes." Gamini turned to Anil. "I'm the family secret."

He pulled the bridge nails from Gunesena's anesthetized hands. Then he washed them with Betalima, a crimson sudsing fluid that he squirted out of a plastic bottle. He dressed the wounds and talked quietly to his patient. He was very gentle, which for some reason surprised her. He pulled open a drawer, got another disposable needle and gave him a tetanus shot. "You owe the hospital two needles," he murmured to Sarath. "There's a shop on the corner. You should get them while I sign out." He led Sarath and Anil out of the room, leaving the patient behind.

'There are no beds left here tonight. Not for this level of injury. See, even crucifixion isn't a major assault nowadays. . . . If you can't take him home I'll find someone to watch him while he sleeps out in Admissions—I'll okay it, I mean."

"He can come with us," Sarath said. "If he wants I'll get him a job as a driver."

"You better replace those needles. I'm going off duty soon. Do you want to eat? Along the Galle Face?" He was talking again to Anil.

"It's two in the morning!" Sarath said.

She spoke up. "Yes. Sure."

He nodded at her.

Gamini pulled open the passenger-side door and got in beside his brother, which left Anil in the back seat with Gunesena. Well, she'd have a better view of both of them.

ADICHIE: What ends up happening to Sarath—did you know it would happen, or did it surprise you?

ONDAATJE: I didn't know it was going to happen. About two-thirds of the way through, I knew something was going to happen to one of them, but I still wasn't quite sure. The book was interesting in structure. I knew it was going to begin with Anil re-entering Sri Lanka and it was going to end with her leaving Sri Lanka. That was the only thing I knew about the structure. Then about three-quarters of the way through, I realized the book couldn't stay with her; it had to stay with the two brothers. When she flies off and leaves the country, she does leave behind a tragedy. It wasn't a story about being someone from Sri Lanka, born in Sri Lanka, but from the West; it was going to be about the place she had come back to.

ADICHIE: For me, it was a lot more about Sarath and Gamini than it was about Anil. I was very moved by the sense of the unknown. Of course I couldn't help thinking about the larger political context behind it and wanted to know what the research process was like for you. Real horrible things were happening and I think you've created art from it. What was it like?

ONDAATJE: First of all, I was not in Sri Lanka at this worst time. I had to ask myself, "Do I have the right to go back and write about it?" This is an issue for a writer morally, even if it's not an issue for other people. When I went back, it was trying to find out about that time. It wasn't about looking at books or newspaper articles, though I did read a lot of Amnesty texts. It was about talking to people. It was that oral tradition—listening to people before stories were lost and then being with doctors and traveling with them to re-witness what they did.

ADICHIE: At this time, what was happening in Sri Lanka? Were the killings still going on?

ONDAATJE: It had pretty well stopped by then. There was some evidence of it, certainly, and the war between the Tigers and the government was still going on. But at the time of this story, we had three elements: the Tigers in the north, the government forces—some legal, some illegal—and the JVP. It was a triangular war.

A lot of political violence in your book is offstage—it's heard by rumor or telephone calls. Even the violence within the family, which is terrible, is intentionally muted by you. The subtlety of the way you depict those scenes between the mother and the father and the violence that occurs there is amazing. I'm also interested in how you write about horrific violence—what was happening in Sri Lanka at this time—and whether a writer has a right to relive and re-explore it fully. Almost unintentionally, writing about a forensic anthropologist, I was able to write without having the actual scene occur. You have someone finding a corpse and then discovering what happened in the past—the week before or a day before or three years before—but there is protection for the reader against reenacting a violence. There is a kind of pornography in violence, I find.

ADICHIE: So do I. You risk losing the reader's faith in you; it becomes, as you said, pornographic, particularly when it's based on what's actually happened. I find that I am dealing with that more now that I'm working on a novel set in Biafra, where horrible things happened. I worry, first, that I am desecrating the memory of people who died by writing about what it was like for them. On the other hand, I feel the story has to be told, but how best to tell it? In *Purple Hibiscus*, I intentionally wanted all of the political violence to be offstage. I felt it was more believable that way, particularly for the narrator. It's how she would experience it—she wasn't likely to be caught in the crossfire during a coup.

ONDAATJE: Even the way she describes the scene on the street: What she notices is somebody's underwear showing, as opposed to what is behind that crowded semi-riot scene. In that last section, they suddenly enter the real world outside the family structure.

ADICHIE: I spent a lot of time reworking that final section, and I changed the tense from past to present continuously. It's actually my favorite section. I ask often about language because I am very interested in language. I find that my writing process is usually that I do the story and then I go back to turn it into what I want it to be, which is art. That's when I think about language and read the sentences and think about rhythm and structure. That's also when I read Michael Ondaatje: to see and get the cadence of sentences.

ONDAATJE: Would you read a bit from the last part? You don't have to give away too much of the plot, but just to show the difference in the voice.

ADICHIE: I'll read a little excerpt.

> We are at the prison compound. The bleak walls have unsightly patches of blue-green mold. Jaja is back in his old cell, so crowded that some people have to stand so that others can lie down. Their toilet is one black plastic bag, and they struggle over who will take it out each afternoon, because that person gets to see sunlight for a brief time. Jaja told me once that the men do not always bother to use the bag, especially the angry men. He does not mind sleeping with mice and cockroaches, but he does mind having another man's feces in his face. He was in a better cell until last month, with books and a mattress all to himself, because our lawyers knew the right people to bribe. But the wardens moved him here after he spat in a guard's face for no reason at all, after they stripped him and flogged him with koboko. Although I do not believe Jaja would do something like that unprovoked, I have no other version of the story because Jaja will not talk to me about it. He did not even show me the welts on his back, the ones the doctor we bribed in told me were puffy and swollen like long sausages. But I see other parts of Jaja, the parts I do not need to be shown, like his shoulders.
>
> Those shoulders that bloomed in Nsukka, that grew wide and capable, have sagged in the thirty-one months that he has been here. Almost three years. If somebody gave birth when Jaja first came here, the child would be talking now, would be in nursery school. Sometimes, I look at him and cry, and he shrugs and tells me that Oladipupo, the chief of his cell—they have a system of hierarchy in the cells—has been awaiting trial for eight years. Jaja's official status, all this time, has been Awaiting Trial.
>
> Amaka used to write the office of the Head of State, even the

Nigerian Ambassador in America, to complain about the poor state of Nigeria's justice system. She said nobody acknowledged the letters but still it was important to her that she do something. She does not tell Jaja any of this in her letters to him. I read them—they are chatty and matter-of-fact. They do not mention Papa and they hardly mention prison. In her last letter, she told him how Aokpe had been covered in a secular American magazine; the writer had sounded pessimistic that the Blessed Virgin Mary could be appearing at all, especially in Nigeria: all that corruption and all that heat. Amaka said she had written the magazine to tell them what she thought. I expected no less, of course.

ONDAATJE: The portrait of the father is amazing. He is such a complex character. Did you have that in mind when you began this book? A man who is extremely violent within his family and also heroic in his politics? It's a really tough portrait.

ADICHIE: I set out wanting to write about a man who was both violent and religious. I wanted the link to be obvious—not so much causative as linked. I also didn't want to have him be easily dismissible. I thought that if he were just violent, we could all simply say, "Oh, he's crazy."

I was keen to write about the kind of people I know in Nigeria. I'm interested in the question of how much literary fiction really does represent reality, because you are often told about the need for characters to be complex. I'm amazed because there are many people in the world who aren't very complex. Sometimes you write about people who exist and what they have done and people say, "Oh, it's not believable in fiction." But on the other hand, we impose reality on fiction. There are many people in Nigeria who are very religious, outwardly so, and who are monsters. I think religion can create monsters.

ONDAATJE: It's interesting how you can have a real person in the real world who is simply too unbelievable for fiction. When I was writing *Anil's Ghost*, a woman working in human rights told me she was driving in Colombo and she looked over to the right and the American ambassador's car came by with the flag, and in the backseat was a clown. She thought she was having a breakdown, but then discovered that the ambassador's wife was a professional clown. In fact, this wonderful woman went around to the villages performing clown shows. If you put that in the book, it will not survive. It will seem like extreme metafiction.

ADICHIE: Your work has been described as "literature of dislocation and displacement," which I find very grand. Usually, the literature of dislocation and displacement is a result of having a complex cultural background—being Dutch and English and Sri Lankan, for instance. Does the question of identity come in when you're writing or editing? Anil and many of the characters in *The English Patient* are in that grey area, nationless. Do you see yourself in them?

ONDAATJE: I'm a mongrel in that sense—I think a lot of us are. I don't think of the word "identity" at all when I'm writing, though I'm sure that I'm preoccupied with it in what I decide to write about. But I don't see the novel as a thesis or an argument for the discussion of identity and nationhood or postcolonialism. We all are governed by what we were as children. Therefore, we tend to refocus again and again on similar things.

ADICHIE: Can I read one of my favorite lines from *The English Patient*? I just savor the sentences. This is Kip: "He moved at a speed that allowed him to replace loss."

IN SEARCH OF THE SENSUAL

Hanan al-Shaykh and Salman Rushdie

SALMAN RUSHDIE: Hanan and I have known each other very well for a long time. Usually we talk about children and dogs, but we'll try and talk about books. I'm going to start by reading a little passage that Edward Said wrote several years ago which may get us kick-started: "In Lebanon, the novel exists largely as a form recording its own impossibility, shading off or breaking into autobiography as a remarkable proliferation of Lebanese women's writing, reportage, and pastiche."

The question is how to create literature, how to preserve its fragilities and its tough-minded individuality in the middle of an explosion. Hanan is the most brilliant of the women writers that Edward was mentioning. In a series of wonderful novels, plays, and other writings, she's attempted to answer these questions that Edward posed in that little passage. I know Edward Said was a friend of yours as he was of mine. I wonder if you want to say anything about his place in your thinking and what that meant to you.

HANAN AL-SHAYKH: I used to always follow Edward Said's books and his reviews, and I never dared to approach him because he was so intellectual and I didn't know how to talk to him. Whenever I saw him, I would hide. But after that article, we met. Edward Said was and still is, although he is no longer with us, a great influence on every acting writer or intellectual. He gave us hope.

RUSHDIE: Edward had different kinds of writing, and I always found the most powerful to be the most personal. He wrote that wonderful memoir *Out of Place* and another book, *After the Last Sky*. I felt an affinity with that personal writing of his and with the way your books work. Edward became a sensual writer when he wrote personally. Other times he was very analytical, but he suddenly displayed his sensuality. If I had to choose one word to describe your writing, "sensuality" might well be it. Are there other writers in the Arab world, or not in the Arab world, who were important to you when you were thinking about how and what to write?

AL-SHAYKH: I was more inspired by my family and neighborhood than I was by books. They used to tell stories all the time. In our house, we didn't have many books. We had only the Koran and we never had a daily newspaper. But I had a neighbor who was older than me (I was twelve or thirteen years old), and I would go to the bookstore with him and read translated books.

I loved *Jane Eyre*. I thought it was amazing because the book started with the heroine talking about how she wasn't beautiful. I come from a society where beauty is so important. If you are beautiful, you can talk and you have something to say. If you are not, then you are put aside. That's why, when I started writing *The Story of Zahra*, I immediately thought I wanted to choose somebody who is plain and not attractive who has a soul behind her.

RUSHDIE: What about the theater? You've written many plays. Was there a tradition of theater in Beirut?

AL-SHAYKH: No, there wasn't at all. There was a man who would read from *The Thousand and One Nights*. The theater in Lebanon at the time was mainly translated plays, especially French plays. I never thought I would be writing for the theater, but I remember the first person who said, "You should try." It was Edward Said. Of course I said, "I don't know how to write."

It happened that the Arts Council at Hampstead Theatre in London wanted to encourage more women. I said I could try and I wrote three plays. Two were staged and the third one, I don't think it has a future.

RUSHDIE: What about movies? Were movies important to you?

AL-SHAYKH: I loved them, especially the Egyptian movies. But you can't imagine how difficult it was to go to a movie. We had to sneak and lie and pretend we were going somewhere else, and then we would go to the movie. I used to sit in the first row, and my sister and my cousin would say, "No, we can't sit in the first row." And I would tell them, "No, I want to touch the actresses. I want to talk to them." I had great passion first for the Egyptian movies, and then later I became very choosy, especially admiring the avant-garde. I think when I wrote *The Story of Zahra* it was like making a French movie in a way, especially the scene between the sniper and Zahra.

RUSHDIE: It's like a Godard movie.

AL-SHAYKH: Yes, a Godard movie: black and white, going down the stairs, and being frightened and trembling, thinking of the sniper and the war around her.

RUSHDIE: So you grew up in Beirut, which has been changed so much. Would you like to say a little about what it was like in those days?

AL-SHAYKH: The Beirut I knew—it is always in my mind—was rich, amazing. The streets were crowded with people—the vendors, the mosques, churches, and synagogues were all bustling. I come from a very, very pious family. But at the same time, Lebanon and Beirut were so open. We used to feel so free. I wasn't very free to do anything, but the atmosphere was so open in Beirut. We would get all the cultures, all the schools. We had English schools, American schools, French schools, universities, everything. It was dramatically changed because of the civil war. The spirit is no more. It's not only because the infrastructure was ruined; it's because the spirit of it has gone.

So many people came to take revenge in Beirut or to help the Lebanese destroy their city. Who didn't come to Lebanon? Who didn't come to, in a way, rape Beirut? Many nationalities of many countries helped us destroy our city. I miss it so much. I miss the old city. My father had a tiny shop downtown in Beirut that I used to visit every day. Can you imagine a family with their daughter at nine or ten years old going from our district to downtown in half an hour? We weren't scared; everything was very safe. There were many Arabs from Syria, Iraq, Egypt even, who, because of their regimes, used to come take refuge in Beirut. Nowadays, it is nothing like that. The literary scene is gone.

RUSHDIE: People used to call this wonderful, famous city the Paris of the East. I remember as a child growing up in India, my family's friends from Lebanon would come and talk about the wonders of Beirut, and it was the place I always wanted to go. Is the vineyard still there?

AL-SHAYKH: The vineyard is still there.

RUSHDIE: Well, that's important. Is there any sign now of rebirth in the aftermath of the conflict? Is there any sign of this world coming back to life—the literary world, for example? Or the spirit of the city, as you were saying?

AL-SHAYKH: Not now, I think. They are trying. But Lebanon is facing a very crucial time. They are at a crossroads over what happened after the assassination of Prime Minister Rafik Hariri. I'm cautiously optimistic because the new generation was brought up after the war, outside Lebanon, so they don't have a grudge or the urge to fight like in 1975, but I'm still waiting. We'll see what can happen.

RUSHDIE: This conflict, of course, has always been there in the background and sometimes in the foreground of what you've written. *The Story of Zahra* is an extraordinary book. In a way, it's a book very clearly divided into halves. The first half has to do with intimate dangers.

AL-SHAYKH: In a war.

RUSHDIE: Yes, in a strife. And the second half has to do with the strife outside?

AL-SHAYKH: Exactly.

RUSHDIE: She's a damaged girl in many ways, Zahra. Even from the beginning, you say she's not attractive, she's constantly laughed at for having acne and picking at it and so on, so you deliberately created a character—

AL-SHAYKH: I wanted to show how society treated unfortunate women. Also, when I thought to write *The Story of Zahra*, I was in London because I left at the beginning of the war. I started thinking, What went wrong in Lebanon? I felt it's not the political faction, not the warlords; it is us now. It was as if the war had a big X-ray machine and we were entering one Lebanese after the other into this X-ray machine and seeing each other for the first time. What do we consist of? Our society, our ideas, our ideals—everything has to be questioned. I felt how the old traditions dealt with womanhood, how they dealt with men who were very prominent and very free. On the surface, it was a very open society, but deep down there were many, many issues: issues of religion, of virginity, and so on. So I thought, This is what I want to do. If the war hadn't happened, I wouldn't have really felt that I needed to talk about a person like Zahra who was damaged by society and by her upbringing and by her dictator-father. And talking about the father, I'm also talking about the warlord in Lebanon.

RUSHDIE: He works on the tram lines. You use that as a wonderful metaphor by saying "these old tram lines." He's a rigid figure who is the Lord of the Trams and can't get off his rails, and is oppressive in many ways to her. She is a person who was abused as a girl, which deranges her in a certain way, and then she comes into this world of larger derangement.

AL-SHAYKH: In the beginning, she thinks the war is freeing her, helping her, because there is no father anymore. When she sees her father frightened, she feels relaxed for the first time and secure that he doesn't have the upper hand. For the first time, she can really look at herself and think, I am a human being, I am an individual, I can do whatever I want. When this book was published and translated in the West—it was translated into languages other than English—many readers didn't think Zahra was a strong woman because they were relating to her from their preconceived ideas. But I think Zahra was a very prodigious girl because she said no to many things, and she became more trapped because she was saying no to her father and her society.

RUSHDIE: From the beginning, you've always written directly and explicitly about women's sensuality, women's sexuality, and you also—even though men are often coarse in their behavior toward women in the books—switch the perspective, and you are able to see inside the man's point of view. You deal very explicitly with what is normally hidden in many Muslim countries—explicit treatment of sexuality and sexual relations.

AL-SHAYKH: It had to do with the war; the war fed me as well. When the war broke out in Lebanon, and when I started writing *Zahra*, I felt free. I want to write what I'm feeling, to expose everything.

What brought us to this war? Why are we in this bloody war? It's because of stifling traditions, our customs, and religion as well. This is why I wanted to expose everything. In the Arab world, in the Muslim household, people seek ideas, but it's a very rigid society. At the same time, sex was everywhere. When I was a child we had a neighbor who always wanted to wash clothes in the garden. She loved to wash the clothes of her family. One time, I was sitting—I used to love her garden—and her husband gave her his trousers to wash and she threw them, and she said, "No, I'm not washing that! You only take them off to be washed!" And I didn't understand; I was so young. So I went home, and asked, "Our neighbor said this. What did she mean?" Then I knew what she meant.

I also remember my grandmother—I don't want to be vulgar, but this is an amazing story; I have to say it. I was very slim when I was young and my grandmother, whom I loved so much, was worried about me. She always said, "Hanan, you should eat, eat, eat. You don't want to stay like this because one day, you will get married and you will have to have children and your womb has to become bigger. You have to eat, you have to eat. You don't want to stay like an ant's cunt." Can you imagine? My grandmother telling this to her granddaughter who was ten years old.

You also can't forget about our tradition. Our old manuscripts were so daring. They talked about sex, about rulers who loved young men, young boys; they talked about explicit things.

RUSHDIE: One of the sad things about the modernist way is that there's a disconnect with the old tradition. The same thing happened in India. There are old temples with erotic carvings; the local villagers won't go because they say the carvings are pornographic and obscene. You say, "These are not American temples! These are not foreign temples. These are temples carved by people in India; it is the tradition of India." They say, "No, no, no. They're too vulgar." In your books, I think that loss of the erotic is foregrounded. How did readers react? With pleasure or with horror or condemnation?

AL-SHAYKH: It varies. In London, there was a Lebanese woman whose daughter used to play with my daughter and when she knew who I was she said, "But you are a nice woman! You are normal and a nice woman! Why would you write this book?"

RUSHDIE: I get that a lot too. When Zahra sees a man she thinks is a sniper, she interposes her body. She uses her own sexuality as a way of stopping him.

AL-SHAYKH: Yes. At the beginning.

RUSHDIE: At a certain point in the book, when she's pregnant, he denies that he was a sniper. He says he never was; he was just on the roof admiring the view or whatever it was. It's unclear whether he is telling the truth. At the end of the book, when she is in the street and she is shot, she believes that he is killing her, maybe because she has said that she is pregnant. Again, we're seeing the story from her point of view, and so we see also that she believes that she has been killed by this man. Do you have a view about whether it's him?

AL-SHAYKH: You are reminding me that when the book was published—in Arabic, of course—I was in Saudi Arabia and an aunt of a friend of mine called me and said, "I can't sleep. Did he kill Zahra?" An elderly woman! "Did he kill Zahra? Was he a sniper? The son of a bitch!" And I said, "What do you want? I want you to go back to bed."

RUSHDIE: I'm with her.

AL-SHAYKH: He was a sniper, and when he knew that she was pregnant, he killed her.

RUSHDIE: But it's very good to leave it ambiguous like that because you really want to know, but the book doesn't tell you. It reminded me of a story about a moment in a Pinter play when the actor who was acting with Pinter wasn't clear about a particularly ambiguous passage, and said to Pinter, "Could you explain what's supposed to be happening here?" And Harold looked at it and gave him back the text and said, "The author's intentions are not clear in the text."

AL-SHAYKH: I wanted to leave it that way. It was like a film; this is how I imagined the whole thing.

RUSHDIE: It's *Anna Karenina*.

AL-SHAYKH: Yes, in a way.

RUSHDIE: Let's go on to *The Women of Sand and Myrrh*. Does that book feel like a long time ago? In terms of your writing, do you still feel close to these books, or do you feel that you've moved on from some of them?

AL-SHAYKH: Unfortunately, I was feeling that I moved on from them, but what's happening nowadays brings me back to them.

RUSHDIE: Because this book felt incredibly contemporary. It was first published twenty years ago. And the condition of the women in this book . . .

AL-SHAYKH: Now, it's the same. Or worse.

RUSHDIE: Do you want to say something about the condition? You don't name the country in this book. One can guess that—

AL-SHAYKH: It's Saudi Arabia, yes. I didn't want to name it because at that time there were many books that were naming the country, and I wanted to keep writing literature. I didn't want people to say, "Oh, she's writing about Saudi Arabia and wants to attract attention to the book." That's why I didn't name the place.

It was amazing the way I thought about writing this novel. I was at the airport on my way to follow my husband, who is Lebanese—because of the war, he had to work in Saudi Arabia and Ghana. The first five minutes at the airport I saw my personality as if I had become a shadow. Not Hanan, not the writer, not the novelist or the mother. I wasn't a woman at all. This is when I thought, Ah, I have the seeds of the novel. Of course, living with women more than men gave me insight about Saudi women—both the very rich ones and the very modest with low incomes.

I thought, the whole time I was writing the book, that I was leading a double life. In my mind, it's my real self, Hanan the writer, who is writing this book. When I close the door to my office and I'm at home and surrounded by closed windows (we weren't allowed to open the curtains and have the sun enter the sitting room; we had to be literally enclosed), I have a split personality. This room, my office, is my true self. When I leave it, I am like the other women in Saudi Arabia.

I think this book created lots of attention in the Arab world. There wasn't any book written by an Arab novelist that talked about these moods and women—as if everything were camouflaged or put in boxes.

RUSHDIE: It's not camouflaged at all. It's very steamy, this book. No one appears to think about anything but sex all the way through it.

AL-SHAYKH: I'll tell you why. In Saudi Arabia, you think about sex continuously—every single person, more than in Europe, more than in clubs in Soho. Even if you want to buy sanitary napkins, you hesitate. You say, "Shall I? Shall I not? If I want to buy it, what is the owner of the shop going to think of me? I better not." Sex was everywhere because it was forbidden. It was everywhere, in the air. The women in my book really want to breathe, and they think through sex they can breathe because maybe if we could have a relationship, we would get something. We miss this taboo.

RUSHDIE: There is also a very explicit lesbian relationship in the book, which on one side appears to be the woman who is genuinely interested in women, and on the other side, it appears to be because there's just nothing else around.

AL-SHAYKH: Absolutely.

RUSHDIE: And the men, also.

AL-SHAYKH: Yes, the men! It is an unhealthy society. It is a very closed society—very oppressive, very unhealthy.

RUSHDIE: And how erotic it gets. People get love potions to capture other people's husbands. I can see why you thought you had a book.

AL-SHAYKH: When it was published in the Arab world, it was banned from a few Arab countries. I remember there was an Arabic bookshop in London. They called me, laughing, and said, "Listen, somebody came to buy this book, and said, 'I want the book of Hanan al-Shaykh.' " And they said, "Which one? She has three or four novels." And she said, "The one she loves women in."

RUSHDIE: The book after that is an extraordinary novel, *Beirut Blues*. It's a very important book. I read it again before we had this conversation and I thought it was perhaps even better than when I read it before. I actually reviewed this book; it was just about the last book I ever reviewed. After this, it was impossible to review other books. It's a portrait of the city in that time we were discussing, that time of its devastation. It's a lament in the way that you have been speaking of here, a lament for a broken city in a broken world. Incredible beauty. In the middle of that, it's also rather old-fashioned. It's a novel in the form of letters, an epistolary novel. The novel began like that. What we would consider to be the first modern novel, Samuel Richardson's *Clarissa*, is also a novel written in the form of letters. It's nearly one thousand pages long—quite boring, actually. All letters.

I was thinking about Saul Bellow. One of the great things about Herzog is the fact that he sends mad letters everywhere. And here is your heroine, Asmaran, coming back to Beirut into the middle of this catastrophe. She's writing letters to everybody she can think of. You had, at that time, also left Beirut and were living primarily outside. Although, of course, you would go back.

AL-SHAYKH: Yes.

RUSHDIE: How did it feel to return to that catastrophe? And was Asmaran your way of understanding what was happening? How did the book come to be?

AL-SHAYKH: I had been away from Lebanon, and after *The Story of Zahra*, I wrote a collection of short stories. I talked about the war as well. I said, "I'm not going back in life; I'm going to proceed. I'm not going to think about civil war and that's it." But every time I went to Beirut, I felt that the city had changed rapidly. When I didn't know a certain street, I became so upset with myself, and I said, "No, I really need to sit and write about the Beirut I knew and what's going on." This is how I started writing it. I felt that I could not write as if I was still there like the other Lebanese writers who were in Beirut. Because I was away in London, this is how it should be: letters.

I wanted to understand the war. With *The Story of Zahra*, the war was new and I didn't know a lot about it. When I wrote *Beirut Blues*, I understood why Beirut became East and West, and about Hezbollah, about the factions, how there were new factions.

RUSHDIE: There are terrible ironies in this book. One of the people she's writing to is her friend who's abroad, and she's saying "You can't understand anything from over there." In a way, she's quite contemptuous toward her for being out. There's the kind of pleasure in return: Now you know who you are because you've returned. Yet she falls in love with somebody who will then take her away again.

AL-SHAYKH: He didn't succeed in taking her away. He thought he was taking her away, but she chose not to go. She said, "If I leave, then all the years I've lived in Beirut are going to disintegrate. How can I do that to myself?" You have to choose between staying and leaving. I was feeling guilty because I left and many friends of mine stayed behind.

RUSHDIE: It seems to me that one of great tragedies of the current situation is the number of Arab writers who are forced into exile. An enormous number of the most prominent Arab writers are, whether by choice or necessity, not living in their country of origin.

AL-SHAYKH: In Iraq and Syria, this is the biggest tragedy. People, intellectuals, writers were forced to leave their country. When they left their country and took refuge in Europe and the United States and in other countries, they were threatened as well. They couldn't, at the beginning, write what they wanted to. There were spies everywhere.

RUSHDIE: A culture that exiles its best imaginative voices—what effect does this have on the culture?

AL-SHAYKH: It is a tragedy. It's really sad when all the intellectuals are leaving their countries. But at the same time, it's very difficult for them to stay. I think intellectuals and writers and artists are the first ones to flee. They have to practice life as it should be. I hope there will be a change, but I'm not optimistic.

AUDIENCE: In Islamic tests, it's written that God gave man one part of desire and women nine parts. Both of you have discussed how there's been a denial of that. Do you see a reclaiming of women's sexual identity by writers and artists who live in the Middle East, or is it only the realm of writers outside?

AL-SHAYKH: Unfortunately, the majority of women in the Arab world are going back to religion. If you see them, even in universities, you only see, like Zorro, a mask—you see only the eyes. I don't think they are questioning desire.

They aren't questioning that they shouldn't show anything, even their names, and they shouldn't use nail polish because it's against religion. I think Islam was hijacked by sorcerers and politicians. The Islam I grew up with wasn't like that at all.

AUDIENCE: I spent some time in Syria and Jordan recently, and when I came back, I found it hard to be objective because my experience there was so great. I know it's influenced a lot because I'm a man, but I was taken into people's homes and welcomed. There's a lot of focus on the problems in the Arabic world. Do you think there is a need to shed light on more of the positive aspects?

AL-SHAYKH: Of course. I think this is the role that intellectuals and novelists should play because they can mend bridges between cultures. In the Arab world, they misunderstand the West. It goes two ways.

RUSHDIE: One of the things that we've been talking about in this festival is the hunger among American readers for information that the news doesn't give us, for stuff we don't get on the TV or the radio or in the press. We find out how many people were blown up today, things like that, but we don't find out what the world is like. I think it's interesting that readers in this country are turning to books for these answers. Like Khaled Hosseini's book about Afghanistan, *The Kite Runner*, and Azar Nafisi's *Reading Lolita in Tehran*. This is something that creative and imaginative writers are able to do. It's one of the great services that literature can perform in this world.

SALMAN RUSHDIE

CONFRONTING THE WORST

Writers and Catastrophe

SVETLANA ALEXIEVICH: I'd like to remember the great Chekhov and his play *Three Sisters*. The main character in that play says over and over, "Now life is terrible, we live in squalor, but in a hundred years, a hundred years, how beautiful, how fine everything will be." And what has happened a hundred years later? We have Chernobyl; we have the World Trade towers collapsing. It's a new age in history. What we have experienced now not only goes beyond our knowledge but also exceeds our ability to imagine.

We are turning into a civilization of fear. Because what is a disaster? A disaster is a high concentration of fear. The commodity that our civilization creates in the largest quantity today is fear. The things that are happening to us today are unbelievable. The human mind is incapable of grasping them: They happen with incredible speed. I worked as a journalist for ten years before I started writing books, and realized that you cannot capture with words and language what is going on. Words and language are smaller than the event.

I don't know what it's like here; I'm not familiar with American culture. But for people who live in Russia and in Slavic countries, the spoken word is extremely important. I began to understand that what I was hearing people say on the street and in the crowds was much more effectively capturing what was going on than anything I was reading in print. And I began to think that it would be impossible for one person to write *the* book that encompasses everything the way that Tolstoy or Dostoevsky was capable of doing in the nineteenth century. We need a book where lots of people can make a contribution; one person may speak half a page, someone else a paragraph or five pages.

I refer to my genre as "the novel of voices," and you might say that my work is just simply lying outside on the ground: I go and pick it up and put it together. If Flaubert said, "I am a man of the *plume*," I can say that I am a person of the ear. It's become increasingly clear to me as I've worked in this genre, which I've done for thirty years now, that there is much about the human being that art cannot convey.

I'm interested in human feelings and turmoil. I try to make a guess about what's going on inside of people, what has meaning for them and what causes them to suffer. Right after Chernobyl, when I made my first trips to that region, I saw dozens if not hundreds of journalists there, and I said to myself, "Those guys are going to put their books out really fast, but the book that I'm going to write will take years." Indeed, I worked on the book for ten years. When I speak of these journalists' work, I am talking about books filled with facts, with medical information. Because try as the Soviet authorities might to suppress that information, it did get out. Chernobyl gave rise to anticommunist books, anti-Russian books, books against the atom, but the most important lesson that we needed to learn from that event took more time to emerge.

All of us found ourselves in terra incognita. Belarus, a patriarchal society based on the peasantry, was suddenly out there in front of the rest of the world. Imagine this incredibly crazy picture: A policeman is walking alongside a woman who carries a basket of eggs. He walks with her to make sure that she buries the eggs in the ground because they are radioactive.

They buried milk, they buried meat, they buried bread—it was like an endless funeral procession for inanimate objects. Thousands of soldiers sliced off the top layer of the soil, which had been contaminated, and they buried it. They took ground and they buried it in the ground. And everyone who was involved turned into a philosopher because there was nothing in the human past that enabled us to deal with this situation. In the Zone, which is what the area surrounding the nuclear stations was called, everything looked as it had before. You had rivers, you had forest, you had earth, but you couldn't walk through the forest. You couldn't wade in the river. You couldn't sit on the ground.

The feeling was that previously in the world, it had been humans who were in charge, who decided what they were going to kill and what they were going to spare. It was as if the earth had risen up and rebelled and was now taking charge. And you felt that you were surrounded by death, but death that had taken on a different guise, which you were incapable of understanding. Radiation is invisible; you cannot see it. It makes no sound; you cannot hear it. It does not have an odor; you cannot smell it. Our five senses, which equip us to protect ourselves, provided no assistance whatsoever.

For the first seven days after the disaster, the bees did not fly out of their hives and the worms burrowed down into the earth. The smallest creatures that creep and crawl on the earth understood what to do and that something was wrong, but we human beings, what did we do? We watched TV, we listened to Gorbachev, and we watched soccer. And we who work in the world of culture, we weren't prepared either; we didn't know how to tell people about what was happening, and people didn't even know how to talk to each other about it.

ELENA PONIATOWSKA: I'm going to read a testimony from a person who helped during the 1985 earthquake in Mexico. It's a boy, about eighteen:

We reached the baseball park in the corner of Qualtemo que Nobrero Mundial Avenues known as Del Capar. I choked up as soon as we arrived. We unloaded our equipment—the formaldehyde, the disinfectant, the spraying hoses, and the tanks. Then I looked at the stadium. It was as if we were in the center of a show, but without an audience. All the seats up there were empty. The actors were all there on the stage, but they were dead. Further back stood three tents covered with spotlights. They displayed signs. The first sign was unidentified bodies, the second identified bodies, and the last one said remains. There were limbs and other body parts in plastic bags that I never wanted to see and thank God I never had to see. These smaller plastic bags were handled with the same care and love and respect given to the bags that contained full bodies. People were coming to identify the remains. As a defense mechanism, I think I started to see myself as a spectator watching a movie. The smell of formaldehyde was very strong.

At the entrance, you could hear the click-clack of the clerks as they typed death certificates. The vans kept arriving with more bundles and more bundles and more bundles, but these bundles were bodies. The first thing we did was to establish a line beyond which no one could go without being fumigated. This is called a sanitary pocket. By the time men, women, and children had been dead for a few days, the process of putrefaction was advanced. We created a layer of plastic and tarp underground to serve as a boundary and as the spot where people would stand and be sprayed. We sprayed the people going in and out—the stretcher bearers, the relatives, the people who brought in the coffins. The doctor in charge ordered, "Start fumigating the corpses. Do it now." Fortunately, I was not involved in the first spray, not even the second. At the distance of some twenty yards, you could see the plastic bags, the dry ice, and the mounds. But those mounds, fully covered with plastic sheets, were bodies. The power hose was so strong that it blew off the plastic sheet, so I thought, I have to overcome my fear. If I don't do this right, I could be spraying all the other workers and cause a problem. Death is part of life; I must force myself to look. . . .

Maybe in the beginning, we were afraid of contamination, but we soon realized that those of us with the formaldehyde were the best protected. A small, skinny brown guy appeared—the typical Mexican, who has had to work very hard from birth. . . .

"And the coffins?" he asked. "The boxes. What's the deal on the coffins?"

He needed three coffins. He wanted to know how much they were. How would he pay for them? The poor bastard.

"Have you identified your family?"

"Yes. They are there. But tell me. How much do those caskets run?"

"No. Coffins are free. We will give them to you right away. Are you here by yourself?"

He was there to take his sister and two nieces, one fourteen and the other nine years old. I was profoundly sorry. I prepared the caskets, a big one and two small ones, and I realized one of them had two nails sticking out, but I said, "Too bad, it doesn't matter anymore." Later, we saw how the skinny man stepped on the nail with his sneaker, and since that didn't work, he got hold of a big board and bent them backward. This simple act restored an old human dimension to the piles of bodies in the stadium, because after four hours I thought that the only real thing was the bacteria. But for the skinny guy, those bodies, even all messed up, were his people, his kin. And his bodies had a right to be in the casket where they wouldn't be hurt by the nails. . . .

"Can we sprinkle the bodies with limestone?" I asked the skinny little guy. "Can I sprinkle limestone on your relatives?"

"Yes, " he said.

The fourteen-year-old had to be transferred out of her casket because she was too big for the other one. As I sprinkled her, I thought of *Hamlet*, when Ophelia, after losing her mind, drowns. Hamlet's mother places violets on her body and says in her mind, "Look, I've come to put flowers on your body, the ones I should have placed on your wedding day." I had exactly the same sensation.

"Girl, I am sprinkling limestone on you so you are all whitened up. You will not live at all." A fourteen-year-old girl. "There you go. All white."

You know, all those mental associations that we have about purity, dignity, and untouched bodies . . . but I could only sprinkle limestone on her, not a single flower, just a little, just a lot, of white dust. And that's how it went.

I think that in extreme situations, people feel the urge to communicate and to be with others. They suddenly have time for themselves and for others. They attempt a new communication with their fellow men and women by improvising their conduct, because barriers and prejudices have been demolished. In doing so, they acquire new knowledge. In September 1985, after the earthquakes, Mexicans witnessed how Mexico City underwent one of the noblest transfers of power in its history: the power that greatly transcended the commitments of mere solidarity, the transformation of the people into government and of official disorder into civilian order. Individuals who were previously invisible became the constructors of a new democracy.

FRANÇOIS BIZOT: In 1971, I was caught by a revolutionary Communist in Cambodia. I was chained and condemned to death and before that, interrogated by a young man who asked me about what I used to do with my father. I wanted to ask him, "What about your father? What about your work? Where were you born? How old are you?" And so on. For three months we spoke together and he chose not to beat me.

I think, as I was suspected to be a spy working for the CIA, he thought it was clever to speak with me openly to see how I would answer his questions. And maybe he thought if he tortured me, I would have a special secret strength in myself, as I would have been trained for that. Anyway, we spoke together every day, and in a few weeks we started to know each other quite well. There were about fifty condemned to be killed in the camp; one by one, I saw them going with the guard. Of course, I was very much afraid. I knew that this young chief, the Cambodian revolutionary with whom I spoke every day, was beating them. And he gave the authorization to kill the condemned.

When we spoke together, I realized, without clearly knowing it, that I was in a very rare situation. He explained to me why he went to the forest to fight the American soldiers. He was a true thinker; he was very involved in justice in Cambodia. He wanted his country to be free enough to have a good life. In a certain way, he was very much like the friends I lived with in Paris who were communist and against the war and against poverty, against injustice.

Going near him every day and seeing sometimes his fragility and sometimes his anger, I realized he was a monster. At that time, he was a small monster. But four years afterwards, I think we can see he was a big one because we recognize fourteen thousand victims. From 1975 to 1979, he was the chief of this huge prison in Cambodia, and organized all the deaths and the torture and the interrogations. To be so near a monster was much more frightening than I had expected. That is the start of the book that I was to write thirty-five years afterwards, because what I saw was not the monster I was waiting for. In fact, he looked like other men, an ordinary person. Sometimes I realized that he was looking a little bit like me. That was much more frightening than what I thought I would see.

After our conversations, he decided I was nuts. He did not want to kill me and so his chief, Pol Pot, ordered, "Let the Frenchman go." That's why I am here now. In 1999, which was a long time afterward, I realized that this person that I'd met thirty years before had given me a tremendous opportunity. We have learned that we should try to identify ourselves with victims, to suffer in our flesh what they suffered. Knowing my interrogator was not married, knowing he was a good scholar, a math teacher, knowing him intimately, I started to identify with him.

That was the reason for the story: I think we should maybe have the courage to identify ourselves with and humanize the torturer. Maybe we should look at ourselves, instead of saying "Never again," which does not work. We could maybe try to ask a new question, as well as a very old one: "How is it possible?" We may find the answers in ourselves.

RYSZARD KAPUŚCIŃSKI: I have been a roaming correspondent in Africa, Asia, and Latin America for a long time, have seen many catastrophes, and have often had to write about them. There is a nexus between the disaster and power. Most of the victims of earthquakes are the poor living in slums and shantytowns. One little earthquake or tropical downpour can raze those poorly built neighborhoods, killing and maiming the inhabitants. Corruption as well as poverty contributes to the number of casualties of natural disasters. Many contractors receive huge government grants to guarantee the cost of safe construction but build cheap, miserable houses that fall apart during the first minor quake.

When dealing with natural catastrophes, the media limits itself to single out-of-context images of rescue teams looking for buried people or relief workers bringing medical aid and food. The context of those catastrophes is far more dramatic than we see on our television or read in the paper. Each disaster has not only direct casualties but also aftereffects.

Two weeks after the 2004 tsunami, a fine photographer showed me some pictures of an Indian town ravaged by the wave. He was in despair because no one wanted to publish them—the event was already considered out of date.

CAROLIN EMCKE: I'm not an expert on natural disaster, but on man-made disaster, namely wars. I assume that all of us have received the same question over and over again: "Why do you do this job? Why do you go to these places where you get shot at, arrested, deported, threatened, or beaten up on a relatively regular basis?" Probably for a complex set of motivations—some personal, many political—and it's difficult to disentangle the various reasons because they are so intertwined with who I am as a person. Whatever explanation we give is somewhat retroactive; it provides a rationalization for something that at the core feels like a need, and reflects an impulse as you would reach out to catch a glass of water that falls off the table. It's really an impulse. For me, it's an impulse to respond to violence and to wars. What I really care about is the relation between violence, trauma, and the loss of language.

Very often, victims of violence are not terribly injured physically, but they're mentally, emotionally, and psychologically injured. What goes along with that psychological injury is the loss of language, the loss of their ability to describe what actually happened to them. I've never in my life—not in one region of crisis or war, not in one area of conflict—met a victim of violence who had lost memory of what had happened to him or her. Not once. Rather than what the contemporary scientific research on trauma wants to make you believe, I've never once encountered a single victim of violence who really could not remember what happened. The first thing you lose is trust in the world. People lose their language or their ability to give an account, to give a narrative of what happened to them, because they lose trust that anybody will care. They lose trust in the sense of community or the sense of belonging to the same world, which is a precondition for talking. It's a precondition for dialogue, a precondition for even making an effort to reach out to another person, assuming she wants to share your suffering and your sorrow.

What upsets me particularly, what makes me go to these areas, is anger at the fact that if people lose the ability to describe what happened to them, the perpetrators win twice. Basically, if people aren't able to give an account or to give an account that we consider intelligible—maybe it doesn't sound reasonable anymore, maybe they can only stutter or mumble—it's only proof that the perpetrator was right.

If we are talking about writing and catastrophe, what the writer has to do is give voice to people who have become silent. It's a creative rush: You have to decipher the broken narratives; you have to try to make sense of something that might sound distorted. No one ever asked me for money, for food, for direct, practical help. But over and over again, people have asked, "Will you write this down?"

In the beginning, I have to admit that I feared they would hope that my writing could change the situation they faced. Over the years, I've come to think it's actually something else. They're not so naïve to think that if I write, something will really change. Rather, people who are victims of violence, of long-term discrimination, of long-term exclusion from society, people who experience injustice and violence over long periods of time, at some point—

when the situation continues and nobody intervenes—they begin to wonder whether what has happened to them might actually be right. At some point, they lose the sense of the injustice. They lose their faith in the world.

So rather than do that, they begin to ask whether what happened to them might be right. What they ask of a writer on catastrophe and war is to say, "No, what you are enduring is not right, it's wrong. It's wrong." This reassures them of their own sense of right and wrong, of justice and injustice, and includes them again in the community that they were excluded from. The writing is also about creating a weave—a normative weave, a moral weave, a weave that is bigger than the realities in these war zones or the realities that these people find themselves in. We somehow all believe in the power of words to ban horror and fear, and yet it doesn't work. Sometimes events and horrors and injustice and wars are just overpowering. And they don't lose their ability to haunt us and traumatize and terrorize us, even if we can describe them properly. That's the paradox of the witness of war: You always fail to reach that state where you can say, "Yes, I adequately described what was going on."

I've written articles as a journalist, as it is my profession, and yet I had this sense of failure. So I began to write letters to my friends, who, I have to say, weren't terribly good at asking questions about where I was, and I wasn't terribly good at describing what I experienced. So, out of that frustration and that sense of failure, I began writing letters that I would send via e-mail to friends across the world—long letters that tried to make sense out of what I experienced in these areas of war, and also tried to reflect on our own role in this. Now it's turned into a book, which is slightly strange because strangers read it and not just friends. It hasn't stopped the sense of failure and inadequacy, but it also hasn't stopped the drive and the need to continue to travel and try to give people a voice.

PHILIP GOUREVITCH: I don't think of myself as a writer of catastrophe, which might sound strange because I've written about Rwanda and Cambodia and other troubled places. I think of myself more as a writer of aftermath. I'm not somebody who, like a combat photographer, stands up when there's shooting to get a better picture. I wait until it's just calm enough perhaps to have a conversation with people again. I like to go in after the press has gone home or the story has moved off the front pages. In that sense, I suppose, part of my work as an aftermath man is to try to slow down our attention span, or at least my own. Writing in long form in our different ways, and ultimately in book form, is a way of trying to accumulate an experience after it has happened, to not let it slip away, and to get a better take on a story than you often get in the heat of the moment—a deeper take.

One question we were asked to consider was "What drew you to the work you do?" I suppose there are several reasons. One, from very early on, would be a sense of family history. Like a lot of Americans, I was part of the first generation of my family to be born here. My parents had come from abroad and, also like many Americans, they came as refugees. A sense of the way that history can intensely shape private lives was always part of my experience as I grew up. What everybody was supposedly yearning for was an extraordinary level of peace and civility and an expectation of more of the same, and there I was, growing up in a New England town with all the blessings you could possibly ask for in that respect. Not to say it was a place without questions, or without turmoil, or without much to scratch one's head or to be outraged about, but it was a place where there was extremely good reason to believe that nobody was going to shatter the fabric of social existence with violence at any moment. One of the other things that made me write is what makes all others write, which is reading. Reading other people's writings and hearing stories from family members from another time, I started to think that maybe I was living outside of history in some strange way. Maybe there wasn't anything going on. Then I started to realize that it was going on elsewhere. But I felt confused when reading newspapers. A lot was going on, but I was feeling that unless I went there I wouldn't have a good sense of it; I wouldn't be able to slow it down and grasp it.

Aside from those personal reasons, there are three words that probably most motivate my reporting on the aftermath of political violence: unimaginable, unspeakable, and unthinkable. These are the reflexive words by which political violence is almost invariably described, and what bothers me is that they give voice to its magnitude without actually addressing it. They are the words by which the press gives you permission to forget and ignore. They are the words by which we let ourselves off the hook. They're supposed to be grand. If I say, in a deep, ponderous voice, "unspeakable," you all shudder and we feel that we've had a shared experience of confronting something, when in fact all we've done is shrugged it off. I noticed that these words were applied constantly to Rwanda. "Unbelievable" is the casual form of all three hooked together. But what are writers to do except to imagine, speak, and think? Or imagine, think, and speak. Preferably, you think before you speak.

This is something I started to realize as I got involved in journalism and reporting and actually going places to see what has happened rather than writing from pure imagination or from pure outrage. And I think outrage is probably a large motivator for everybody here, whether it's personal or not. Some of the books that first inspired me were novels, works of the imagination. Then I began to understand that reporting, too, is a work of the imagination. That does not mean that it is not also necessarily factual. Facts are problematic; facts can be abused; facts can be distorted; facts can be misunderstood; but facts are nevertheless the essential touchstone that distinguishes fiction from nonfiction. Both fiction and nonfiction will be judged by whether they are truthful. The real trick in nonfiction is to be stuck with facts and somehow be truthful, and for that you need a certain amount of imagination. And you also need other people's stories. It often requires imagination to understand the parts that they aren't telling you. People do want to speak. I think they want to speak for some of the reasons that have been addressed; I think that they want to speak so as not to be annihilated. Often in situations where there is a sense of doom, a sense of crushing forces very close to the bone, I think people speak simply to exist, and when we go to them as reporters we are amplifiers of that existence.

At the same time, I'm also quite skeptical of the idea that anything we do has an immediate effect. I've never believed it did. I've never thought of what I do as human-rights reporting. Yes, human rights have been violated, but I find that to be a very narrow, technical rubric in which the only real question is the assertion of blame. It assumes there is a perpetrator and a victim, and the question gets complicated when you have a conflict in which there is no clean side. That does not mean that both sides are equally unclean. I think that can be an easy refuge for journalists—this fiction that the vantage point of neutrality is always the wisest one. Objectivity is obviously wise and useful, but neutrality in the face of genocide seems to me obscene. It's a kind of complicity. Neutrality can be used to let us subtly off the hook.

Part of our job is not just to imagine and not just to speak, but also to think along the way and to pass judgment. There is no accurate reporting that isn't based on a series of difficult judgments. That's why I think it is worthwhile to do what I do even though there is a kind of existential futility in it from the short-term, activist point of view. The activists who say, "I will go, I will make visible what is invisible. I will speak for those who are voiceless and things will change," are going to almost always end with a certain level of frustration. The history of wars is pretty much inseparable from the history of humanity. I think that conflict will always be with us. You can say, "If conflict is going to be with us and if horrible things are going to perpetually happen, why do this?" I think there is a cumulative effect—that if we stopped what we're doing, the world would be worse. And if you believe that at all, you have to accept that there is value in the cumulative power of truth-telling, of making and keeping a record, and keeping track of what has happened.

In that sense, I think the project we're all involved in of writing in the longer form and writing slowly over time—ten years for a book on Chernobyl, thirty years for a book about an experience in Cambodia—implies a consistent view of history. Probably most of us are a bit pessimistic about history. You see the things that we've seen, study the places that we've studied; it's not chipper stuff. But alongside that pessimistic view of history, implicit in the kind of activity we're engaged in, is a sense that over time this kind of record informs, instructs, and is absorbed in some way that's a part of the balance for the good. If the world's a crushing, horrible place filled with nasty people doing terrible things, it's not a bad way to spend your time.

NON-MILITARY STATEMENTS

1
Yes, I did write in my letter
that I would wait for you forever.
I didn't mean exactly "forever,"
I just included it for the rhythm.

2
No, he was not among them.
There were so many of them!
More than I've seen in my life
on any television screen.
And yet he was not among them.

3
It has no carvings
or arms.
It always remains there
in front of the television
this empty chair.

4
I dream of a magic wand
that changes my kisses to stars.
At night you can gaze at them
and know they are innumerable.

5
I thank everyone I don't love.
They don't cause me heartache;
they don't make me write long letters;
they don't disturb my dreams.
I don't wait for them anxiously;
I don't read their horoscopes in magazines;
I don't dial their numbers;
I don't think of them.
I thank them a lot.
They don't turn my life upside down.

6
I drew a door
to sit behind, ready
to open the door
as soon as you arrive.

—**Dunya Mikhail** (translated by Elizabeth Winslow)

ZAKES MDA

AFRICA AND THE WORLD

Writers at Home and Away

BREYTEN BREYTENBACH: If one mentions the word "Africa" in a global context, it tends to evoke many responses and perhaps even some obsessions. People tend to project on the continent strange emotions either of unconditional hope, allegiance, and support or unalloyed horror at what they perceive as the terrible things taking place on the continent. Nobody is left unmoved by Africa. But, of course, it's a huge continent. The people here on stage are either from Africa or they're writers for whom Africa resonates because of descent, involvement, or interest. I'm not sure what they have in common, but I think that we will be enriched by the vast diversity of experiences, of backgrounds, sometimes of languages, certainly of histories.

Africa is filled with powerful contradictions. There's perhaps no other continent that is so rich potentially but also actually in its cultural expressions, its history, its religions, its myths, and which is at the same time so abysmally poor—more poor than any other part of the world if you take the continent as a whole into consideration. There's no other continent where human solidarity, solidarity within family, clan, age group, and even sometimes with the enemy, is as developed, functional, important, and maintained. Yet, as you know, there's no other continent so wracked by civil wars, uprisings, terrible plagues, things falling apart. There's no other continent that has taken as easily to some of the manifestations of globalization. Yet there would seem to be no other continent that is as impervious to change. There's no continent where the word, the tongue, the exact image is as important—talking, reading, oral culture carrying on the traditions, telling the stories. Yet it would seem to be a continent that is blissfully neglectful of its riches in languages. You know from the history of people like Ngugi wa Thiong'o, here with us tonight, how much struggle there has been on the continent for the recognition of African languages, and yet we don't seem to be any further advanced now than we were decades ago. There's no other continent where the flames of liberation and independence have burned as high, and perhaps there's no other continent that so demonstrably illustrates the bankruptcy of our dreams and the bankruptcy of our idealism.

The one thread that runs through, I think, is perhaps the preeminent characteristic of the continent, the sense of humanity, the importance of being human. It's not "Why are we going to change the world?" It's not even "How are we going to become rich in the world?" It's not "How are we going to become powerful in the world?" All of that comes much later. Sometimes I remember in a very early story, I imagined that one would go as a subversive agent for Africa all over the world and scribble on the walls, in the dark of night, graffiti saying: "AFRICA LIVES."

ACHMAT DANGOR: History. We all have our stories.

Forty years ago, at the eager age of sixteen, I had to appear before a race-classification board in Pretoria, South Africa, because of my mixed heritage. Let me describe that: One ancestor, great-grandmother or great-grandfather, was brought to the Dutch as a slave from Java or Malaysia; we're not sure. Another came as a merchant from India. I have a great-grandmother who came as something else, from the Netherlands. And I was speaking Afrikaans as my mother tongue and, because I grew up in a mixed township, my second language was Isizulu. So can you imagine the confusion of those race-classification people? In the end, they classified me as colored. Of course, there is nothing wrong with being classified, but in a race-obsessed society, everyone had to have an identity. Now, we have a new kind of identity.

In the past few weeks and months, I've been reading from my book *Bitter Fruit* in various parts of the world—in London, in Antwerp, in Amsterdam, in New York, in Toronto—and I get the same question every time: Are you a Muslim writer? So here I am, with a new identity: I am a wine-drinking, Muslim-born writer who writes in English. I'm equivocally African.

I'm going to read from a story, a section of the novel, which I hope will perhaps demonstrate that ambiguity. This novel is about a young man, Michael, who discovers that his biological father is a security policeman who raped his mother. He discovers this due to the Reconciliation Commission process, as I called it, and he decides that he will not forgive and forget. He decides to execute his biological father. And the night before he does that, he wanders through the streets of Johannesburg thinking about these things.

Daybreak, when the Bilal bhangs.

Michael had heard the expression from Sadrodien, a mixture of Arabic and Malay, describing the call to prayer that the Bilal makes at each of the five prescribed prayer hours. Michael had since learnt that one of the Prophet Mohamed's first adherents was a black man named Bilal (a faithful servant, a freed slave?). For his foresight and courage—those were dangerous times, the first Muslims had many enemies—Bilal was accorded the honor of calling the fledging band of faithful to prayer. Now, everywhere in the world, five times a day, a man—European travel brochures call him a "muezzin"—climbs a winding staircase to the top of a tower, supporting his bony knees with his hands, so that it seems he has added an extra element to the ritual of worship, and proclaims to the world: Allah u Akbah! God is Great. Bilal the man has been transformed by time and myth from person into concept.

Not all Bilals are black, Michael thinks. But here in Newclare of course, he is, a Somali émigré, poor and pious. Michael is there, at the gates of the Griffith Street Mosque, when the Newclare Bilal bhangs the dawn salaat. He watches the faithful arrive, they smile indulgently: so this is the prodigal son that Imam Ismail is trying to bring back into the fold!

When the Moulana arrives, surprise flickers in his eyes. "Wait for me in the classroom," he tells Michael.

Michael sits on the floor, his knees drawn up against his chest. He is exhausted, light-headed from lack of sleep. The place and the hour, as well, bring upon him a dreamlike euphoria.

He remembers: he had taken a taxi from Julian's place, long before the party ended, was dropped off outside his home in Berea. But the world beyond that door seemed small, Lilliputian. He imagined that the house had become a labyrinth of narrow tunnels, booby-trapped, rigged with concealed trapdoors through which the unsuspecting visitor might fall. Alice in Mandela's Wonderland. Why Mandela? That came later, he thinks. He had turned away from the house, carefully retreating as if trying to allay the fears of some suspicious watcher.

He had walked down the hill to Louis Botha Avenue, then to Norwood, where a street party was taking place. Dancing and drinking in the street, loud music, glass against glass like the clash of metal, a loud, mad-hatter merriment, party-goers with smiles permanently painted onto their faces.

He remembers: Lydia lying on the billiard table, that young Mozambican, João, perched above her, birdlike, a heron, uncommonly black, his awkwardness given grace by her arched body. Silver shadows lighting up the loveliness of their coupling: green upon her olive skin, deep blue against his dark, dark back. She held him, no more than that, moored him, as if to prevent him from drifting into space, his head in her hands, whispering in his ear, as if instructing him in the art of sex. On the other side of the room, lit up by a full moon, stood Silas, staring intently, like a voyeur. Then he stumbled away, as if intoxicated.

He remembers: he had wandered away from Grant Avenue, away from the theatrical, staged revelry, along dark streets, until the world was quiet again, and he could hear the wind rustling in the trees, a true and solitary peacefulness. Somewhere, what seemed like hours later, he had come upon a small convoy of cars pulling up outside a house. Some important person in a Mercedes-Benz. Blue lights began to flash on the roof of the leading car when he stopped to watch. A warning: move along. But he stood still, watching as the cars waited for gates to trundle open on a rail.

Who is the VIP? he wondered. It would be easy to assassinate him. What else are they good for but dying famous deaths. The Mercedes-Benz had darkened windows. They became famous in order to crave privacy.

Then a window in the car rolled down, and Nelson Mandela smiled at him. "What are you doing out so late, young man, and all alone?"

He was stunned, tongue-tied. He must have walked all the way down to Mandela's residence in Houghton. He wanted to extend his hand, offer a greeting; then, incongruously, he remembered the gun in his pocket, and stepped back.

The President looked at him quizzically. "Are you afraid of me?" he asked.

"No, sir."

"Do you need help?"

"I'm not far from home," he remembers stammering, before waving to the President and his increasingly restive bodyguards, and walking away. To the freeway. A passing motorist had stopped, looked him over carefully, then offered him a lift (perhaps his stooped, shivering stance, that vulnerable look he instinctively assumed when he was being examined, made him appear harmless).

Through the rest of the night, he remained aware of the gun in his pocket, pressing its presence on him. He had practiced pulling it out rapidly, because that might be the only way he would get close enough to Du Boise. Would he really have shot that grand old man, he wonders now, as something in his mind was subliminally suggesting when he stood before Nelson Mandela's open window?

ELIZABETH ALEXANDER: I've been asked very loosely to think about the relationship of African writers and Africa at large to American writing. An enormous topic, of course, but I'll offer a few thoughts. Even before 1922, when Countee Cullen wrote his famous poem "Heritage," Africa was a monolith, an idea for most Americans. We know that through the so-called idea of Africa, many white Americans have found their imagined antithesis, their aesthetic inverse, their thrilled fantasies. Even, or perhaps especially in children's literature, for example, one still encounters vulgar stereotypes such as bones through the nose, wild-eyed savages, and darling knaves in contemporary garb. But what of the African American writer's relationship to her African predecessors, heritage, and peers? That for me is a richer and more interesting question.

In the poem I mentioned, "Heritage," Cullen wrote: "What is Africa to me: / Copper sun or scarlet sea." He echoed William Blake's metrical and rhyme patterns from "The Tyger"—"Tyger Tyger, burning bright, / In the forests of the night; / What immortal hand or eye, / Could frame thy fearful symmetry?"—in writing the African American self, the temporal relative to the immortal, the African American relative to the imagined African self. For Africa as such was no more real or known to Cullen than it was, say, to Picasso when he first saw those sculptures at the Trocadero near the turn of the century and was so radically rocked at the aesthetic and philosophical root, his entire artistic project and European art history changed forever.

We know from the landmark 1925 anthology *The New Negro* that many African Americans were seeing and imagining Africa for the first time when this art and these artifacts made their way to the Western world. So Africa was, for those writers, also new, and their relationship to it opened for exploration and investigation. Yet the African American, of course, has a different history, a different journey to explore, a different relationship to Africa that emanates from the interruption, the violent fissure of the Middle Passage and its subsequent soul-annihilating indignities. There is a melancholia about the unresolved slash, the never-to-be-known homeland that coexists with the great and limitless possibilities of reinvention, which gave the world, for example, jazz—a music that is heavily influenced by Africa but utterly, purely, completely African American, which is to say, American.

We died at the bottom of the ocean, and then at the hands of the brutal slave system, then due to the privations of Jim Crow, then at the hands of the police and of each other. That's a lot of unending blues. I think of Gwendolyn Brooks's wonderful words that strive to connect the dots between Africa and Afro America: "I am black. I am one of the blacks. We occur everywhere. Don't call me out of my name." And her wish to be called "black" links her to other African people, diasporized and not. Does that linkage hold? Is our wish for it to hold sentimental? How do we locate motherland in our art forms? The African retentions, as the art historian Robert Ferris Thompson called them, of bottle trees and shell-studded graves.

In poetry, you see the continued effort of black American poets of almost all stripes to keep their ears open, both for the literal sounds of our different Englishes—formal and vernacular—and for our oral traditions and whatever is left of proverbial logic and structure, ancestral mythos, musicality, the African *something*—the genius that occurs when spoken word successfully marries literary form. We see African Americans now sending our cheek-scrapings and hair strands to genomic projects at Howard University in hopes that we can learn not so much what we have, how much of what we have in us, but rather names, names that will tell us something about what we come from, give us something to start with.

I wonder, in that particular search for roots, do we overlook that which we have, skip right over to the easier work of romance and iconography? Perhaps we look past what we have already made, skip over the added challenges of being an American in the world with civic responsibilities and an urgent need to have our say in our country's role at home and in the rest of the world. I think about moments of contact and cross-pollination: the mutual-admiration society, for example, of Toni Morrison and Chinua Achebe; the relationship of the late poet and scholar Melvin Dixon to Senegal and his fine, definitive translation of the poems of Senghor; Langston Hughes's anthologies of African short stories and poems, which brought African writers to U.S. audiences in the 1950s and 1960s; Robert Hayden's winning the Grand Prix for poetry in 1966 at the African Arts festival in Dakar; Louis Armstrong giving a trumpet to the young Hugh Masekela; Stevie Wonder and Sounds of Distinction covering Masekela's "Grazing in the Grass"; James Brown and Fela Kuti riffing back and forth endlessly, fiercely.

For many of us of my generation, the anti-apartheid movement was a way to connect with African writing, politics, and history in the making. That civil-rights battle for desegregation and human dignity resonated, of course, with our own history. In the United States in the 1980s, affirmative action was under attack, and the Reagan era was changing the country's winds from the Great Society in the 1960s. The "Free South Africa" movement kept our eyes on the prize and fueled our own ongoing struggle. The movement gave us a certain kind of clarity; its writers gave us the gift of clarity as we moved through that transitional period in African American civil-rights history.

Today I'm particularly interested in the population of young black people, like many of the ones I teach at university, who are as likely to have been born in Lagos or Port of Spain as in Los Angeles. The diaspora is alive and well and

creative and has a new face. The black kids now—as my own children, whose
father is Eritrean—describe themselves: When he was four, the eldest said to
me, "Mommy, you're an African American, right?"

And I said, "Yes."

And he said, "And Daddy is African, right?"

And I said, "Right."

And he said, "So we're *African* American."

So, I think that generation of *African* Americans in American universities,
that is to say, young Americans of immediate African descent, are the ones
whom I'm very eager to hear from in the arts and in literature. I think that's
the next very exciting thing. And I know we're going to hear from them loudly
and in large numbers.

Being a race warrior, being a race worker, or even just being a race scholar
in the American context is exhausting work. Sometimes the mind's portals
fill up and may seem unresponsive to the necessary knowledge that awaits us
around the world in conversation. I say without hesitation that from African
people and African literature, I have learned—and many of my companions
have learned—certain essential aspects of these following large categories:
beauty, grace, patience, profound woe, and capacity for joy. And so resonates
the blues. There is more for us to find in the width of that sky. I want to close
with two poems of mine that deal in some way with this contemporary diaspora
as it "occurs"—to use Brooks's wonderful verb—all over the world, but from my
vantage point, here, in the United States, in this new century. This first one is
called "The African Picnic":

> World Cup finals, France v. Brasil.
> We gather in Gideon's yard and grill.
> The TV sits in the bright sunshine.
> We want Brasil but Brasil won't win.
> Aden waves a desultory green and yellow flag.
> From the East to the West to the West to the East
> we scatter and settle and scatter some more.
> Through the window, Mama watches from the cool indoors.
>
> Jonah scarfs meat off of everybody's plate,
> kicks a basketball long and hollers, "goal,"
> then roars like the mighty lion he is.
> Baby is a pasha surrounded by pillows
> and a bevy of Horn of Africa girls
> who coo like lovers, pronounce his wonders,

oil and massage him, brush his hair.
My African family is having a picnic, here in the U.S.A.

Who is here and who is not?
When will the phone ring from far away?
Who in a few days will say goodbye?
Who will arrive with a package from home?
Who will send presents in other people's luggage
and envelopes of money in other people's pockets?
Other people's children have become our children
here at the African picnic.

In a parking lot, in a taxi-cab,
in a winter coat, in an airport queue,
at the INS, on the telephone,
on the crosstown bus, on a South Side street,
in a brand-new car, in a djellaba,
with a cardboard box, with a Samsonite,
with an airmail post, with a bag of spice,
at the African picnic people come and go.

The mailman sees us say goodbye and waves
with us, goodbye, goodbye, as we throw popcorn,
ululate, ten or twelve suitcases stuffed in the car.
Goodbye, Mamma, goodbye—
    The front door shut. The driveway bare.
Goodbye, Mamma, goodbye.
The jet alights into the night,
a huge, metal machine in flight,
Goodbye, Mamma, goodbye—
At the African picnic, people come and go
and say goodbye.

Then to close, a short poem, a funny poem with a title that's meant as a joke,
which makes itself clear in the poem—an American poem, with an African
American story in it that's also an African story. The poem is called "Ars
Poetica #28: African Leave-Taking Disorder."

The talk is good. The two friends linger
at the door. Urban crickets sing with them.

There is no *after* the supper and talk.
The talk is good. These two friends linger

at the door, half in, half out, 'til one
decides to walk the other home. And so

they walk, more talk, the new doorstep, the
nightgowned wife who shakes her head and smiles

from the bedroom window as the men talk
in love and the crickets sing along.

The joke would be if the one now home
walked the other one home, where they started,

to keep talking, and so on: "African
Leave-Taking Disorder," which names her children

everywhere trying to come back together and talk.

TSITSI DANGAREMBGA: When I think of myself, I don't think of myself as an African writer. I think of myself as Tsitsi Dangarembga. The place I live that people call Africa is actually to me the place where children run in the garden, where the water starts ebbing away out of the taps at six in the morning only to come back at six at night, if we're lucky. So this place that people call Africa probably means something quite different to me.

I thought that rather than talk about the role of the writer, I'd read an article I wrote. It was a commissioned article, and from that you may be able to deduce what, for me, my role as a writer from Africa is. The title of the piece is "Electing Zimbabwe."

My heart is in turmoil and I am in great pain. What is the world coming to? When will Zimbabweans not be afraid to say, "I am a Zimbabwean. And this is what I believe in"? There is a lot at stake, as I know only too well. As Zimbabweans, we live on a continent and in a country where people die of easily curable diseases, where people still die of hunger. In this situation, few of us are willing to give up what little political security we may have eked out for ourselves, for fear of losing what little we have. . . .

I am Zimbabwean and proud of it. I was born in this country. When I was very young, my parents relocated to England for several years in order to pursue further education. It was in England that I first learned to smile when sweet old ladies called me "pickaninny." That is, until I went home one day after having smiled many times, after receiving sweets and pats on the head or pennies for my cuteness.

"I'm a little pickaninny," I told my mother proudly. Mum wasn't amused.

"No, you're not," she said tersely. And my mother was at that time a gentle, nonabrasive type, not often employing terseness. I knew something was wrong, but it was good to be found cute and sweet and to be given sweets.

"Why not?" I asked. "That's what the lady called me."

Mum made time to explain the derivation of the word from the Portuguese for "little child," and its generic usage to denote any child of color.

I had another run-in with "pickaninnies" several years ago at a writers' festival in Durban. The festival organized an essay competition for local Durban secondary schools. The prizewinning essays were read out at one of the ceremonies during the festival. The essay that won third prize was written by a young white girl, and it was the story of a maid on her Sunday off. This maid, too, ran past pickaninnies. I picked up on this, as well as on several other points, during the Q & A, when I asked the judges whether they had considered that they might offend young people from indigenous secondary schools, or that such offense might have easily been avoided by a change of language. Apparently, no one had considered these possibilities, which to me were very self-evident. In fact, I was censured for attacking and traumatizing the young writer. Actually, I was quite traumatized by the event, as I believe were all the young girls from indigenous schools sitting in rows at the front of the auditorium. Time has healed the trauma, but I remember the tears I didn't shed.

Slowly, I and some of the people involved revisited this incident. I was told, for example, that *pickanin* was a Zulu word for little child and the Zulus used it themselves. At this information, a lot became clearer. First, it was a question of intention when an act is committed. If a person does not intend to commit an offense with words or action, can he or she be blamed for using that particular word or action? Second, it was a question of ignorance versus knowledge. We know what we have experienced. If no one has reacted against the use of a word or action, then how will another know the word is offensive? The way I see it, objections have to be raised as and when necessary. In the context of *pickanin*, or its more correct original, *pickanina*, the phrase is a term that was used by the early Portuguese in this part of Africa to denote a little black child. It soon became a generic term, much as the word *boy* did. It connoted people who are looked down upon by the users of the term and furthermore is not used to generically describe their own children. By raising the objection and hearing other people's points of view, I began to realize how the young white girl had used the word without any awareness of its roots or racism or the relegation of African people to positions of inferiority. I did not condone her usage of the term, but at least, by challenging and listening, I was on my way to deeper understanding.

I'm feeling in a similar situation today after Zimbabwe's sixth election, and I'm dealing with the entire crisis in my country the same way as I have dealt with the question of being a *pickanin*: trusting personal and collective experience to inform me. This was why I returned to Zimbabwe in December 2000, to live at home permanently: to continue shaping my perspective on the situation of my country through firsthand experience. I left Zimbabwe for Germany in 1989 to take up a course in film and television studies in Berlin. Although I completed my course in 1997—by that time I was married and had children—my husband and I had not saved enough to relocate to Zimbabwe and make a living there, so we stayed in Germany. I was perpetually homesick.

Then in 2000, the land invasion started in Zimbabwe. This is what finally compelled me to act. There was widespread coverage of the invasions on German television. In June 2000, *ARD*, which is the main German program, showed footage of some young men throwing a burning log into a farm outbuilding. The commentary deplored the violence taking place in Zimbabwe. A little later, the same footage was used, this time to decry the escalating violence in Zimbabwe. Finally, the same footage was used a third time to talk about the absence of all law and order in the country. One newspaper compared President Mugabe to Pinochet; one blamed him for the plight of the Tunga, who had been displaced when the Kariba dam was built in the 1950s.

Finally, a professor from the university I was enrolled in for my doctoral thesis on the reception of African film told me she had been approached by a journalist who was looking for a Zimbabwean who took a different view from the pervading doctrine in the German press. The journalist wanted the Zimbabwean to write her or his point of view as passionately as possible. She thought I would do a good job. With much misgiving, but as I was broke, I agreed to write the article. Imagine my surprise when it was published alongside one by Peter Godwin of *Mukiwa* fame and the headlines suggested Zimbabwe was in a black-white conflict. I was terribly angry that I had not been informed. It was then that it became clear to me that I could not stay away from home and retain my national integrity. Without preparation, without work, with practically nothing, my husband and I and two small children relocated. Luckily I had a one-semester teaching job at MIT, so I was able to keep the family afloat.

Many people in Cambridge were interested in my perspective on Zimbabwe. I told them what I knew, how my father had always pointed out a big tree when we took a trip to our rural home in the beautiful eastern highlands. He told me that he had been born under that tree, but he and his family vacated the land when it was taken for cheap sale to British World War II veterans. I told my audiences of the members of my family who had been killed during the liberation struggle, including an older cousin who had cerebral palsy and had not understood the village order to take cover. Instead he had been told never to let the cattle stray, so when the alarm sounded, he ran around to round up the cattle. The Rhodesian security forces shot him in the back. My aunt found him later with his intestines spilling out. She heaped them back in, but he died in the general hospital.

These are the stories I tell because they are what I know, and I believe they have not been adequately heard. My point is that there has been a lot of suffering all around. Suffering is not limited to one group of human beings, yet it seems to me that some suffering carries more human weight than other suffering. It is not so much a case of "Do we not bleed?" as everyone, I believe, agrees we do. It is rather now a question of "Is our blood worth as much as yours? And do the wounds pain us as badly?"

ZAKES MDA: I will read a passage here from *The Whale Caller*, which is a novel set in South Africa in a small town called Hermanus. Hermanus is well known for whale watching. This is a love story, you know, the eternal triangle: man, woman, whale.

He has taught her to waltz to the songs of the whales. These are the most exhilarating moments of his life. Sharisha has gone back to the southern seas, but other southern rights are still here, providing the music. Sometimes a humpback visits and adds its thrilling notes. At dawn the Whale Caller wakes Saluni up and together they go to the Voelklip beach. Sometimes, more often of late, it is Saluni who wakes him up, since now she has got into the spirit of things. If the whales happen not to be there that dawn he calls them with his horn and they respond. He gets ahold of Saluni and together they float on the sand as if they are riding the clouds, as he used to float, albeit the rocky surface, during his days at the Church of the Sacred Kelp Horn.

At first Saluni was not too excited about these early morning frolics. But she decided to indulge him, especially after he had deserted her for the whole day and night to be with Sharisha on the eve of her departure.

Saluni had only been staying with him in the Wendy house for about ten days when one night the Whale Caller had a nightmare: Sharisha was being attacked by hordes of killer whales. The deadly orcas were concentrating mostly on the callosities, biting the chunks away. The water around was red. He woke up screaming. He knew at once that Sharisha would be leaving soon. Nightmares were her way of communicating that to him. He rushed to the bedroom and woke Saluni up to tell her of his fears. She was not pleased at all; especially because her head was pounding from a hangover. The previous night she had finished a whole bottle of wine brought from the mansion, while watching the Whale Caller cook his staple of macaroni and cheese. The drinking had continued while they ate the supper and while he washed the plates and pot. He had gone to sleep in the kitchen as usual, leaving her sitting on the bed, pretending to be in some tavern; singing colorful songs and cracking dirty jokes to herself, then rocking the Wendy house with her gruff laughter. To be woken up so early in the morning on account of bad dreams about whales was not something she was ready to entertain.

She shouted: "You and that ugly fish! I hope it goes away. . . forever! Maybe we'll have some peace when it's gone."

Without another word, the Whale Caller dressed up in his tuxedo, took his horn and left Saluni in bed nursing her precious hangover.

This time he went to his peninsula where he knew the curious could only watch from a distance. He blew his kelp horn, praying that Sharisha had not migrated yet. Her head emerged from the water, only fifty meters away. She rose out of the water and then crashed down with a loud splash. Refreshing droplets sprayed him. She rose again, turned in the air above the water, with yet another louder splash. Seagulls flocked to pick up from the surface of the water pieces of skin that she shed as she breached. There would be some lice to pick up too, now that she had been infested. Sharisha breached like that repeatedly, increasing the pace as the Whale Caller got more excited.

The rising sun found him sitting on a rock and blowing his kelp horn. Sharisha responded with her own love calls. She rocked in the water in a mating dance. The Whale Caller stood up and rocked on the rocks. He raised his left leg, turned and twisted on one spot, then stamped the foot down. He did the same with the right leg. He repeated this dance in a rapid succession for a long time, whilst blowing the sounds of the whining wind. People gathered on the shore and watched. Even those who had regularly watched the Whale Caller at his antics with the whales had never seen anything like this before. He did not seem to tire. He just went on and on raising his legs, spinning his sturdy body in the air, and then stamping his feet on the rocks. Sharisha did not seem to tire either. She was creating a whirlwind on the water by making a complicated combination of rocking, breaching and lobtailing. The rocking part—moving from side to side, and then forwards and backwards—fascinated the onlookers most for they had never seen a whale do anything like that.

By midday Saluni was getting very worried about him. She could hear the horn from the Wendy house. . . . [She] had not reckoned with the power of the whirlwind that Sharisha was generating in the sea, locking the Whale Caller tightly in her embrace. The sun was about to set and the Whale Caller had not returned. Saluni swallowed her pride and went down to the shore. The biggest crowd she had ever seen at his whale-calling events had gathered. People were clapping their hands in accompaniment to the kelp horn. And to Sharisha'a grunts and groans. It reminded Saluni of the charismatic church services that were sometimes held in circus-like tents by visiting superstar pastors. People babbling things whose meaning no one could fathom, then falling on the ground shouting the name of the Lord and foaming at the mouth. When they woke up they were saved and their road to Heaven was guaranteed. Only here the things they were babbling had nothing to do with the Lord. While some were egging the Whale Caller on, others were directing their encouragement to the whale. There those were just screaming and whimpering as if they shared the ecstasy of the man and his whale. . . .

The next morning the dance continued. Spectators returned and found the Whale Caller drenched in sweat. Both his horn and Sharisha were groaning deeply like out-of-tune tubas. Both were breathless as the dance seemed to be slowly fizzling out.

It was almost midday when Sharisha sailed away waving her flipper and the Whale Caller found his steps back to the shore. The crowd was going crazy, screaming, making catcalls and applauding. As soon as he reached the shore he fell on the ground in utter exhaustion. He was drenched in sweat and other secretions of the body. The front and the seat of his tuxedo pants were wet and sticky from the seed of life.

He opened his eyes and smiled at the wide eyes that were looking at him from above. The people went even wilder with applause. Saluni was among them. But she was not participating in all the excitement. She just stood there, arms akimbo, shouting at him: "You have shamed yourself . . . and me!"

CONTINENTAL DIVIDES

Joseph Lemasolai Lekuton and Cornelia Funke

JOSEPH LEMASOLAI LEKUTON: I'll begin by reading from my book *Facing the Lion: Growing Up Maasai on the African Savanna*:

> During the middle of the night, I woke to this huge sound—like rain, but not really like rain. I looked up. The starlight was gone, clouds were everywhere, and there was a drizzle falling. But that wasn't the sound. The sound was all of the cows starting to pee. All of them, in every direction. And that is the sign of a lion. A hyena doesn't make them do that. An elephant doesn't make them do that. A person doesn't. Only a lion. We knew right away that a lion was about to attack us.

I wrote this as a memoir about a small village in northern Kenya where my mother still lives in a cow-dung hut. She's never seen a television, a radio, or a telephone. I wrote it to describe my growing up in a nomadic environment where, without cows, any Maasai is like a zebra without stripes. Everyone wants to own as many cows as possible. It is the same cow that helped me come to America: I got a full scholarship to come to the United States to study but I didn't have airfare. So the village got together—some gave a cow, some gave a goat, some gave a sheep. They sold all those animals and bought me a ticket to come here.

It is in one of those cow camps where I faced my first lion. We all have our own lions; everyone here has a lion. The first one was a real lion that I faced with my spear and my club. I'm always trying, in my books, to tell American kids that you must face your lions; you cannot run away from them. The challenges that are constantly in front of American kids—from the cutthroat competition, to drugs, to peer pressure, everything—those are the lions American kids face. I attempt to tell my story of my own lion, that journey from there to here.

In Kenya, I went to school because it was forced on us. The government came and told us that each father must send one child to school. So I will read the part of my book that describes the day that started the journey that eventually led me to the United States.

The way the government people reckoned a child's age was to ask him to lift his arm, reach over the top of his head, and touch his opposite ear. A small child can't do that: His arms are too short. So they asked me, "Touch!" and I stretched, put everything into it, and just about reached—or at least got close enough to satisfy the police. It solved the problem for them and my father and my brothers.

I have two older brothers and my father pointed at brother number two, and the next morning he ran and hid behind a dam. For my brother, going to school was horrible, and he said he'd rather be beaten than go to school. So they found him and brought him back. He was so small, a lot of hair, chubby. They told my father, "Choose one," and he chose me—there was no one else. The villagers said, "There's something called jail, and it's very bad. If your father refuses, they'll take him to jail and he'll never come back to the village." So I said, "Don't worry, I'm going."

The next day I went to missionary school, where there was an American lady from California. The first thing this lady did was give me candy, and that was it. I had never eaten candy before in my life, so it was like magic. I stayed. And every morning I went there to get more. But in Kenya school closes every three months, and you have to go look for your family, who can be as far as fifty miles away. By the time I was ten, I was walking twenty miles by myself in the middle of the savanna with my small spear to look for my family every three months. I would sleep in trees in case there were wild animals, and I would eat small game and wild fruits, and keep looking until I found my family. Very tough life. There have been kids trampled by elephants. Animals are everywhere and you have to be very smart to avoid them.

In Kenya, the Maasai is always the bottom stratum in education. We don't have good education because we don't value it. So when I went to high school, I was looked down upon as a Maasai, a herdsman. People said, "What does your family do?" and I would say, "We have *cows*," and for me, it was such a pride to say. Other students would say, "What? Cows?" And you grow up with that. One thing I always say in my book is that you've got to be proud of your culture. My brothers have a lot of cows and each cow has a name, each of them. You can have two hundred cows and each one has a name. When the cows came come home in the evening, my brother stands on a small raised place, and in two minutes he knows which one is missing. That's incredible knowledge.

Two years ago I graduated from Harvard, and in the *Harvard Gazette*, they wrote about my graduation and how the only graduate whose parents are not proud today is me. It's true, because they don't know what it is. My mother cannot comprehend what school is. She has no idea. How can you know what a degree is if you do not know what a television is, or a radio, or an amusement park? I have pictures in my book of my mom. If she saw the book, she would say, "Oh, this is me." That's all she knows about the book.

CORNELIA FUNKE: So how does it feel for her to be in the book?

LEKUTON: She doesn't know what a book is. I show her and she says, "Oh." Don't think she isn't proud of me. She sits with all the women in the evening making beads and every time the radio says "overseas," she says, "Oh, my son went over the water."

FUNKE: Tell us about the Pinching Man.

LEKUTON: At home every village has a Pinching Man, who disciplines all the kids. The Pinching Man is this guy with a long beard, very dirty, and he chews tobacco all the time. He makes sure the tobacco saliva comes onto his beard. His nails are long and dirty. I don't know how many times I cried before I ever got pinched. Looking at him is scary. In every village, there is one.

FUNKE: I have to ask you, how do you become a Pinching Man?

LEKUTON: You have to fit that image. I'll tell you a good story about the Pinching Man. I was seven or eight, and every kid had a responsibility. Mine was to bring the cows out a mile away from village in the savanna, all the little cows. You have to take care of them and make sure they eat the grass well and then bring them home to the village. I told a man, "Listen. I've not seen a friend of mine who's four miles away in the middle of the savanna. Can you take care of my cows today and tomorrow and I will return the favor?" So he said, "Okay, go." I started running, and I was really, really chubby, but I didn't care. I kept running.

I met face to face with the Pinching Man, and he looked at me and his hands came out, and I wanted to die before he pinched me. He said, "Where are you going?"

I had to make up something quickly. I said, "My mother asked for sugar."

He said, "At this time?"

I said, "Yes."

He said, "Go to your mother's hut."

This was not good because my mom expected me to be with the cows from six in the morning until six at night, no lunch in between. I said, "Okay, bye." So he took off. I waited until he went around the corner. So I thought, I can't go on the lane because there's only one path. If I cut through the bushes, I could be killed by an elephant. I decided I'd rather be killed by an elephant than run into him again, so I cut through the bushes, ran to the village, and before he got there—he was such a slow guy, he took his time—I went and told my mom everything. She said, "You're a very bad kid." I said, "It won't happen again." The Pinching Man came and said, "How are you?" And my mother said, "I'm doing well. Come in." He said, "By the way, I saw your son running. Did you send him to get some sugar?" She said, "Yes, I did." So she covered for me.

But not all the time. I liked imitating people when I was small. And one day, I was imitating a warrior and said, "Who struts like this?" I made fun of him all day, and the kids were laughing. All the boys had taken an oath—the moment you're seven, no one knows what you do as boys because that's how you train yourselves to be warriors. No one knows your secrets. It's is a fraternity between warriors. But I had a cousin in the group, and she told the warrior what I did. I was inside my mother's hut and the warrior came in the evening after all the cows came home.

I came right out and said, "Where do you want me to go?" because I loved for people to send me to go get things for them.

He said, "Come here." We went to the bushes and he had a long, thin branch tied around his waist and I didn't see it. I said, "Where do you want me to go? Which village? Tell me; I'll run."

He told me, "Come here. You've been making fun of me all day." He took this whip and whacked me everywhere. My mom was in the hut, listening. So after that, I called a meeting with all the boys because I didn't realize my cousin-sister told on me. That's a big part of being a Maasai child: You cannot disrespect an elder and everyone has a right to correct you. Every village has a Pinching Man. You grow up as a child of the village. The village becomes you and you become the village.

Getting ready to come to America, to go over the water, I was very scared. I was afraid of what would happen to me. I worked so hard in Kenya to get good enough grades to come to America, and I was told, "America is very dangerous—many dangerous things. The most dangerous are the women."

So I said, "Yeah? How?"

"Because of the little bags women carry. They have guns this small, and if you scare them they shoot you."

So I spent a whole month, when I went to college, looking at the ground when I saw girls.

Someone also told me that you have to be well dressed in America, because if you don't, then everyone will laugh at you. So I said, "How can I make an impression?" I went and bought myself a three-piece woolen suit. It was ninety-two degrees in New York. I was walking around JFK airport, and feeling very good in my suit, very proud, and people were staring at me. I was thinking, Hey, I made the right choice—they really like my suit.

I say this here because I want to put a human face on Africa. I tell my students: Close your eyes and tell me the first thing that comes to mind when you think of Africa. Only animals and forests. No human beings. I wrote my book because I want people to understand that Africans love their culture. I decided to show them my journeys, and every summer I bring one to Kenya. It's part of teaching; it's a part of extending that culture from there to here.

FUNKE: This is from *Inkheart*.

Rain fell that night, a fine whispering rain. Many years later, Meggie had only to close her eyes and she could still hear it, like tiny fingers tapping on the windowpane. A dog barked somewhere in the darkness, and however often she tossed and turned Meggie couldn't get to sleep.

The book she had been reading was under her pillow, pressing its cover against her ear as if to lure her back into its printed pages. "I'm sure it must be very comfortable sleeping with a hard, rectangular thing like that under your head," her father had teased the first time he found a book under her pillow. "Go on, admit it, the book whispers its story to you at night."

"Sometimes, yes," Meggie had said. "But it only works for children." Which made Mo tweak her nose. Mo. Meggie had never called her father anything else.

That night—when so much began and so many things changed forever—Meggie had one of her favorite books under her pillow, and since the rain wouldn't let her sleep she sat up, rubbed the drowsiness from her eyes, and took it out. Its pages rustled promisingly when she opened it. Meggie thought this first whisper sounded a little different from one book to another, depending on whether or not she already knew the story it was going to tell her. But she needed light. She had a box of matches hidden in the drawer of her bedside table. Mo had forbidden her to light candles at night. He didn't like fire.

"Fire devours books," he always said, but she was twelve years old, she surely could be trusted to keep an eye on a couple of candle flames. Meggie loved to read by candlelight. She had five candlesticks on the windowsill, and she was just holding the lighted match to one of the black wicks when she heard footsteps outside. She blew out the match in alarm—oh, how well she remembered it, even many years later—and knelt to look out of the window, which was wet with rain. Then she saw him.

The rain cast a kind of pallor on the darkness, and the stranger was little more than a shadow. Only his face gleamed white as he looked up at Meggie. His hair clung to his wet forehead. The rain was falling on him, but he ignored it. He stood there motionless, arms crossed over his chest as if that might at least warm him a little. And he kept on staring at the house.

AUDIENCE: You speak very good English, yet you write in German. How does it feel to read your work in translation?

FUNKE: I love to taste English on my tongue. I take delight in it. I love the language. I think it's a very singing one. It's quite different than German. You have to work hard to make German sing. You can do it, but it's very hard.

AUDIENCE: I find it interesting that both of you started with rain, or what seemed like rain.

FUNKE: Yes, Lemasolai said to me, "In my country the people are so happy when they hear the sound of rain." I come from a northern country, and for us, it means gloominess, fog, melancholy. It means too much rain. If he were to tell my story to an African child, the child would think, She must be so happy. I would have to use a different image.

AUDIENCE: My question is about the cows. What are their names? Are they named after plants?

LEKUTON: No. They're named mostly after mountains and hills and rivers. Every cow knows its name. When you call it, it will come to you. My brother is very good with them. He knows everything about them. It can be the middle of the night, pitch black, five hundred cows, and he just goes and touches and knows the cow's name. He knows everything. Right now, I have a student who started a program called Cows for Kids. We're trying to buy cows for those children who have lost a cow because of drought. If you don't have a cow, you're nothing. These kids will go to school and other kids will ask them, "How many cows do you have?" If you say none, you're crushed. You have no dignity.

FUNKE: How much money do you need for a cow?

LEKUTON: One hundred dollars for a cow.

So now we're buying cows in Ethiopia. They have to be driven from Ethiopia to where I am—two hundred miles. We give them the names of the places they come from. But the kids also give them names. I told them, "You buy a cow, you pick a name." So five years down the road, there will be a lot of cows called Virginia.

AUDIENCE: Where do you get the ideas for your books?

FUNKE: That's probably the most difficult question ever. My head is so full of ideas that I have to write them down all the time. I have lots of files on my shelves for all the stories I want to tell, and I'm sure I can't do it in one lifetime. We're surrounded by ideas. Lemasolai will give me ideas now that I've met him. So everyone I meet and everything I see give me stories.

AUDIENCE: Your reading really reminded me of *The Sandman* by E. T. A. Hoffmann.

FUNKE: This is interesting. When I got published in England, I always thought, I'm so much in the Anglo-Saxon tradition, and then the English said, "You're completely wrong. You're in the German tradition. You're Hoffmann and the Brothers Grimm. That's what we find in your stories. It's not English." I suddenly looked at my own stories and found my own culture in there. Lemasolai is proud of his culture and he has many reasons to be. But I am German. This is something you can't be proud of, right? All of the Germans in this room know what I'm talking about. We have a different approach to our culture and we have to learn again to be ashamed of what's wrong with it but also to see the things that are wonderful. For example, we were big storytellers, once upon a time.

POWER STRUGGLES

Tsitsi Dangarembga and Achmat Dangor

YVETTE CHRISTIANSË: I'm going to begin by asking a broad question about beginnings. Tsitsi, if I may start with you: I know you were born in a small town in Mutoko, but you moved back and forth between Zimbabwe, what was then Rhodesia, and England. I was wondering if you could talk about the kinds of educations you had, both formal and informal, and how that influenced you as a writer.

TSITSI DANGAREMBGA: The formal education wasn't that different between Rhodesia and England because we were a British colony and all the practices were very similar. In fact, the informal education was quite similar as well. I think one learns early where one's place in life is meant to be and one has to decide whether to occupy that place or not. Luckily, my parents encouraged me not to occupy a set place.

CHRISTIANSË: Achmat, could you speak about the kinds of formal and informal influences you had in South Africa?

ACHMAT DANGOR: I had three kinds of education. The first was obviously the formal government schooling. My mother tongue was Afrikaans but my father said there was no future in the language and forced us to go to an English-speaking school, so I went to school and didn't understand a word. Simultaneously, we went to madrassa, which is where I learned to read the Koran in Arabic, and I didn't understand a word in Arabic. So I guess I compensated by finding an informal education, which was my grandmother's stories. That's where my love of literature came from. I think I loved the third part more than anything else.

CHRISTIANSË: Tsitsi, could you talk about the place for a young woman in the Rhodesia of that time and switching over to Zimbabwe?

DANGAREMBGA: It's really difficult for me to answer that question because I didn't conform to anything but I also wasn't consciously rebelling. The way I managed this—I see it in my daughter and I get frightened—was by going into my room and closing the door and reading. I could have been reading D. H. Lawrence at the age of ten. The next book might have been lighter, but this was the place where everything was happening.

CHRISTIANSË: Yes—the Famous Five. It's the colonial curriculum of another kind. You must know the Famous Five as well, Achmat.

DANGOR: Yes, I had another peculiar advantage in that in my grandmother's household, where I lived, there were her children, my uncle, and my aunt. My uncle, unbelievably in those days, was gay though he never announced it. He had a Jewish boyfriend, and that was also never announced. They trafficked in unbelievably wonderful literature, so, like you, Tsitsi, I was, reading books I never should have read at my age. Maybe that's what formed my imagination, reading *The Origin of Species* at the age of twelve. Then going to madrassa the next day and listening to these guys talk about how God created the world literally in less than seven days because Muslims always do it quicker.

CHRISTIANSË: At what point did the reader become the writer?

DANGOR: I think I always knew I would be a writer, but when I finished high school and for the first time resisted my father's will and didn't become an accountant, I went to Cape Town. I lived in District Six. For those of you who know South Africa at all, District Six is almost a mythical place. It was the one place apartheid had to destroy as a symbol of multiracialism. I lived in a room above Hanover Street and watched the world go by, and I had to record it. In a year, I had finished a monstrously big novel, which took me ten years to turn into something publishable. That's when I knew—sitting there and recording what I saw in front of me.

CHRISTIANSË: In *Waiting for Leila*, there's a sense that the character walking through District Six, which is about to be dismantled, is reminding himself of the streets, for his writing, because his place is about to vanish. Were you aware of what the fate of District Six was to be?

DANGOR: Not consciously. We all knew that the apartheid laws were coming in, that there was a Group Areas Act, and that this would be a designated white area. But for me, what was frightening was to watch how systematically the bulldozers pushed down this little city street by street, road by road, house by house. I saw history being made in front of me.

CHRISTIANSË: Tsitsi, you're quoted as saying you returned to Zimbabwe out of a sense of political and national service. And Achmat, I know that you have also done what one could call national service through your various involvements—the Youth League, the Kagiso Foundation. You're now at the U.N. in Geneva working on increasing awareness, activity, and action around the issue of AIDS. I wonder what role, if any, you perceive literature to have played in the struggles in which you have both engaged?

DANGAREMBGA: I made that statement a long time ago and I'd probably be less dramatic now. I think it wasn't so much the political sense of service, but the home instinct, if you like. I was in England and there were events taking place in Zimbabwe. This was 1979 and 1980—the country was becoming independent. Lots of Zimbabweans had left Rhodesia under schemes for displaced people and now the country was opening up. One didn't have to be displaced anymore so it made sense for me to go back and see what I could do in this place that was my home. This has happened again a second time now. It's funny how one's life repeats itself. I hope it's not going to happen a third time.

When I was in Berlin in 2000, unrest was beginning in Zimbabwe, and I felt compelled to go home, simply to be at home while all these things were happening, partly because by then, I had realized I was going to make narratives about what I experienced. It seemed important as a maker of narrative that I should be where the things are happening in order to witness it later on.

I think of myself as a storyteller. Maybe later on when I'm a bit older and experienced, I may think of myself as a writer. Now, I think of myself as a culture producer, someone who produces narratives.

CHRISTIANSË: So, your film *Mother's Day*: Are film and the written word just part of a continuum for you?

DANGAREMBGA: I find that. I also find that, given my character, it's good to have both. I really cannot take the isolation of being a writer; it just floors me and I haven't got the discipline. In between takes, ideas come while I'm busy with something else. I find that the two complement each other very well. I also find that one can do things in film that one can't do in prose and vice versa. It's interesting for me to be able to delineate what belongs to the realm of prose and what belongs to the visual realm.

CHRISTIANSË: What is it that film can do and what does literature do? It's a huge question, but humor us.

DANGAREMBGA: A film like *Hard Earth* is basically about the early months and years of the land issue in Zimbabwe; I shot that in June 2000. There's one scene where a man who's a landowner rides over to his estate on his horse with a film crew. I had a friend from New Zealand doing the shooting at that point; I thought it would be best if I didn't appear. So the man invites the crew back and as they're going into a huge Cape Dutch–style farm house, an old woman appears and the man starts laughing and says, "Oh, I know that woman. Her husband used to work on the farm. Look, she's really funny, I'll show you." He greets her and he says, "Mother, dance." She begins to dance and it's gruesome. He's standing there and the camera's running; the man *knows* the camera is running and he's laughing and saying, "I told you! She's so funny!"

This kind of thing cannot be written, or it takes a very different way of writing. But when people see that it's real, they can't accuse you of having staged something. It has a great impact. That particular scene always makes white people mad at me, I'm sorry to say.

CHRISTIANSË: Achmat, could you speak about the role you perceived literature to play during the struggle?

DANGOR: We must first remember that apartheid was an absurdity in which there was no such thing as normal life, and those of us who love the world, who love literature, who were exposed to literature, would have preferred just to continue writing. We had to put aside our personal ambitions just as people who wanted to be doctors had to put theirs aside. We became involved in the political struggle because the apartheid government gave us no choice.

I remember my emotions the day we watched Nelson Mandela walk out of prison. I thought, Perhaps we'll soon all be able to live a normal life because the leaders can run the country, they can get involved in the political struggle. We can go back to doing things we love. Writing and literature in South Africa during the anti-apartheid years, became, in the words of activists, a "cultural weapon." You had to use it to fight apartheid and some of us resisted that. How can you use your language? How can you use your creativity? But in the end, you recognize that you are facing a government that has absolutely no scruples about using culture and art to oppress you and you have to respond.

CHRISTIANSË: When you were publishing, you had access to—in fact, you were a founder of—Ravan Press. What other kinds of spaces were available for writers, particularly non-white writers in South Africa during this time?

DANGOR: We started a collective called Ravan Press, which became the vehicle for publishing many writers. But more important than formal publishing were the innumerable magazines and township samizdat newspapers. My work, even when I was banned, was being published under pseudonyms in newspapers, leaflets, and magazines. We used to distribute subversive little letters, cyclostyles. We made our own space because the apartheid regime denied it. There was no such thing as black literate culture.

DANGAREMBGA: In Zimbabwe, when we were going through the revolution, in the late '60s and '70s, people of color—indigenous Zimbabweans—didn't have the means to start up a press. Where did you get the money you needed?

DANGOR: A lot of people collected money individually. Writers like Nadine Gordimer contributed, so we had the big-name writers and some funding from external donors. Without the Dutch government and people in the Ford Foundation, Ravan Press would not have survived. The funny thing is that Ravan actually kept the bookstore alive; it sold. We were amazed at how hungry South Africans were for books. Ravan Press, by the way, was bought by a big conglomerate and has since disappeared.

DANGAREMBGA: Zimbabweans didn't have the money. We didn't have a culture of indigenous people who had been in an economic system for maybe a century. Also, our Rhodesian community did not have that long tradition of being in the country. They hadn't built up their own literary traditions.

One reason film seemed to be an appropriate medium for the kinds of things I wanted to do goes back to the liberation struggle. Literature did not play a big role. People had the standard Marxist texts at that time, but what was coming out of Zimbabwe was literature that had been ratified by the Literature Bureau—stories about witchcraft and wives and evil stepmothers. For me, the revolution in narrative came from the more indigenous forms of narrative—a lot of singing, messages put through songs. "The Voice of Zimbabwe," a radio station in Mozambique, really moved me every evening. My dad would tune in and you could hear songs and little stories: "It's Mom and Dad. We've gone out of the country, we're in Mozambique. But don't worry, we'll be coming back." That was a whole narrative in one song.

I think Zimbabweans are now looking for ways to bring that kind of feeling into what we're putting out. The written word, especially prose, is a bit constrictive. Sometimes I think one needs to bust out a lot more. Dambudzo Marechera was trying to do that in *The House of Hunger*. But I don't think all of us can actually get to that level, so other forms are also useful.

CHRISTIANSË: Could you compare the Zimbabwe of the moment you were writing *Nervous Conditions* with the Zimbabwe of now, when you're making your new films?

DANGAREMBGA: Psychologically, the space I walk in is very similar because a lot of the things that needed to be said about that time still need to be said. Maybe in South Africa more has been said in the sense that the racial issues of the conflict have been looked at. At least you're allowed to talk race in South Africa; in Zimbabwe you're not allowed to talk race. If you're black and you're talking race, you're a reverse racist. We never had that purging process, which I think the Truth and Reconciliation Commission began. What happened in Zimbabwe is that people had been bombing each other for about fifteen years, and then suddenly they said, "Let's be reconciled." People looked at each other and thought, "What's going to happen?" or "It looks as if it's going to be okay. Let's be reconciled." So everybody was walking about in the same little space they'd occupied before and nothing could actually happen. With the conflict now, we see that all these things are coming up again, whereas if we had dealt with them properly earlier, we might have resolved the issues.

In Zimbabwe, most publishers are putting out educational textbooks. They claim there isn't a market to sustain any other kind of publication. That could be true, especially in recent years with devaluation of the Zimbabwean dollar and everything becoming so expensive. But Zimbabweans are not really very conscious of literary standards. I think we need a lot of education to improve the standard of writing and then, when the writing is good enough, maybe we can persuade more people to publish.

The other problem we have in Zimbabwe is that we have an equivalent of a ban in that very few people are given money by foreign sources to make literature available, and usually the money is given to people whose points of view are sympathetic to what I call the Anglo-Saxon Axis. There are lots of other writers who may not be sympathetic to the goals of the Anglo-Saxon Axis, who are saying things that are relevant to Zimbabweans, things that the world needs to know about.

The problem with Zimbabweans is not that we don't read. We do. Anyone who's been to Zimbabwe has seen the second-, third-, and fourth-hand book-stores on the street. One book is being read by about twenty people. They might even be paying money for it and the price is decreasing each time. I really don't know what we can do about that. You really can't expect people to pay a lot of money for a book when milk has to be bought as well.

CHRISTIANSË: Achmat, what effect did the ban have on your writing?

DANGOR: I was included in a group of about twenty writers who came together and printed a book called *Black Thoughts*. Quite arrogantly, we thought we would combat the entire apartheid propaganda machine, which claimed there was no such thing as black culture and black writers. This was the 1970s, and postcolonial literature was coming to the fore, so we not only read our subversive poems to township audiences and anyone who would listen to us but we also read the books that were coming out of Africa. We were reading the first wave of neocolonialist skepticism—*Things Fall Apart*, books like that. We were taking into the townships culture that students and ordinary people were denied and this was deemed subversive. It was deemed more subversive than standing on a platform and saying "Stand up against apartheid." So they banned us.

The ban meant that I and the other twenty, along with eventually twenty thousand people, couldn't be in company with more than one person at a time. That was a social gathering; we were forbidden from participating in social gatherings. No newspaper could quote me, which meant I couldn't be published. Even worse: The wording said I couldn't prepare anything for publication, which meant I couldn't write. But it was probably my most productive year; I wrote and wrote and wrote, and we found ways of hiding and distributing things. We had pseudonyms. We wrote under enormous pressure because we could be found guilty, believe it or not, under the Suppression of Communism Act for being found at home writing. In many ways that was my most creative period.

CHRISTIANSË: Tell me about Buurmansdrift, which is a little town that some might know from South African history called Mafikeng. I know Buurmansdrift was really significant in your life as a writer.

DANGOR: Buurmansdrift means "neighbors' little town." It was a small little enclave on the way to Botswana. In fact, it was the route the so-called "terrorists" (the A.N.C. insurgents) used when they crossed the border from Botswana to South Africa.

My uncle had a small holding there, a little farm store. He was mixed like me, mixed Asian and everything. For some reason, the government didn't expropriate that farm. Every December, my family used to come from

Johannesburg to this place for a holiday; there was no cinema, there were no lights. The township was incredible in many ways, but at least there were lights; there was sound; there was music in the street. In Buurmansdrift, you had nothing but absolute silence, nothing.

I began to see what I called the many layers of our society. Conservatism had spread across the color line. If you spoke to the white farmer and you spoke to the black foreman and you spoke to my uncle, you couldn't tell the difference between them. Each hated the other. If they had prevailed, there would have been no reconciliation. For me, it was the dark side of my imagination. It did help my writing later on, my critics said, but not much.

ACHMAT DANGOR

QUIXOTE AT 400

A Tribute

SALMAN RUSHDIE: We're gathered here to praise what many people would call the greatest novel ever written: *El ingenioso hidalgo don Quijote de la Mancha* (*The Ingenious Knight, Don Quixote of La Mancha*). When there was a poll in Europe last year—I don't know if Americans were involved—well over a hundred writers were asked to name the greatest works of literature. *Don Quixote* came first, and poor old Shakespeare had to settle for second and third place. But just remember that the author of *Don Quixote* and the author of *Hamlet* and *King Lear* were born on the same day in the same year. Actually, *Don Quixote* was published in the same year as the story of that other mad old man, King Lear, so it was a great year for mad old men. There are more jokes in *Don Quixote*.

There's a sense in which India can take a little bit of the credit for this great novel. The clue to that is in the use by Cervantes of a narrator, a fictional narrator, an ostensible narrator who is not himself, but in fact a Moorish narrator, Cide Hamete Benengeli. Now, Benengeli is a very interesting figure in the book because in Volume One of *Don Quixote*, the book is episodic; it's full of little tales and actually it looks very like *The Arabian Nights*' framed narrative. You have the framed narrative of Quixote and Sancho Panza and inside that are set any number of wonderful tales. And to have that told ostensibly by an Arab narrator is, in my view, an obvious homage by Cervantes to the Arab origin of the wonderful tale. Now you have to remember that the Arabs didn't make it up; the Arabs got it from India. The Arabs had algebra; they can settle for that. But the wonderful tale came from India into Arab culture, from Arab culture to Spain, from Spain into the *Quixote*, from *Don Quixote* to Latin America, from Latin America into García Márquez. And so, you see, it's all India, really.

In part two of *Don Quixote*—in my view a better book than part one—Cide Hamete Benengeli changes: He becomes a very unreliable narrator; he keeps getting things wrong; he gets things wrong about the story; he gets things wrong about Don Quixote. And Cervantes has fun at his expense, which may be Cervantes's way of saying, "Well, okay, it's Arab up to a point, but I wrote this book." One of the reasons to celebrate this great novel is that it stands as the unifying novel between the literatures of the East and the West: It is the novel into which things poured from the East and out of which things poured to the West. The history of the literature of the world comes out of this single novel. And what better reason to celebrate a book?

LAURA RESTREPO: It is no coincidence that Don Quixote and Hamlet—the two literary characters who prefigure modern man, one from the Spanish language and the other from the English—are both crazy, or pretend to be. Both Cervantes and Shakespeare resort to this peculiar narrative recourse of making their respective protagonists mad, with the result that in the centuries following their works, the concept of the madman gradually came to be a hallmark of modernity, of otherness, of a subjective ironic vision of the world. It encompasses a freedom to err, to make a fool of oneself and of others, to doubt, to fail—which is to say, a freedom for human foibles to get their own way. But what is the symbolic connection between madness and modernity? Why should modern man end up recognizing himself in the words of a lunatic?

As Cervantes himself indicates again and again, the main cause for Don Quixote's madness is his reading of books of chivalry. This obsession leads him to lose his identity and to consider himself no longer as simply a person, but as a character. On the one hand, there's the everyday Alonso Quixano and on the other, the vision he has of himself as knight errant and righter of wrongs. To reinvent himself in the very likeness of what he has read, he gives himself the false name of Don Quixote, invents a suitable alias for his horse, conjures a fair lady out of thin air, and contrives a monumental love for her.

From his birth, Don Quixote's nature, as modern man's will be, is branded by culture and media. It is not by chance that Don Quixote is born at the same time as that first means of mass communication known as the printing press, which in turn fostered the widely disseminated literary expression: chivalric romance. Don Quixote rants on and on as he invents himself, and readers find him strange, find him crazy. But at the same time, they recognize themselves in him, and that's when the great transformation is revealed. For between Don Quixote and the world surrounding him, a powerful cultural mediator—language itself—has suddenly appeared with its immense power to shape reality and, not infrequently, supplant it. Don Quixote, the first modern man, goes from being a mere natural being to a cultural entity. With Hamlet, something similar happens: His madness is basically theatrical to the extent that he is *acting* as if he were mad. He sees the world as a scenario. In *Hamlet*, this new cultural reality assumes a power that finally imposes itself over the old other reality—the real one—which slowly unravels and is seen to be systematically suspect. Both *Don Quixote* and *Hamlet* confront us with a new type of human being who is no longer obsessed so much with reality as with the representation of reality through culture.

We are here today still traveling along the trail blazed by those two characters. It should be noted that maybe we're not discussing so much the influence of *Quixote* on people, but on the culture that human beings have generated. We cannot be accused of madness on this account. What for Don Quixote was madness is today a standard component of modern man, who mistrusts this faint element we call reality and even doubts its existence. We feel more comfortable trusting the symbolism of the real and its representations. We're no longer very interested in dealing with reality as raw matter, as we feel more on solid ground when we do battle with our own creations—the system of signs that constitute culture itself. In the seventeenth century, this peculiar form of epistemology erupted so unexpectedly that Cervantes had to call it madness. But lately, it has achieved a rare stature in the dominions of reason. Don Quixote believes himself to be a knight errant, yet he isn't. Cervantes undertakes to reveal to us his true face through a play of double articulation, a reflected vision that turns out to be typically modern. Between the man and the vision he has of himself, there is a disparity that induces vertigo.

With unlimited possibilities thrown into play and a nearly unmanageable dose of ambiguity, ultimately there is irony. This new type of human being suspects that there is an undoing, a mismatch between the self and the universe, between the subject and that which surrounds him, and it is precisely from this misunderstanding that modern irony emerges, with its Hamlet-like mistrust of the possibility of action. To conceive of the new man, one has to proceed through doubt, methodical doubt, according to the first modern philosopher, Descartes, but also through mockery. Cervantes makes fun of his characters, makes a grotesque creature, a freak. A similar tool of modern mockery later converts the Gregor Samsas of contemporary literature into beetles. In this way, man overcomes his own ingenuousness when he turns upon it this new disassociated ironic look. By overcoming such ingenuousness, he leaves childhood behind. Whoever allows himself to doubt and laugh leaves behind flat, decipherable reality to penetrate a more troubling zone, populated by chiaroscuro figures, by twist and turn, by double entendre, by resounding ambiguities. Doubt and humor imply the end of heroism; irony tends to paralyze the ancient faith that made action possible. Thus, Hamlet as avenger is such a failure and Don Quixote as knight errant is such a caricature. In these two characters, modern man recognizes himself as having recast the path of his own destiny and taken two steps back for every step forward, as getting tangled in one's own cape or pissing in your own soup. To put it in the words of Cervantes himself: "We recognize ourselves as having set off for the world through the wrong door."

The decisive game has ceased to be played on the terrain of reality and is mediated rather in the terrain of culture. As a result, we come to view certain attitudes imbued with too much reality as ingenuous, pre-modern, and passé. Too occupied with the avatars of the real, we find heroism suspect, not to mention any excess of passion or conviction or giving one's life for a cause or dying for love. Such attitudes are considered beyond the spectrum of what is reasonable. Serious writers have given free rein to a tendency to view social dramas, regional grammars, ordinary human grammars of flesh and blood—which is to say, the kind we see on the street, the kind that offend our sensibilities—as anachronism. We prefer to deal with it after it has been filtered, catalogued, and in some way tamed through obstruction. With the end of believing in any form of heroism, we have also exiled grandiloquence, pedantry, and melodrama.

But not everything has been profitable in this evolution of modernity. What we earlier termed methodical mockery turned out to be a devilish device that has ceased to obey us; once we have set it in motion, we run the risk of not being able to stop it. Irony opens decisive doors, but also carries within a burden of exhaustion, of disbelief, of paralysis, against which Rilke warned in his *Letters to a Young Poet*.

There is a fable from postwar Japan that tells the story of an octopus, left abandoned in an aquarium, forgotten by everyone, and unfed by anyone. Overcome by unbearable hunger, the creature begins to eat its own tentacles, day after day, devouring itself until it disappears completely. Then the aquarium appears to be empty, but the octopus continues to exist there, invisibly imprisoned by the same insatiable, perpetual hunger. For me, the idea of this octopus devouring itself, eternally hungry, invisible, yet fiercely there at the same time, is extremely disturbing. We may ask ourselves if our famished and voracious process of culturalizing everything doesn't resemble in some sense this unfortunate octopus. I ask myself whether we have had trouble so far along the path trodden by Don Quixote, whether by pure dialectical inversion, we may have already inadvertently spun so out of control; what was madness for him, for contemporary man turns out to be a privileged form of reason.

Nowadays, every windmill is some sort of giant invented by reason—or, as Goya phrased it, "The sleep of reason produces monsters." To believe in the real existence of windmills has turned out to be mere naïveté, or even worse, an unpardonable form of kitsch. We give free rein to our tendency to construct culture as if it were some kind of lasagna, layer upon layer upon layer. Cultural representations support previous cultural representations, and in turn generate subsequent cultural representations. And in the process, where is any link to reality to be found? Where has our old friend life itself gone? Like the octopus of legend, a culture that only feeds on itself runs the risk of disappearing up its own ass. The protagonist of Umberto Eco's latest novel, *The Mysterious Flame of Queen Loana*—who has lost his intimate personal memory while keeping intact his encyclopedic cultural memory—laments while attempting to recall his grandson: "I knew all about Alexander the Great, but nothing about Alessandro, the tiny, the mine." Perhaps he's lost his soul, to sum up the problem in his own words.

It's possible this may be the moment to reconsider, or at least to question, that which in the seventeenth century was such a discovery. That is why on this four-hundredth anniversary, we say with all our hearts, to our great Don Quixote, long life. May he live at least another four hundred years. At the same time, I believe we must recover from oblivion that which was once so healthy: the old, solid windmills of reality. We mustn't forget they also exist. Or who knows? Do they really exist? I have to confess, I suspect they might not anymore, except in the Netherlands of course, where they have been reduced to mere cultural ornaments.

ANTONIO MUÑOZ MOLINA: Becoming, not being, is what the novel as an art form is all about. And that is why we regard Don Quixote as the first modern fictional hero. In epic poems and tragedies, the task of the hero is to fulfill his destiny. According to Bellow, the be-ers are those who try their best to remain forever the way they are, who are content with their lives, with their names, with the places they live in. Becomers always feel ill at ease with the world as it is and what they love are not the certainties of being, but the adventures of becoming. There is always another life they would rather believe in, another country or distant city where they suspect a better life might be possible, another job, more beautiful or passionate lovers, more exciting friends. Personal identity is not their home but a prison. Identity, this celebrated mantra of contemporary culture, is not what they are in search of, but what they are very often fleeing from. That is why the heroes of so many modern novels are liars, deceivers, fugitives, impersonators, impostors, becomers—perpetually unsatisfied with their lot in this world, forever trying not to be what other people have agreed or decided they are, but something else, somebody else. For them, Arthur Rimbaud wrote, "True life is elsewhere." But then, Rimbaud was a fugitive himself, a poet and an outcast, who gave up poetry altogether and became an arms trader in Africa.

Nowadays, as in Don Quixote's time, social pressures compel us to conform to an established identity, to be part of a group and proudly proclaim what we already are, not what we have done or what we would like to be or do. Through our blind allegiance to an original culture, to our sexual pressure or national being, we are expected to achieve a better self, the only possible one for each of us. This seems to be a time for be-ers, not becomers. But that is precisely why *Don Quixote* is so relevant, especially to those among us who are not willing to abide by any fixed laws of identity. That is why we love to read novels in the first place and also why some of us like to write them.

In our time, to break through the boundaries, we are not supposed to trespass, to escape beyond the limits of the self, the frontiers of the space, in what Vladimir Nabokov called "the prison of time." Novels, stories, and plays are almost always about someone who is eager to escape, who sets out on a journey toward an uncertain destination. Like a spy or like an actor, the gentleman Alonso Quixano provides himself with a false identity before taking to the world. Chanting the name that was given to you at birth is the first step toward starting on a new life. After having read so many adventures, Alonso Quixano is ready to enact a new one that has yet to be written, namely the adventure of becoming one of the heroes he has read so much about. The author and master of his own story, like any other, he has to begin by choosing the right names for his characters—for himself, for the lady he has decided he must be in love with, even for his horse. Of course, we know he's a ridiculous old man, grotesquely caught up in homemade armor, so intoxicated by what he has read in books that he can no longer tell reality from fiction. We laugh at him because we know he's bound to be defeated again and again, to be taken in by his lack of attention to the hard facts of reality and his stubborn reliance on the lies told in books. But these are the dangers every becomer has to face. Not only the heroes we have learned to love in novels, plays, and films but also each one of us, who cannot say like Don Quixote, "I know who I am, and who I am in my heart of hearts has nothing to do with your ideas and your expectations about me." Our highest aims seem very often a ritual, and the same imagination that allows us to identify them exaggerates the hardships we will have to confront in order to achieve them.

Being is comfortable; becoming is risky. And there is always the chance that we may tilt at windmills, mistaking them for frightful giants. This is the second lesson we learn from Don Quixote and, through him, from Cervantes's wisdom and irony: You should have the courage to desire, but also the shrewdness to look very carefully at things so as not to get lost among the mirrors of your imagination. This book of laughter is also a book of sadness, and in its celebration of the power of desire and the joys of fiction lies a serious warning about the boundaries between self-invention and self-delusion. Having been a failure himself most of his life, Cervantes knew what he was writing about.

Many appearances are deceiving, as we readers of Don Quixote's adventures know all too well. Failure and success can be as deceiving as windmills and giants. Miguel de Cervantes was really only an obscure Spanish writer, a failed playwright, a handicapped veteran, a survivor of poverty and misfortune. What is it that has brought so many of us here tonight to remember his name and pay tribute to his masterpiece?

MARGARET ATWOOD: I'd like to speak briefly about a small piece of *Don Quixote's* posthumous life: the recent opera by Cristóbal Halffter, which premiered in Madrid at the Teatro Real in the year 2000. I saw it completely by accident. It was what was on; I knew nothing about it. This is an unmediated-by-media view of the opera; I didn't read any reviews.

This opera is one more installment in the continuing saga, the centuries-long afterlife of a literary creation. There's a book called *Dead Elvis* about the after-death activities of Elvis Presley—his appearances in parking lots and so forth. But a much thicker book could be written about the posthumous lives of Don Quixote. Don Quixote and Sancho Panza have been painted by artists and sculpted by sculptors and turned into ballets; they can be bought on eBay in many forms, including fridge magnets, posters, centennial trays, and ladies' cowboy boots. And a large number of operas have been written about them.

Halffter's surprising and audacious new opera is episodic rather than linear. As the audience takes their seats, a bulldozer is pushing piles of books into a huge hole in the middle of the stage. Cervantes enters, dressed solemnly in black, and makes his way to his writing desk. The writing into being of *Don Quixote* takes place in the vicinity of a memento-mori skull. Cervantes must die, as all human beings will, but then another image is presented to us: an enormous mountain of outsize books rises up through the stage. The small, buried, dead books have given rise to huge living books and as we watch, the covers of the books open and some of the characters of *Don Quixote* climb out of them. Two women are wheeled on in two gigantic red high-heeled shoes. I liked that part. They sing the roles of Dulcinea and Aldonza, the two aspects of the same person: the peasant girl Don Quixote decides is really a noble lady. In this scene, they also act as muses, inspiring Cervantes to create not only his novel but also themselves. This doubling of the heroine is repeated in the hero because the Don Quixote figure, who arrives from the air, a luftmensch in a monoplane, is the other self of Cervantes.

Next, the mock knighting of Don Quixote in the inn is accompanied by a chorus extolling the mindless life of the senses. The windmill scene follows; the windmills are giants for Don Quixote and windmills for Sancho Panza, but for Halffter, and thus for the viewer, they are giant, ruling, newspaper-printing presses. I was happy they weren't printing books, just newspapers, thus representing, says Halffter in his notes, "power exercised from banality by the liar, the mediocre, and the miser." Don Quixote fights them in the name of truth and justice and is defeated. In the next scene, Don Quixote's familiar domestic circle, the niece, the barber, the scholar, and the priest—well-meaning folk in the novel, but in the opera a more sinister bunch—denounce the books they feel have led Don Quixote into madness. The list includes, not only those authors named by Cervantes but also a great many others, including Joyce, Freud, Kafka, and Cervantes himself.

Then in come the two flocks of sheep, which for Sancho Panza are sheep, for Don Quixote armies, and for Halffter the forces of military might and the masses who obey them. This sheep chorus starts helping the domestic circle in their preparations for book burning. By this time, the mountain of outsize books is smoldering; these, we recall, are the books from which the characters themselves emerged. The characters are thus destroying the basis of their own reality.

The last scene in the opera is the death of Don Quixote. The books lie in ruins. Cervantes tells Don Quixote that he is not allowed to die; he is not a man but a myth, and his role is to fight, to right wrongs, and to bring justice to the world. At the end of the death scene, it is thus the Cervantes character who dies. The chorus of sheep happily believes it has triumphed over books, reading, and the imagination, and that it is now a mindless, homogeneous flock. But a cracked bell continues to sound: "the symbol of Don Quixote," says Halffter, "and all that was attempted to reflect through him: utopia, culture, tradition, chivalry, idealism, interpreted reality, creative fantasy, literary creation, and a lengthy et cetera."

There have been many other *Don Quixote* operas. The best known is probably Massenet's, in which Don Quixote is a persecuted Christ figure, too good for this earth. Halffter's intriguing version is closer to the spirit of Beckett and to the Ionesco of *Rhinocéros*. The Don struggles on against forces that are too vast and malevolent for him, but he struggles nonetheless. He does not win; the sheep are not destroyed. But he doesn't lose completely, either, since his cracked bell continues to sound. This is about as much sustained hope as we can handle here in the twenty-first century: the sound of a cracked bell ringing. What will Don Quixote become next? It's hard to say. But he will become something, for he is a figure of many lives, always transforming. In his multiplicity is the secret of his immortality.

PAUL AUSTER: In *City of Glass*, a man named Daniel Quinn, whose initials are D. Q., has taken on a job as a private detective under the name of someone called Paul Auster. He meets Paul Auster, who turns out not to be the detective at all. And they're having a conversation—this Auster that he meets is a writer, of all things—and during this conversation they have, I will quote, he begins to question Auster about his writing. Auster is somewhat reticent about it, but at least he concedes that he is working on a book of essays. The current piece is about *Don Quixote*:

> "One of my favorite books," said Quinn.
>
> "Yes, mine too. There's nothing like it."
>
> Quinn asked him about the essay.
>
> "I suppose you could call it speculative, since I'm not really out to prove anything. In fact, it's all done tongue-in-cheek. An imaginative reading, I guess you could say."
>
> "What's the gist?"
>
> "It mostly has to do with the authorship of the book. Who wrote it, and how it was written."
>
> "Is there any question?"
>
> "Of course not. But I mean the book inside the book Cervantes wrote, the one he imagined he was writing."
>
> "Ah."
>
> "It's quite simple. Cervantes, if you remember, goes to great lengths to convince the reader that he is not the author. The book, he says, was written in Arabic by Cid Hamete Benengeli. Cervantes describes how he discovered the manuscript by chance one day in the market at Toledo. He hires someone to translate it for him into Spanish, and thereafter he presents himself as no more than the editor of the translation. In fact, he cannot even vouch for the accuracy of the translation itself.
>
> "And yet he goes on to say," Quinn added, "that Cide Hamete Benengeli's is the only true version of Don Quixote's story. All the other versions are frauds, written by imposters. He makes a great point of insisting that everything in the book really happened in the world."
>
> "Exactly. Because the book after all is an attack on the dangers of the make-believe. He couldn't very well offer a work of the imagination to do that, could he? He had to claim that it was real."
>
> "Still, I've always suspected that Cervantes devoured those old romances. You can't hate something so violently unless a part of you also loves it. In some sense, Don Quixote was just a stand-in for himself."

"I agree with you. What better portrait of a writer than to show a man who has been bewitched by books?"

"Precisely."

"In any case, since the book is supposed to be real, it follows that the story has to be written by an eyewitness to the events that take place in it. But Cide Hamete, the acknowledged author, never makes an appearance. Not once does he claim to be present at what happens. So, my question is this: Who is Cide Hamete Benengeli?"

"Yes, I see what you're getting at."

"The theory I present in the essay is that he is actually a combination of four different people. Sancho Panza is of course the witness. There's no other candidate—since he is the only one who accompanies Don Quixote on all his adventures. But Sancho can neither read nor write. Therefore, he cannot be the author. On the other hand, we know that Sancho has a great gift for language. In spite of his inane malapropisms, he can talk circles around everyone else in the book. It seems perfectly possible to me that he dictated the story to someone else—namely, to the barber and the priest, Don Quixote's good friends. They put the story into proper literary form—in Spanish—and then turned the manuscript over to Simon Carrasco, the bachelor from Salamanaca, who proceeded to translate it into Arabic. Cervantes found the translation, had it rendered back into Spanish, and then published the book *The Adventures of Don Quixote*."

"But why would Sancho and the others go to all that trouble?"

"To cure Don Quixote of his madness. They want to save their friend. Remember, in the beginning they burn his books of chivalry, but that has no effect. The Knight of the Sad Countenance does not give up his obsession. Then, at one time or another, they all go out looking for him in various disguises—as a woman in distress, as the Knight of the Mirrors, as the Knight of the White Moon—in order to lure Don Quixote back home. In the end, they are actually successful. The book was just one of their ploys. The idea was to hold a mirror up to Don Quixote's madness, to record each of his absurd and ludicrous delusions, so that when he finally read the book himself, he would see the error of his ways."

"I like that. "

"Yes. But there's one last twist. Don Quixote, in my view, was not really mad. He only pretended to be. In fact, he orchestrated the whole thing himself. Remember: Throughout the book Don Quixote is preoccupied by the question of posterity. Again and again he wonders how accurately his chronicler will record his adventures. This implies knowledge on his part; he knows beforehand that this chronicler exists. And who else is it but Sancho Panza, the faithful squire whom Don Quixote has chosen for exactly this purpose? In the same way, he chose the three others to play the roles he destined for them. It was Don Quixote who engineered the Benengeli quartet. And not only did he select the authors, it was probably he who translated the Arabic manuscript back into Spanish. We shouldn't put it past him. For a man so skilled in the art of disguise, darkening his skin and donning the clothes of a Moor could not have been very difficult. I like to imagine that scene in the marketplace at Toledo. Cervantes hiring Don Quixote to decipher the story of Don Quixote himself. There's great beauty to it."

"But you still haven't explained why a man like Don Quixote would disrupt his tranquil life to engage in such an elaborate hoax."

"That's the most interesting part of all. In my opinion, Don Quixote was conducting an experiment. He wanted to test the gullibility of his fellow men. Would it be possible, he wondered, to stand up before the world and with the utmost conviction spew out lies and nonsense? To say that windmills were knights, that a barber's basin was a helmet, that puppets were real people? Would it be possible to persuade others to agree with what he said, even though they did not believe him? In other words, to what extent would people tolerate blasphemies if they gave them amusement? The answer is obvious, isn't it? To any extent. For the proof is that we still read the book. It remains highly amusing to us. And that's finally all anyone wants out of a book—to be amused."

CLAUDIO MAGRIS: Once, at school, when I was fourteen, a brilliant and controversial teacher of German questioned me on the relation between *Faust* and the French Revolution. When I, showing off somewhat, began to answer with the words, "Well, I think . . . " he stopped me at once. "What could you think, you wretch? Learn and repeat," he exclaimed, and then delivered a shock lesson on the fatal German imbalance between its extraordinary cultural flowering and its political backwardness, the source of world tragedy. "And on all this, Magris will ponder and perhaps will be so generous as to present us with the fruits of his thought."

We all realized immediately that this was a genuine paradoxical exhortation to *really* think, which does not mean to parade one's own opinion, but rather to draw close to the subject, putting brackets around the humors of one's own small self. The greater the subject, the more insignificant the personal reactions become. We may have our own personal opinions of an average writer, but in front of *Don Quixote*, we are all interchangeable. Conscripts of fate line up in front of love and death, the enchantment and the impossibility of living. I share Dostoevsky's hyperbole, according to which *Don Quixote* would be enough to justify the ways of man to God. It is a book that contains everything: the sublime and the base, the sacred and the scandalous, trust in man and religion, faith and chaos. Such all-inclusiveness would seem to authorize everyone to take the form of the book that pleases him most. That is not possible, however, seeing as those opposites are inseparable, like the two sides of the same coin. The cheese squashed under the helmet, which soils and mocks the knight of the sorrowful countenance, is also Christ's sweat of blood. Don Quixote, knight errant, who believes that he is of the old order, is par excellence the hero of the modern.

He sallies forth not so much to conquer the world as to search for and verify its meaning. This meaning does not exist and his obstinate search brings upon the knight disasters, beatings, unseemly humiliations, yet does not affect his profound need. Cervantes's masterpiece demonstrates the indissoluble unity of utopia and disenchantment. Utopia gives meaning to life because it insists against all proofs to the contrary that life has a meaning. Don Quixote persists in believing against all the evidence that the barber's bowl is the helmet of Mambrino and that Aldonza Lorenzo is the enchanting Dulcinea. He is wrong, and Sancho Panza sees that the helmet is but a bowl. Sancho understands that the world is neither complete nor true if there is no seeking for that shining beauty, the need for which reflects its own light upon rusty bowls and confers on reality the splendor of meaning.

When the knight recovers his wits, Sancho feels lost and maimed without those bewitching adventures and he becomes the true Don Quixote. But Don Quixote without Sancho Panza would be both empty and dangerous. Empty because he would lack the concreteness of existence. Dangerous as utopia is when it violates reality, confusing it with its own dream and brutally imposing that dream upon others, as is usually the case with political totalitarian utopias. When Sancho, hearing his master extol the prodigies and marvels seen in the Cape of Montecino, tells him that probably it's all eyewash, Don Quixote agrees. It is this capacity to believe and not to believe, to unite inextricably enthusiasm and disillusionment that enables us to live. Cervantes's masterpiece is the basis of modern narrative—its symbiosis of novel and novelistic theory, each merging into the other. It shows how attempts to redeem the world fail ridiculously, but also how the need to change and improve the world reasserts itself after each defeat.

Knocked about and yet indomitable, Don Quixote has faith not in life, which does not know what it is doing, but rather in books, which do not seem to recount life, but give it meaning, its banners. For these banners, he fights and is regularly and comically beaten, since almost always good loses and evil triumphs. But not even when he is unseated does he doubt those banners. When the bachelor of arts Sampson Carrasco fails him, he declares that his weakness does not compromise the truth of what he believes in. It is this awareness that enables us to live despite continual defeats. Sancho, no less great than his master, reminds us that men, namely us, are, as he says, "as God has made them, as God has made us, and sometimes, even a bit worse." Simply by knowing this, when some individual or indeed the world at large informs us, "You do not know who I am," we have the right to reply with the humble firmness of Don Quixote, "I know who I am."

NORMAN MANEA: We are celebrating four centuries since the birth of a masterpiece, author, and hero. In the last four hundred years, the irresistible errant and dreamer Don Quixote and his Sancho Panza have been accompanied by numerous relatives and successors and by many similar buffoonish couples made of the boss and of his servant. You may imagine the boss as the President, the General Secretary, the Chief of Army, the boss of your marriage or of your building, whatever you think. You immediately discover the servant. Even the history of the circus is focused on such a couple: the vain, dignified white clown and, august as a fool, the humble and humorous loser, kicked in the ass by his stiff and pompous partner. In Cervantes's narrative, the role of each is interchangeable with the other. The hilarious and wheedling companionship continuously varies the fascinating dynamics.

For somebody coming from the much-troubled area of Eastern Europe, it is not easy to ignore the connection between the history of the circus and history itself. The Communist Manifesto announced the specter of the great utopia haunting Europe, but failed to warn us against its bloody tyranny. The always deceived Sancho Panza was meant to take a deceptive dogma of the revolution as an entitlement and start the brutal war against everybody. Don Quixote's dream of bettering the world was to be used as a cover-up of a farce that didn't affect only the misleading irony of buffoons believed to be missionaries, but instead destroyed generations of victims—the specter of Communist totalitarianism and the nightmarish Nazi totalitarianism of the world's twentieth-century history.

We are paying homage to this great book in a time when we are reaching a routine cohabitation with a very different outrageousness: religious fanaticism and terrorism, political manipulation, the cacophony of perverted simplification, the belligerent marriage between a new messianism and an aggrandizing quixotic blindness. With a free market carnival, nothing seems visible unless it is scandalous and nothing is scandalous enough to be memorable. Yet we are celebrating a book. As long as we are still entertaining this childish ritual, perhaps not everything is lost. We never have been interested in our neighbors called Sancho, Dulcinea, the barber, the priest, or even the old madman, self-appointed great Hidalgo, as much as we were and still are in love with the characters impersonating them in this essential book about our not-too-idyllic human destiny. And we are grateful to our young Spanish colleague and master, Don Miguel de Cervantes de la Mancha.

ELIF SHAFAK

THE WAY WE LOVE NOW

Who Wrote the Book of Sex?

WAYNE KOESTENBAUM: This panel's title pays oblique homage to the late Susan Sontag, whose 1986 short story "The Way We Live Now" itself honored Anthony Trollope's 1875 novel, *The Way We Live Now.* "Now" is always a seductive concept, and it is always shifting. Love, too, is what semioticians might call "a shifter," a pivot term—empty, unstable, and meaningless, subject to contextual tides of history, temperament, and locale. Sontag's story showed how AIDS tore holes in our speech, introduced circumlocutions. To be polite, to be linguistically mild-mannered, she suggested, was to substitute the placebo of bad faith for the brutal elixir of truth-telling. This is the love panel. This is the sex panel. And this, perforce, is the perversity panel. Doesn't the word "love" always bring wrongness, errancy, and deviation into play?

To salute perversity I'll read two brief poems by Sontag's contemporaries Adrienne Rich and Frank O'Hara, North Americans who wrote straightforwardly, which, in their cases, means queerly, about ardor's incommunicability and whose candor about erotic disobedience preceded this country's reactionary turn away from free speech and free love. Here is "Poem XIX" from Adrienne Rich's *Twenty-One Love Poems* of 1976:

> Can it be growing colder when I begin
> to touch myself again, adhesions pull away?
> When slowly the naked face turns from staring backward
> and looks into the present,
> the eye of winter, city, anger, poverty, and death
> and the lips part and say: *I mean to go on living?*
> Am I speaking coldly when I tell you in a dream
> or in this poem, *There are no miracles?*
> (I told you from the first I wanted daily life,
> this island of Manhattan was island enough for me.)
> If I could let you know—

two women together is a work
nothing in civilization has made simple,
two people together is a work
heroic in its ordinariness,
the slow-picked, halting traverse of a pitch
where the fiercest attention becomes routine
—look at the faces of those who have chosen it.

And here is Frank O'Hara's poem "You Are Gorgeous and I'm Coming," an acrostic for his lover Vincent Warren, written August 11, 1959:

Vaguely I hear the purple roar of the torn-down Third Avenue El
it sways slightly but firmly like a hand or a golden-downed thigh
normally I don't think of sounds as colored unless I'm feeling corrupt
concrete Rimbaud obscurity of emotion which is simple and very
    definite
even lasting, yes it may be that dark and purifying wave, the death of
    boredom
nearing the heights themselves may destroy you in the pure air
to be further complicated, confused, empty but refilling, exposed to
    light

With the past falling away as an acceleration of nerves thundering and
    shaking
aims its aggregating force like the Métro towards a realm of encircling
    travel
rending the sound of adventure and becoming ultimately local and
    intimate
repeating the phrases of an old romance which is constantly renewed
    by the
endless originality of human loss the air the stumbling quiet of breathing
newly the heavens' stars all out we are all for the captured time of
    our being

ELIF SHAFAK: I will talk about how I interpret the relationship between sexuality and fiction writing and the relationship between sexuality and the fiction writer. Most of my remarks will be inspired by my experience as a woman novelist in Turkey. Geographical location is important. In Turkey, we do not like to see ourselves as a Middle Eastern nation. We prefer to call ourselves a European nation. However, as those of you who come to Istanbul know, at the one end of the Bosporus Bridge is written "Welcome to the Asian Continent," and at the other end of the bridge is written "Welcome to the European Continent."

The Turkish nation is a threshold society. Although the Turks would like to see themselves as a European nation, we do share many things with the Middle Eastern cultures. When we talk about Middle Eastern cultures and sexuality, especially in the West, almost immediately two things happen: First, it is always women we start talking about. Women become the object of our attention, the object to scrutinize as if there were no other actors or forms of sexuality to talk about. Second, sexuality becomes problematized, if not trau-matized. We start talking about honor killings, virginity tests, homophobia, and the colossal issue of the veil. I'm not saying that these things should not be talked about; they should certainly be critically evaluated. However, we oftentimes fail to recognize that this is not what sexuality is all about in the Middle East.

In the Middle East, sexuality is also about delight, pleasure, and yes, sexual perversion and the delight you derive from that. It's also about not knowing your limits. There's a long tradition behind that. There's a long tradition of eroticism, erotic literature, and especially homoeroticism. The interesting thing that happened in Turkey is that in the name of modernizing, secularizing, and Westernizing ourselves, we cut our ties with that erotic literature. This didn't affect the tradition of the poem, the genre of the poem, very much, but it did influence the genre of the novel because it is a very recent genre, and when it came, it brought us the voice of Westernization. The novelist, oftentimes the cultural elite, did not have any contact whatsoever with that old tradition of eroticism and homoeroticism. For instance, when we look at the Ottoman Empire, books on sexuality—*The Perfumed Garden*, not to mention *The Thousand and One Nights*—were circulated widely and widely read. So we lost that connection in a way.

The second source through which sexuality could be expressed was Sufi thought, different interpretations of Islam. We tend to regard Islam as if it were just one monolithic terrain. However, there's a big discrepancy between a more orthodox interpretation and a mystical interpretation of Islam. The latter is very much open to eroticism and the notion of desire and delight. There are many literary examples of this as well, but to tell the truth, it has a resonance with my personal life and my background.

As a child, I grew up with two different grandmothers. I lived with one of them for a short period and with the other for a longer time. At first glance, you would say there is no difference whatsoever between these two women. They come from very similar class backgrounds, they are both Turkish women, they are both Muslim women, and they both read the Koran. However, I think they read it in very different ways and with very different eyes. My grandmother in Smyrna had a god based on fear, the Muslim God. It was like a celestial gaze always watching you from above with a very paternal, patronizing gaze, seeing every sin you committed or you were even thinking about committing. I remember coming back from Smyrna pretty traumatized and not being able to go to the bathroom because if God is always watching you, you don't want to be seen naked.

The other grandmother was a different story. Again, of the same age group, a Muslim, Turkish woman, she was a woman of folk Islam and superstitions. She would say, "Yeah, the clergy is like that. Religion is like that. But they are bricks and you are water, so they will stand in your way, and you will flow." Her understanding of Islam was based on love, not fear, and in that understanding there was so much scope for delight and pleasure.

I think that is part of what differentiated me from many other Turkish novelists. The cultural elite in Turkey is cut off from these two traditions, both eroticism as a tradition and the Sufi tradition. My first novel, for instance, is the story of a hermaphrodite dervish with very heterodox views about Islam. He falls in love with an impossible lover—impossible in that he is in love with another man, who is Greek. It is, in a way, transgressing national and ethnic boundaries at the same time.

It was interesting to see how many veiled women brought me the book so I could sign it. Obviously they liked this book. I sometimes ask myself if I had told the same story in a different language, would they still accept that story in their houses? Because I do, as I said, use the tradition of Sufi language, an esoteric language, and the language of eroticism, which already existed in Ottoman times. By using these two traditions, I was able to enter people's houses, maybe through the back door.

I would like to say a few words about how I interpret the relationship between sexuality and the writer herself. Especially in Turkey, gender is of course a big, big, big criteria. But so is age. We come from a culture in which youth is not a good quality and is not respected. Age is respected. It's also a society that is very writer-oriented, rather than writing-oriented. When you write about sexuality, or anything else, they read the book but they think they are reading you. People don't discuss the book, the novel; they discuss you. It puts the writer at the center of attention, which can be suffocating if you do want to write about sex and sexuality.

Women novelists, in Turkey in particular, but in other parts of the world as well, have found three ways to cope: First, they do not write about sexuality until they are old. They wait, they wait, they wait. Then, when they're safe, they all of a sudden publish this book that is almost pornographic. The second strategy is that you do write about sexuality, but you desexualize yourself. You try not to look feminine, to look more masculine if possible, but to look, in any case, as desexualized as possible so you can be respected. The third strategy is to speed up the flow of time so you can age as quickly as possible. We age very quickly. We jump from the category of virgins to respected old women, and there are many women in their thirties acting as if they're in their sixties. You derive strength and respect from aging quickly. I try not to follow these three strategies. I try to develop my fourth strategy by going back to the tradition of eroticism and the tradition of Sufi thought.

ANTOINE AUDOUARD: "The Way We Love Now." I mean, who is "we"? Emily Dickinson: "That love is all there is, is all we know of love." Okay? That pretty well does it. So ladies and gentlemen, thank you very much for your attention and see you next year. This is going to be about my love, my life.

For many years, I led the life of the invisible man. As a child, I was kept silent by my father's wonderful talent for storytelling. As an adolescent, I always managed to pair myself with some other guy whom I thought brighter or funnier than me, who would run the show while I could play peeping Tom. As I grew older, I realized that in the company of real men, the self-effacing aspect of my personality was never a problem, that the world was full of people who needed to talk and be heard, and that my career, like a fly on the wall or a goldfish opening its mouth without emitting any sounds, was off to a good start.

The only ones who seemed to take notice of me were girls—nice girls, plump girls, skinny girls, dirty girls (never enough of those), romantic girls. While others were busy with the lofty task of changing the world or making serious money, I seemed to care only about two things: read every book I could put my hands on that established the tragic nature of my condition, and fall in and out of love. The in part was always the best. To be looked at with those eyes made me emerge from the mist of my invisibility and feel real—well, real enough until the real thing, which became very unreal as soon as it was over and done with.

I was a second-hand Don Juan. In my A to Z catalogue there were only 103 girls instead of the legendary *mille e tre*, a magic, impossible number—the human equivalent in the world of seduction of infinity in the world of mathematics. And yet, I promise you, I never played hard to get. It's not that I wanted sex that much. I sincerely felt the pangs of something I called love, for want of another word. What would I call it now? Infatuation? Boredom? The unbearable lightness of being? Whatever my efforts or my illusions or my perversity, I was lucid enough to feel like a bit part in a B-list romantic comedy, like the one where the guy says, "Hold me tight, make me feel real, " and then leaves without notice.

You must bear in mind that I was under the influence not of Dr. Ruth but of Franz Kafka, who let us establish the impossible nature of marriage or even of serious relationships and the irrelevance of any kind of romance. So I followed my impulse, as much as girls let me, only to write telegrams that went, "Sorry I skipped our second night. There will be no other night. Will explain later." As you would guess, later would never happen. It did once, twenty years later to be accurate, and I got slapped in the face as soon as I opened my mouth, but that's another story.

Some cried and called me a jerk; some just shrugged and let go. Some insisted on saving me—wonderful women, endlessly hoping that they might save us from ourselves. One day as I was trying to break up with an astrologer, she looked at me intensely and said, "I'm sorry, you can't leave me. I've been working all night on my astral software. And this is it. Your black moon is just in line with my sun. I'm the one you need." Although I didn't doubt for a second that she was right, I said I was sorry and I left all the same, only a wee bit faster. On my low days, I try to imagine all that would have happened between my black moon and her sun and this zodiacal bliss I nearly made.

Between the ages of twenty and twenty-four, I managed to publish three novels. War, love—I had it all figured out. I was invited to the literary program of Bernard Pivot, the creator of *Apostrophes and Bouillon de Culture*, but I was not formidable enough to be asked my favorite question: "If God exists, what would you like to hear him say?" The smartass answer I would have given: "Come along, angel, and meet the thousand and three virgins." Sorry—wrong god. Having made myself noticeable for a short while, I wisely decided that I'd said it all and proceeded to erase myself from the surface of the world. Invisibility is a good life. We all know that no one really cares about us. Only when you are invisible can you address your own nothingness with the needed care. Plotinus used to say we have to work relentlessly on our inner statue— chiseling, chopping off. I did just that, reaching moments of emptiness lighter than the air, heavier than water. I was a publisher, you see, and that helps. I didn't need to walk down the staircase of humility like Benedict (not XVI, the first). Any sales meeting would do the trick. My life was going to be spent like this: girlfriends, work, marriage, children, adultery, divorce, girlfriends, back pain, insomnia, more girlfriends.

Then, eleven years ago, something strange happened: I fell in love. I know, the big L word again. I will say with my shy, invisible man's voice that this time, it was different. I've been in love with the same woman for the last ten years, and I will be for the next hundred or so that are left for us. I fall in love with her every morning and I'm surprised she even recognizes me. Every time she leaves, I'm pretty sure she has abandoned me, which would be only natural, all things considered. But there she is.

As a result, I felt my invisibility receding into my soul, feeling real, day after day, loving to touch and be touched. Feeling unhappy made me write, and feeling happy made me write again with a sort of innocent joy that I thought was reserved for others. At first I'd write at night to make sure no one would see me, then I got bold and wrote in broad daylight. I still have guilt about this, always remembering that I should have some more serious occupation.

It's no accident that the narrator, in fact the real hero of my novel, makes himself invisible. I'm sorry I had to summon such formidable figures as the great Peter Abelard and the beautiful, unforgettable Heloise, to actually write my autobiography. The legend goes that when Abelard's tomb was opened for Heloise to be buried with him, he opened out his arms to welcome her. If, God forbid, it was to be reopened again, I fear they would both sit up in their graves, dust and loving bones, and curse me for using their tragic fate for such selfish purposes. My poor William is a man who sees and feels and thinks but is incapable of action. What's left for him except to become a writer? A failed life, or the feeling of a failed life is, for most of us, the best material for a good book, and for a bad one as well.

Most days I feel like those Vietnamese folklore spirits, neither truly human nor ghost but somewhere in between—wanderers traveling back and forth according to the breeze, the constellations of stars, or the crosstown traffic. Only when I open my eyes in the morning and I want to hold my wife and she wants to hold me do I feel fleetingly real and I think, as I do every day of my life, I know this is soon going to end. A hundred years from now for me, a few million years for our species, a few billion for life itself—I know nothing is going to be left of it, and nothing remembered. But God forgive me, and also Allah, Vishnu, Buddha the merciful, the compassionate pagan gods and goddesses of springs and winds, and I'm sorry if I forgot anyone, there is no offense meant. Let me tell you, it was worth it.

NATSUO KIRINO: Eroticism and its various definitions exist in paradox. It's the nature of human beings to be held captive by eroticism. Even while longing to be set free, we still seek to be held captive. It's a strange desire that tears the heart apart. Perhaps it points to the true state of being human. Based on this observation, I would like to discuss my work and some relevant issues within Japanese society.

In recent years, I have depicted in my novels mostly the losers in the game of eroticism. I am more interested in exploring the heartbreak and misunderstanding that sex triggers in both heterosexual and homosexual relationships, as well as its aftereffects, including despair and disappointment. In my novel *Grotesque*, which is currently being translated into English, there are two sisters, one who is incredibly beautiful and the other who is ugly. The youngest sister, Yuriko, has an otherworldly beauty, which has triggered men to pursue her ever since she was a child, but as she enters junior high, she becomes a prostitute. Why? Yuriko harbors an emptiness in her soul. Each time she has sex with men, she realizes that she exists solely as an entity to be taken from. And what is taken from her? When she realizes that the men themselves don't even know what exactly they are taking from her, she comes to the understanding that she can never escape from the emptiness.

There is another girl who is a friend of both sisters. She is a smart girl who is average in all other ways. The girl's name is Kazui, and she is the main character of the story. Kazui is a hard worker who tries to get good grades in school to secure a position at a prestigious company. She works equally hard at the company but she comes to a realization soon after she turns thirty: No matter how hard she tries, men maintain a standard that judges her on physical beauty, rather than on merit. She will never be judged for the qualities that lie within.

Kazui, who had worked hard all her life, finds but one path that will set her free: She decides to become a prostitute. This side job that Kazui keeps ends up splitting her apart. Day job and night job—her identity during the day and her identity at night. As the story unfolds, Kazui becomes anorexic, eventually losing so much weight that she physically morphs into a monstrous creature and is murdered by a customer. Yuriko, who is a professional streetwalker by then, is also murdered by the same man. The murderer is not simply a criminal but a man who symbolizes exactly what Yuriko has been robbed of. The man, for his part, does not understand what he is taking from prostitutes or what exactly he detests about them.

In this way that *Grotesque* encompasses the topic of eroticism and women, women and work, social context, the Japanese education system, and other issues. The point I was trying to make in this work is that perhaps there are no winners in this game of eroticism. I do understand that it is not simply a matter of winning or losing. When Yuriko, who has been a streetwalker for quite some time, bumps into Kazui, they have this dialogue:

"Yuriko, you really despise men, don't you? I always thought that you couldn't help yourself from loving men."

Yuriko responds to Kazui: "I dislike men, but I like sex. It's the opposite for you, isn't it?"

Kazui responds that she likes men, but dislikes sex. There is no way out for her.

Yuriko's response: "If you and I together became one woman then we could probably have a good life. But a good life means close to nothing as long as we are born a woman."

It's precisely here where readers notice that love is nonexistent in my novel. I took careful measures to eliminate love from the very beginning. Sex and love have two separate identities in Japanese culture. The reason I write about losers in the game of eroticism could be because I was born a woman in Japan. Japan had long had a system of authorized prostitution—places called *yuukaku*, which were licensed whorehouses. Men drank, bought women, and went home the next morning. Men who considered the *yuukaku* their playground were often thought of as cool and clever and even lauded for their behavior.

Of course there are no longer any *yuukaku* in post–World War II Japan, but they do remain in existence in a different form. It would not be an exaggeration to say that these *yuukaku* are responsible for building what would be considered Japan's culture of eroticism. In other words, the healthy love and romance that is born of modern male-female relationships is not the kind of eroticism that is desired. Instead, what is desired is a culture of eroticism that is strange in form, dependent on the woman establishing a separate identity from her everyday self. Love and sex form separate identities, and even if there is a period of happiness where they come together as one, it's in complete isolation from everyday existence. Japan showed us this strange culture at its root, and this was why, in *Grotesque*, I depict women who mainly long for the reunion of sex and love in bed. In addition, I depict the men who watch the besieged women in bed unable to make a move.

I don't think there have been any changes to better this situation. In recent years, there has been an increase in crime aimed at virgins—partly because the culture that kept love and sex as separate entities was internalized, and women started to step out into society, which caused men to develop a fear of the mature female. These men who rob women of their virginity are also losers in the game of eroticism. I intend to keep observing and gazing at these losers straight in the face.

MEIR SHALEV: When we talk about love, it's part of an international conspiracy: Writers know something about love that readers do not. The same way rabbis and priests and imams know things about morality and faith that simple believers do not. The same way we believe that psychoanalysts know something about the human soul that we patients do not. This is not true. The only thing writers know better is how to tell a story, a love story; how to phrase it, build it, put it in a way that will make the reader think differently about love. But we do not know about love more than you do. Right now, I can see at least twenty faces of men who have more experience and knowledge in love than I have, and at least ten women and three men with whom I have no chance. So I have to be modest in speaking about love. I write in Hebrew, which I can proudly say is one of the oldest languages still written in the same way, and is the language in which the very old love stories were written—Adam and Eve, Jacob and Rachel, David and Bathsheba, Samson and Delilah, all stories that can be read by Hebrew readers of today in the text of three thousand years ago.

So we write love stories for three thousand years and we still have no solution. We can just describe more and more love stories. We have no ideas, no clear understanding of love, and on the other hand, all of us know exactly what love and passion and desire and longing are until we are asked to describe love in words. But we know when we are in love. We know when we do not love anymore. We know when we feel lust, or longing. It is only the writing or expressing or the verbal part of love that is difficult.

I want to tell you the story of how my parents met for the first time because this is the story that created the way I understand love: It all takes place in 1946. My father was a young teacher and poet in Jerusalem. My mother was a young country girl from a village in the north of Israel. She came to Jerusalem with a group of other young high-school graduates to complete some courses at the university. She was eighteen, and there was a young man in this group who was after her, and they were walking together in the center of Jerusalem in Jaffa Street, one winter afternoon. Suddenly, a terrible, heavy, very strong, rare kind of rain poured down from heaven. They got soaked to their skins and this young man said, "My cousin lives very close by. Let's run away and find a shelter in his room."

They ran to the room, two hundred meters away. The young man was my father. For years he believed that this rain came down just for him. He even wrote a poem called "What Would Have Happened If This Cloud Did Not Come Over Jerusalem?" When I was about seven or eight and my sister was four, he used to sit with us at the table and we'd say, "Tell us the story," and he'd say, "Now, children, what would have happened if this rain had not come down on Jerusalem? I wouldn't have met your mother, and you wouldn't have been born." This is a sort of cruel story to tell children. I felt a little dizzy. And then he said, "Or, you would have been born to other people and then you would not have been yourselves." This is the conception of love I grew up on: something completely random. Most of us meet our future partners from a limited sample of the population. Statistically speaking, the best way to find your ideal match is to stay home and never leave, because the one who is looking for you knows where you are.

I want to read a short piece from my book *The Loves of Judith*, a story about a woman who comes to work in a village in the valley of Jezreel, where three men fall in love with her. Ten years later, she gives birth to a child who resembles all three men. Nobody knows who the father is. All three men claim the mother's love and the fatherhood of the child. One of them is Jacob Sheinfeld, a chicken grower. His hobby is canary birds. He talks to the little boy, who may be his son, and who narrates the novel:

> "You don't need big things to be friends. And to hate, too, very little reason is enough, and even to love."
>
> Jacob's voice cracked a moment. "You don't need big reasons to love a woman. And the size of the love has nothing to do with the size of the reason. Sometimes one word she says is enough. Sometimes only the line of the hip, like a poppy stem. And sometimes it's how her lips look when she says 'seven' or 'thirteen.' Look and see, with 'seven' the lips are starting out like with a kiss. Then you see the teeth are touching the lips a moment to make the 'v.' And then the mouth is opening a little . . . like this . . . se-ven. See? And with 'thirteen,' the tip of the tongue is peeping out for the 'th.' Then the mouth is opening and the tongue is touching the top of the mouth at the end."
>
> He stared at me as if he wanted to see if I caught the meaning of his words.
>
> "To understand that thing, hours I stood looking at the mirror. I stood there and I said all those numbers real slow, and I watched real careful how every number looks on the mouth. And once I even said to her, Tell me, Judith, how much is three and four? just to see the seven on her mouth. But she probably thought I'm nuts. And sometimes, listen, Zayde, just the eyebrows, just the eyebrows of a woman can grab a man for a whole life. . . . You can love a whole woman for a whole life just because of one terrific little thing she's got. Just remember that women don't know that, and you shouldn't tell them."

HANIF KUREISHI: I'm absolutely delighted to be invited to speak about sexuality, eroticism, and love. As my wife was saying to me the other day, "These are things you know a great deal about. You are clearly a world expert on this subject, and you've been invited to New York to lecture to the American people about sex, eroticism, and love." My wife is very sarcastic. As I lay on the sofa in my writing position, considering what she was saying, I went into a terrible panic. I know nothing about this. Not only do I know nothing about this but I've also managed to make other people whom I've been in love with feel worse than they would have felt if they'd never come into contact with me.

As I was thinking about this, I began, as one obviously would, to think about the Pope. I have the TV on in my writing room and there was the Pope, looking very good, very cute in his Nazi uniform. It suited him as a young man. I began to think, Well, who would be an expert on sexuality? I began to think about the Pope and the effect of religion on the sexual lives of young people around the world. I began to think that some of us in the West are able, in literature, in the cinema, in our meetings with one another, to have a space in which we can think and talk and explore our sexuality. When we think and talk and explore sexuality, what is it we're really talking about? We're talking about telling the truth, about lying, about fidelity, about infidelity, about homosexuality. Everything is connected to this primal act.

I began to think that our religions, not only Islam but also, obviously, Christianity, think and talk about sexuality all the time. Watching this chap Ratzinger and one of his cardinals on the TV, I heard an incredible word I'd never heard before, which really shocked me, in fact made my blood go cold: the "re-evangelicization" of Europe. I began to think of Catholicism as a huge corporation that was intending to re-brand itself in the West, and that there would be masses of propaganda. I began to be very, very afraid. I began to think of the writers of the last century who had run into enormous trouble with the religious authorities: Joyce, of course, Lawrence, Nabokov, Henry Miller, and our host, Salman Rushdie.

It often seems to me that a writer's job is to be irresponsible—we are not politicians; we don't stand for anything but our own imaginations. But keeping the spirit of sexual inquiry alive is very, very important. There is great danger with the rise—let's say the re-rise—of the new Middle Ages that we seem to be reversing into very rapidly at the moment. It seems ironic that we in the West are exporting democracy daily but we are also importing more and more religion, and that this act of social intercourse around the world is causing a new age of darkness. We, not only as artists but also as citizens of the world, need to think and talk with each other very carefully about the terror of religion, which is more or less entirely fixated on sexuality. These guys never do it, but they know all about it, and they're ready to tell you about it. Can you imagine? Would you ask someone to come and fix your car who had never seen a car before, had never looked inside, had no idea how it worked, but somehow had become an authority on cars?

It's a new era of darkness and I think that religions with their massive authority and their authoritarianism are very dangerous. In order to think about our sexuality, to think about our families, to think about how we want to live, the kind of relationships we want to have, and the kind of people we want to be, we at least need a space that's free of religious morality. If, at this conference, we have the opportunity to think of the relationship between the freedom to be a sexual being and literature and authoritarianism, we will at least be heading in the right direction.

PETER STAMM: I wanted to talk about love in Switzerland, but the country is so small, there's really not much to say. Only one detail: In Swiss-German "love" is not a verb; it's only a noun, whatever that means. When I thought about love, I thought about love stories. I thought about TV. Most of the love stories we see are on TV. Like murders, we see thousands of them on TV, but we don't usually see one in real life. This somehow takes the complexity out of love. The media teach us how to show our feelings. That's my fear: to end up feeling like people feel on TV.

There was a TV quiz on in Switzerland about twenty years ago, and when someone won a big prize he would just say, "Oh, thank you," and today he jumps up and down and screams. We have learned from American shows that this is the way you show joy. In my novels, I try to give back the complexity of love and to show love not only as a positive feeling but also as something quite complex. I'm going to read you a short passage from *Unformed Landscape*: A woman is traveling after a man. They finally meet and are staying in the same hotel room, but nothing has happened yet. They have a beautiful dinner in a Paris restaurant and now are back in the room.

> It was her turn to go to the bathroom. She got undressed, and looked at herself in the mirror, which was still steamed around the edges. Considering my age, she thought, and then, bah, who cares, whatever will be will be. She ran her hands over her hips, as if to sculpt fresh curves. This is me, she thought, this is my body. That's all there is.
>
> Kathrine washed with a cloth, she didn't feel like having a shower anymore. It was cold in the bathroom, but an English nobleman showered even when it was cold. He ignores the cold, she thought. He doesn't allow it. She combed her hair, tied it up, and then shook it out again. She plucked a few eyebrows, sniffed her armpits, and washed her feet in the bidet. She squirted a bit of her new perfume on her throat. It smelled of a different country, of night and of love. Why not, she thought, he didn't insist on having a second bed, after all. An English nobleman, she had once read, used the sugar tongs, even if he is all alone. She had never seen sugar tongs. She pulled on her panties. Then she took them off again, and stepped into the room quite naked.
>
> Christian was lying in bed. The television was on. An old film

starring Catherine Deneuve. Kathrine slipped in beside him under the blankets, and pulled them up to her throat. Christian didn't look at her, only moved a little to the side to make room for her, and turned the volume down. She felt his nearness, and the warmth of his body. He asked if she wanted him to turn off the television. She said it didn't bother her.

"Isn't she beautiful?" he asked.

"What film is it?"

"*Belle de Jour*. Catherine Deneuve."

"If I was French, my name would be Catherine too. What does the title mean?"

"Beauty of the day," said Christian. "It's the story of a bored woman."

He looked at Kathrine. She smiled. She had never been bored, even though her life was monotonous, even though nothing happened in the village. Her favorite days had been the ones where everything was exactly as always. Only Sundays had sometimes bothered her.

Shots rang out on the television, and Christian turned to see what was happening. She turned away and shut her eyes.

They finally make love five pages later, but it is on a night train, and night trains have no TVs.

THE FIRST NOVEL

Be my heroine, whispers the Novel to the Novelist.
Love me and die for me! orders the Novel to the Novelist.
Poetry, please lend me your blade, cries the Novelist.
It is as voluptuous to behead the one you love as to offer him your own head for a trophy, smiles Poetry.
The Novelist then writes:
One winter, I was traveling in a night train. All the windows of the dining car glimmered with the crystalled frost. A stranger sat down opposite me. Troubled, I dined with him, in silence...

—*Shan Sa*

HANIF KUREISHI

A HISTORY OF TRAUMA

Khaled Mattawa, Hanan al-Shaykh, and Fadhil al-Azzawi

KHALED MATTAWA: What's ringing in my ear now is the adverb "originally," and I want to discuss with Hanan and Fadhil the issue of origins. My question for them is about their early readings, their exposure to literature, and what led them to writing. There is a moment, an original moment, when one moves from being a reader to being a writer, and I want to see if our authors can tell us about when they discovered their literary impulse.

HANAN AL-SHAYKH: I used to read everything, especially inscriptions found with medicines, and I thought they were amazing. I used to love the words that I didn't understand. I used to also read the names of the shops, at a very early age, when I was walking in Beirut. There was one called *Nâr Wa Nûr*—"Fire and Light"—and these two words used to fascinate me. I would go every day just to look at the two big words.

At that time I was reading, like any young girl or boy, books for children taken from *The Thousand and One Nights*. But I never thought I would be a writer, except for one time when I was visiting my mother—she left my father and divorced him when I was five and a half or six. We weren't allowed to see her the first months after the divorce, but once she took my sister and me to the mountains. I was about eight years old and I heard my mother singing while I was in the bathroom, and all of a sudden I was so happy. I thought, I want to capture this moment, because I wasn't seeing her a lot. So I got a pen and paper and started jotting down these feelings—I didn't want the feelings to disappear. I remember putting the paper in my pocket, and every time my mother was sitting in front of me and talking to me, I'd get the paper and read what I wrote. I knew that the next day or the next I was going to leave her, so I was so happy that I had this letter with me.

Since then, whenever I was moved, either by something very nice or very sad or unknown, I would write it down. When I was fourteen years old, I started writing to our newspaper, which had a special page for the students. So whenever my brother wouldn't let me go out, for example, I would write something and send it to the newspaper, and this is how I started writing.

FADHIL AL-AZZAWI: I discovered literature very early when I was still in school, and I wrote my first poem when I was nine years old. I read Arab literature, Arab poetry, and I learned a lot of poems by heart. After reading and learning all these poems, I tried to imitate some poems in my schoolbook— which is how I wrote my first poem. Some of my schoolmates told my mother, "Your son is a poet." She called me, "Come, Fadhil. What a shame. Are you going to be a poet?" I said, "Yes, what is the problem?" She told me, "That is impossible because poets in the Arab tradition praise the government. Are you going to praise the king or the governors?" That was my first lesson: The poet must be not with these people but against them.

MATTAWA: Hanan, you seem to have begun as a poet by writing your feelings down. Another idea is that writers begin by trying to fill a gap, something they feel is missing in the world. Was there something missing in the world that hadn't been told?

AL-SHAYKH: No, I didn't feel that at all. I started writing my first novel, *Suicide of a Dead Man*, when I was nineteen years old, when I was a student in Cairo. It was after a big love affair. I was interested in words, not only as an expression of my feelings. I could have expressed my feelings in other forms. But I was really interested in literature, especially when I was in Cairo. The atmosphere in Cairo then was captivating. I didn't want to write to teach anything or anybody. I just felt I wanted to write about this episode at that time in my life, but from a man's point of view. The narrator was a man because I said, "I'm not going to be like all the other female writers in the Arab world." They were known—this is what the critics thought—to have one story, their life story. They're going to write it and that's it; they're not going to write again. I thought, No, I should be the man. My character was a man talking about existentialism, of course, and about his love for the woman, his sickness, and this girl who is young. I was talking about, in a way, how to get old, how you feel when you get old. And I was nineteen.

MATTAWA: Fadhil, you started out with experimental writing after your homage to classical poetry when you were nine. Was that your sense of the gap? Can we still approach this idea, this need? Was there something that you wanted to say when you were young?

AL-AZZAWI: Literature for me depends on the point of view. My first book was avant-garde and experimental. Why did this happen? Because at that time, I saw Arabic literature as very traditional. It spoke about old things and old emotions. I wanted to do something to attempt to renew the language. It was very important for me. I have read the old Arab literature, but I have also read Western writers—from T. S. Eliot to Ezra Pound to the Beat Generation.

AL-SHAYKH: Do you read them in translation?

AL-AZZAWI: I read some in translation, but also in English. Another source for my writing was Turkish literature. I'm from Kirkuk, which is very multicultural. In this city, we speak four or five languages as children. I speak Arabic, Turkish, Kurdish, English—English because the famous British oil company IPC is in Kirkuk, where many people worked, including my father.

I wrote once about the drunks in Kirkuk, the men who sing. There is in Kirkuk a kind of Turkish poem, only four lines but very, very beautiful. When the drunk people return late at night, they sing in the street—not old songs but new ones. They create in the moment. They sing very loud and everybody hears it. Another drunk in another city maybe hears it, then answers. And then another one, and there you have a dialogue of people with the people they hear, and this becomes part of literature and heritage without knowing who created the poem.

MATTAWA: You both seem to address and be concerned with issues of trauma. You are both interested in what happens after major events, in the aftermath. Why is fiction a better way, or the way you've chosen, to tell the truth about trauma, whether it's the postwar period or the period after a dictatorship or even the end of the world? Why is fiction the way to tell the truth about trauma, rather than documenting trauma itself?

AL-SHAYKH: I think I chose the written word to express certain things in the world—the violence in the world and the violence inside me. I cannot ask myself why I chose this form of expression; I feel that I always wanted to express myself by writing.

Before *The Story of Zahra*, I wrote a book called *The Praying Mantis*. It was the first time I lived in Saudi Arabia. I became a bride and my husband had work in Saudi Arabia, so we went there for one year. For the first time I felt that I was an Arab, a Muslim, and that this country was an Arabic country. I'm from Beirut, and Beirut was very cosmopolitan. So I wrote *The Praying Mantis* about being in Saudi Arabia. It made me go back to my childhood, to my early days and what I felt about religion—how my father wanted me to become religious. He was never a fanatic, but he was a very pious man. Because religion was strong in Saudi Arabia, it made me go back, and I felt that I wanted to express certain things about the status of women in Saudi Arabia and religion vis-à-vis myself and my upbringing.

From my second novel until now, I express things so I can feel that I have a solution. When I wrote about the war in *The Story of Zahra*, I was like a wounded mare; I couldn't believe that this is what the Lebanese were doing to the country. I couldn't believe that all the streets I loved one day became different streets—streets of violence and despair and crime. I thought, I have to sit and write a book because I want to be stronger than the warlords or I want to be at their same level so I can understand why they are doing this. I wanted to understand the war. I wanted to express how upset I was in a violent way. I wanted to write about a sniper because I was terrified of sniping and snipers. I couldn't believe that there could really be a man like me, from flesh and blood, who would perch on a roof with a pistol or a Kalashnikov and snipe people he doesn't know. So I chose to talk about all these traumas by writing.

MATTAWA: Did you go back to Beirut after you left?

AL-SHAYKH: Yes, I left in 1976 because I was so frightened of the snipers, and I wrote *The Story of Zahra* while I was living in London. Nobody wrote anything at the beginning of the war. We had only one question: life or death. You had to save and protect yourself. I kept going back to visit, and the second book I wrote, in 1994, was also about Lebanon. The war took another shape altogether in my novel *Beirut Blues*.

MATTAWA: Fadhil, I think your work responds to two historical events. One is the 1958 revolution, which had a great deal of violence and the other the 1963 coup, which toppled that leadership and also incurred a great deal of violence in Iraq, after which you spent some time in jail. This is where I position some of the sources of trauma in your work. How much did both of these experiences direct your vision, your material, or where you were going as a writer?

AL-AZZAWI: The whole history of modern Iraq is a history of trauma. It was 1958, I was very young, and I saw the destruction of the country, of the people. I knew a lot of writers in the world and I wanted to be one of them. It was impossible for me to be with the executioners. I was arrested many times and spent more than two years in prison. I was still a student in the university. I saw the hell in Iraq; in prison I met victims, young people destroyed, families. Of course I wanted to stand against that, to write, to do something. That was my challenge.

There are three levels of trauma. One is personal: the trauma I experience with violence. Then there's national trauma. And there is also a trauma for the whole world. I tried to write about that in *The Comedy of Ghosts*. I tried to rewrite Dante's *Divine Comedy* in a very modern way, to write a human comedy, an earthly or worldly comedy. Adam tries to reach Paradise but he has to go through hell, and this hell was the hell of Iraq, my hell, and the world's hell.

AL-SHAYKH: The trauma you're talking about is also living in an oppressive society. You feel it, as you said, on a personal level. If you write about it, you want to express certain feelings and if you write about it, you are somehow taking revenge—you understand that and you have to write about it as if you're fighting it or taking revenge.

AL-AZZAWI: I wrote about my prison experience in *The Fifth Fortress*—that was our prison, the Fifth Fortress—and about how innocent people are captured and destroyed. They didn't accept the book for publication in Iraq so I published it outside of Iraq.

MATTAWA: In shaping these experiences, both of you also experiment with the shapes of the novel. Hanan, you have the epistolary form in *Beirut Blues* and the multiple points of view and characters in *The Women of Sand and Myrrh*. Then you have a fast, almost cinematic pace in *Only in London*. These are markedly different undertakings. Did you set out to make sure your novels are all shaped differently? Is this a conscious decision? How do you go about choosing which form will fit and why? Can you take an example and tell us why one form was appropriate?

AL-SHAYKH: It depends on the novel and what I want to say in it. In *The Story of Zahra*, because of the sniper and the trauma of the beginning of the war, the first sentence made me carry on. I knew what I wanted to do because of the first sentence. When I decided to write this book, I was walking in London and I said, "What is the most traumatic experience I can visualize or think about?" And I thought about a girl not understanding what's going on. This was a parallel to my world because I still didn't understand what was going on in Beirut. So from that sentence, "We stood trembling behind the door—", I knew the novel should be about a mother and daughter, and I knew it should have a first-person narration.

With *Women of Sand and Myrrh*, I chose four women to talk about their experiences in the desert. In the first version, it was about God talking, or in the third person, and somehow it wasn't immediate; it was a bit artificial. So I thought that these four characters of mine should talk. It should be very immediate, because they are all in an oppressive society— I didn't name the place, but because I lived in Saudi Arabia, I based it on Saudi Arabia. The Lebanese girl, the American woman, and the two Saudi Arabian women—one of the Saudi Arabian women is still very naïve, very kind, but determined to change her life for the better, and one is decadent. I wanted to really hear their voices.

With *Beirut Blues*, because I was in London and the war was still going on in Lebanon, I thought, I can't talk as if I'm still in Lebanon; it has to be in letters because something should stand between me and what's happening there. I can be cunning when I'm writing, but deep down I'm a very honest person, even in writing. I thought, I don't deserve to write about the war in Lebanon while I'm away. Lebanese writers who are still living in Lebanon can write about what's going on from day to day while I'm in London, sitting facing the trees in a calm atmosphere.

In the last novel, *Only in London*, I started to reveal my hidden personality, the comic one, or the lighthearted one. That's why it's rapid and the tempo is hurrying; this is how I saw the Arabs in London—hurrying and trying to live another life and trying to change themselves. They all meet on a plane; their lives interact as well. It's culture. It's East and West, and this is the way I thought it should be.

MATTAWA: Fadhil, you mentioned *The Comedy of Ghosts*, and I see that even in your poems, the earth seems to shift under people's feet. The time and place are unfixed. It seems everything is linked to Iraq in one way or another, but time and place keep changing.

AL-AZZAWI: I read *The Thousand and One Nights* maybe twenty times before I was twenty. It is a fantastic book, and I have learned to mix reality, adventure, imagination, and different worlds. Picasso says that reality is not only this material reality—it's in our heads, in how we think about the reality. When I go to my head, I see the times and places mixed with each other.

We talked about trauma, but there is also humor in my works. Nietzsche says that inside every artist is a child playing. For me it is important to enjoy my work, to play in my work. But it is also important politically and culturally to create a new form and a new language. I wrote my first book when I was between twenty-five and twenty-seven years old. It's a mixture of novel, short story, poetry, essays, imagination, reality, and super-reality.

MATTAWA: Both of you have been living away from your countries. Almost half of your lives have been spent abroad. I don't know if you're post-national or not—you keep writing about your native places in one way or another—but you are living abroad and being translated and so forth. What is your sense of being a post-national or international writer, or this notion of being a writer of "world culture"?

AL-SHAYKH: When I sit to write, I don't think, except about what my characters are going to say and where I'm going to lead them. I face the empty page and I don't think about being the Arab who is living in London and still writing in Arabic. I just write—as simple as that. I continue to write.

MATTAWA: In Berlin, there isn't a big Arab presence—

AL-AZZAWI: There is, but they have no interest in the literature. The important thing for me is that I have lost my country. For nearly twenty-eight years, I didn't visit Iraq. I live outside Iraq. My readers are not only in Iraq but also in the whole Arab world. I consider myself an Arab writer—I write in the Arabic language—but I want to reach everybody. I want to write for all the people, but I write about what I know.

THE LAST IRAQ

Each night I sit Iraq on my table
and pinch his ears
until his eyes fill up with tears
of joy.
Another cold winter, crisscrossed by jet fighters.
Soldiers sit on a hillside
waiting for history
to rise from the darkness of Ahwar,
a rifle in its hand
shooting out angels
training for the revolution.
Each night I place my hand on Iraq,
and he slips through my fingers
like soldiers fleeing the front.

—*Fadhil al-Azzawi*

PACO IGNACIO TAIBO

INTERNATIONAL NOIR

Breaking Out of Crime Time

ROBERT POLITO: Noir is commonly thought of as an American genre, if it's in fact a genre. The films "noir" was first used to describe back in the 1940s were American; I'm thinking of the initial French writings in 1946 about a few films like *The Maltese Falcon, Double Indemnity, Laura, Murder, My Sweet,* and *The Lost Weekend,* which French critics were viewing for the first time, and the novels and stories that these and later films were based on also were American. But of course *noir* is obviously a French word, coined most likely in the model of *Série Noire,* the black-jacketed French crime novels. So this American genre with a French name was, right from the start, international. That internationalism is one of the assumptions of this evening's panel.

Another assumption, I think, of this evening, is that almost no one ever really plans to write a film noir; it's a term that's usually applied retrospectively (and maybe only *can* be applied retrospectively). Over and over in interviews with the great noir directors, you hear them refuse or at least deflect the name, saying they never set out to direct something called "noir." And the same is still true, I think, of most contemporary noir writers. The reason I say noir can only be applied retrospectively is that if you set out to write something called "noir," you almost invariably end up with pastiche, parody, or nostalgia. I prefer critic James Naremore's sense of noir as not so much a category of items with common properties, but a looser, more slippery network of relationships and associations that develop and change over time.

That said, I want to conclude by just glancing at some of the obvious achievements of American noir. The first is that historically and in the present, noir is one of the great sources of the American vernacular and the demotic. The film and sound editor Walter Murch told Michael Ondaatje in his great book *The Conversations,* "I spent a lot of time trying to discover those key sounds that bring universes with them." To focus for a moment on James M. Cain: The sounds of Cain's sentences, particularly his first-person fictions of the 1930s and 1940s, vividly shadow pure-product American characters. A concoction of carnality in California, highways, cars, fast food, and lunges at stardom, this Cain universe is instantly tangible, rooted in objects and work, fascinated by road signs, tabloids, radio, and insurance tables, yet tilting toward fable, even surrealism.

That leads, I think, to the second achievement of American noir: It's always been a home for experimentation. Think of the self-consuming narratives of Jim Thompson's novels, or the notion that the only American writer that Gertrude Stein wished to meet, during her triumphal American tour after the great success of *The Autobiography of Alice B. Toklas*, was Dashiell Hammett. Stein esteemed Hammett as a crucial American novelist; she invoked his writing as a counterpart to her own experiments in the stripping away of nineteenth-century psychology, character, even plot from twentieth-century fiction. The following year, she would observe in her book *What Are Masterpieces*, "It is curious, but the detective story, which is, you might say, the only really modern novel form that has come into existence, gets rid of human nature by having the man dead to begin with, the hero dead to begin with, and so you have, so to speak, got rid of the event before the book begins."

And last, noir is also a home often for radical politics and for novels of political and social history. As we say in the festival program, "From Hammett through Chester Himes, Jim Thompson, Charles Willeford, and on to James Ellroy and Walter Mosley, crime novels inscribed a black-mirror twentieth-century America far more dishonest and bloody than the country of official chronicles." In Europe, until recently, despite writers like Simenon, the push for secret history and covert historical reckoning tended to surface instead in espionage fiction. But much as once all politics famously were local, from now on, all crimes probably will be global. So there is at least one salutary effect of globalization—international crime, which leads us directly to tonight and to the search for other traditions, for other histories.

from **IDIOTS** by Jakob Arjouni (translated by Anthea Bell)

Ohio rose from his desk and, limping slightly, went down the hall, past four other rooms, and into the kitchen to make himself a cup of tea. The apartment seemed quieter and emptier every day. In fact it was full of furniture, some of which was inherited from his grandparents, and a collection of pop art posters. The expensively framed Warhols and Lichtensteins were all propped on the floor, leaning against bookshelves and walls. He had seen this effect in a documentary film about Picasso: pictures all over the house but none of them hanging. He had begun collecting the posters sometime in the seventies. At that point

Ohio had hoped for a while that with the new interest certain German publishers and newspapers were taking in American crime novels and light literature, he might finally join the ranks of those authors who were taken seriously. And because the people interested in this kind of literature were mostly young and modern, he began creating himself a new lifestyle, even though he was over fifty. Instead of listening to whatever was on the radio, drinking beer, and buying naïve paintings from Lake Constance, he suddenly began going in for French chansons, jazz, white wine, and pop art. He spent a whole summer going to readings by long-haired young authors, he visited exhibitions in damp cellars where bottled beer was drunk and New York bands played, and in the evenings he went to the Charlottenburg bars frequented by students and artists. He had a three-day affair with a girl student of American literature; it lasted until he gave her one of his novels. She read half of it, told Ohio his American Indians were racist clichés, and threw him out. Other acquaintanceships that he made that summer never lasted any longer than three days either. Sometimes a discussion in a bar about comparative structures of narrative in novels and movies would go on until eight in the morning, sometimes he spent the afternoon by the lake with a group of art students, all stoned out of their minds, who kept sending him to the kiosk every half hour to buy chocolate bars and pretzels, and once he was invited to a private porn movie show, which made him, apparently unlike everyone else, feel first embarrassed and then, also apparently unlike everyone else, horny—at least, after the show they all drank tea and discussed the difference between sex and eroticism. Ohio could do what he liked: be curious, interested, serious, ironic, get drunk, stay sober, boast, talk big, listen, chauffeur people through the Berlin night in his Cadillac, stand them drinks in bars, buy pictures from young painters, which his wife immediately stowed in the cellar, praise poems of which he understood nothing except that they mustn't rhyme, watch films of young people sitting on sofas, looking out of windows, and breakfasting half naked, take note of more and more new music groups, whose disks he bought and listened to in the afternoon so that he could join the discussion of them in the evening—but all the same, at the end of that summer he was still the weird old guy in cowboy boots, jeans, and denim jacket who wrote some kind of Wild West nonsense.

He put the kettle on the stove, took a teabag out of its packet, hung it in the cup and waited for the water to boil. It wasn't really quiet in the apartment either. Some kind of modern music echoed up from the floor below day in, day out, and there'd been renovations in progress on the floor above for the last three weeks. All the same: an empty, quiet apartment. Since his last mistress, Marita, moved away from Berlin, he had had exactly nine visits in four years. Four times, always at Christmas, his widowed sister came. She'd hated him ever since, in that hopeful summer in the seventies, he had described her husband, a police officer, as a Nazi and a petit bourgeois (he really did it only on account of the student of American literature, so that he could feel close to her once more; that was two weeks after she threw him out, and he hadn't seen her again). Twice he had a visit from his son, who worked as a head of department for the Karstadt chain of stores, speculated on the stock exchange as a side line, and spent his visits sitting on the sofa following the share prices on television. Once his daughter came with her new boyfriend, about the fifth since her divorce; the boyfriend's parents had emigrated from Turkey and he kept making jokes about the Turks, which first irritated and then infuriated Peter Ohio. And finally there were two visits from the Giselle Publishing concept manager, aged thirty-one, who wanted to persuade him to lend his name to a new series written by a young team. The central character was a kind of Greenpeace version of James Bond, who in the course of the first twelve episodes turned out to be the disowned and repudiated son of an Arabian royal house. Brought up as a child by a lonely old Christian lady, he had seen so many accidents at oil wells and pipelines in his native land that when he reached twenty he decided to save the earth. Meanwhile, he appreciated good champagne and would remain a bachelor for the time being, breaking hearts but never a promise to God.

"What utter tripe!" said Ohio. "Who reads that sort of stuff today?"

"Oh, Peter!" The concept manager succeeded in giving him a smile that was both admiring and superior. "You may have changed, but the world hasn't. People still want this kind of thing. Come on, do yourself a favor, you'll get a quarter per cent, and what do you have to lose?"

My name, Ohio almost said, but he saw the trap just in time. "You probably won't understand me, but all the same: I've been writing this stuff for forty years, and there's no realistic prospect of the name Ohio being connected with anything but cowboy adventures, but it's been my pseudonym for over forty years, and at least once I want to write a real book under it."

JAKOB ARJOUNI: *Idiots* is not a crime noir story; I mean it's about a noir crime writer, a Western writer. My relation to crime writing, it's funny that I say "crime writing" and not "noir" because "noir" for me is so French—I don't know what this word means in New York. For me, I think there was never a big difference between noir novels and non-noir novels. Maybe at the beginning, when I was very young, it was a kind of alternative literature to the school literature. My first contact with literature, by chance or by accident, was a noir novel, when I was ten years old. Dashiell Hammett's *Red Harvest* was a shock at this age—a good shock, a wonderful shock. I didn't understand anything, but I felt there is something behind the mountains that I don't see, but it must be wonderful, and one day I will understand it. And then I was going on and reading all this stuff, Hammett especially, who is still one of my most important writers, not because he writes crime stories, but because he is a wonderful modern writer. So then I continued to read Chandler and Himes, and later Charles Willeford was one of my favorites. When someone told Chandler, "There's so much crap in crime novels," he said, "Yeah, but in every kind of literature there's a lot of crap," and I think he was right.

But then I wrote other things, novels and short stories and even fairy tales. I think the only difference in literature in general, in storytelling, is that you have two kinds of suspense: One suspense is what happened and the other suspense is how it happened. The suspense of "what happens" happens more in crime fiction. I don't know how many possibilities there are for "what happened," but there are five billion possibilities for "how it happened." And the suspense of "how it happened" is in good crime novels, as in all good novels. This is what I'm interested in as a reader and as a writer. For a lot of people, the suspense is "what happened." I think the "what happened" suspense is a kind of adolescence. When you are between or not so sure with your sex, when you're "figuring out a lot of things," then the "what happens" suspense counts a lot. People who don't make things clear are working with the "what happened." Now I have the impression that my English is definitely a "what happened" suspense.

So anyway, in the end, I just want to say I think there's wonderful literature in crime writing and there's wonderful literature in non-crime writing, and the only difference is that the frame is different. But in the end, it's always about people and relations between people and societies. And there are good books and bad books, like Chekhov said.

from **OUT** by Natsuo Kirino (translated by Stephen Snyder)

She got to the parking lot earlier than usual. The thick, damp July darkness engulfed her as she stepped out of the car. Perhaps it was the heat and humidity, but the night seemed especially black and heavy. Feeling a bit short of breath, Masako Katori looked up at the starless night sky. Her skin, which had been cool and dry in the air-conditioned car, began to feel sticky. Mixed in with the exhaust fumes from the Shin-Oume Expressway, she could smell the faint odor of deep-fried food, the odor of the boxed-lunch factory where she was going to work.

"I want to go home." The moment the smell hit her, the words came into her head. She didn't know exactly what home it was she wanted to go to, certainly not the one she'd just left. But why didn't she want to go back there? And where did she want to go? She felt lost.

From midnight until five-thirty without a break, she had to stand at the conveyor belt making boxed lunches. For a part-time job, the pay was good, but the work was backbreaking. More than once, when she was feeling unwell, she'd been stopped here in the parking lot by the thought of the hard shift ahead. But this was different, this feeling of aimlessness. As she always did at this moment, she lit a cigarette, but tonight she realized for the first time that she did it to cover the smell of the factory.

The boxed-lunch factory was in the middle of the Musashi-Murayama district, facing a road that was lined with the gray wall of a large automobile plant. Otherwise, the area was given over to dusty fields and a cluster of small auto repair shops. The land was flat and the sky stretched in every direction. The parking lot was a three-minute walk from Masako's workplace, beyond another factory, now abandoned. It was no more than a bare lot that had been roughly graded. The parking spaces had once been marked off with strips of tape, but dust had long since made them almost invisible. The employees' cars were parked at random angles across the lot. It was a place where no one would be likely to notice someone hiding in the grass or behind a car. The whole effect was somehow sinister, and Masako glanced around nervously as she locked the car.

She heard the sound of tires, and for an instant the overgrown summer grass that bordered the lot shone in the yellow headlights. A green Volkswagen Golf Cabriolet, top down, drove into the lot, and her plump co-worker, Kuniko Jonouchi, nodded from the driver's seat. . . .

"Let's go," Masako said. Sometime after the New Year, she'd begun to hear talk of a strange man hanging around the road that led from the parking lot to the factory. And then several of the part-timers had reported being pulled into the shadows and assaulted before barely escaping; so the company had just issued a warning that the women should walk in groups. They set off through the summer darkness along the unpaved, ill-lit road. On the right was a ragged line of apartment blocks and farmhouses with large gardens—not particularly appealing but at least a sign of life in the area. On the left, beyond an overgrown ditch, was a lonely row of abandoned buildings: an older boxed-lunch factory, a derelict bowling alley. The women who had fallen victim to the attacker had told of being dragged in among these deserted buildings, and so Masako kept careful watch as she and Kuniko hurried along.

NATSUO KIRINO: I debuted as a novelist twelve years ago. Before I became a novelist, I studied screenwriting, wrote for magazines, and also wrote books aimed at young adults, including storylines for *manga* or graphic novels. Since then, I have published fourteen novels, three short-story collections, and a book of essays, which brings the grand total to eighteen books. I have one book out now that has been translated into English, and two books, *Grotesque* and *What Remains*, are being translated into English as we speak. It's my hope that they will be available next year.

Upon hearing that I have written eighteen books in twelve years, some of you may think, "My, does she work hard." But in fact, among Japanese novelists, this is not an excessive amount of work. Novelists in Japan write a whole lot. Once you are a published professional novelist, work requests become rampant. In Japan, there are a total of seventy thousand published items per year. Literature composes one-sixth of this total, which brings the number to twelve thousand; that includes magazines, paperback books, as well as children's literature. But even so, there are few countries in the world that can say they publish a thousand literary books and magazines a month. I must point out that foreign books in translation are included in this number as well. Books in translation make up 15 percent of the total, though recently there are signs pointing to a decrease. I believe it's still quite a significant percentage.

Since modern times, Japan has made an effort to bring many books originating in Western cultures to the forefront. Indeed, a good number of the World Voices participants' works have been published in Japan, not to mention the fact that most books deemed as foreign classics and masterpieces have repeatedly been introduced over the years. I can confidently say that though the Japanese may not be good at communicating face-to-face, we excel at taking words under careful consideration and have a keen ability to comprehend and express them in graphic form, as in *manga* or animation. We have a large domestic market and therefore even more competition. This is why even the experimental attempts are highly coveted. It's my hope that there will soon come a day when the Japanese novel will cross the language barrier to be read by many across the world, and that one day it will not just be Haruki Murakami who is read by fans of Japanese literature.

Out was published eight years ago in 1997. It depicts four housewives who work the midnight shift at the factory stuffing ready-made lunch boxes sold at convenience stores. Each of the four women are suffering and have different repressing elements in their lives as they continue to work under the demanding conditions of the factory to make ends meet. One of the women, in a fit of fury, ends up killing her negligent husband and asks her co-workers for help in disposing of the body. The women come together to chop the body up into little pieces and dispose of it as common garbage. After the fact, instead of repenting, the women start a business disposing dead bodies, make a lot of money, and run headfirst into a life of crime. As you can see, the story is quite shocking, and when the book was first published, I received both praise and condemnation. Most of the criticism was from people who could not believe that the wife would kill the husband. Or there were those who were frightened that anybody would chop up a body into little pieces. Though it was nominated for a book award, it did not win on account of its antisocial views.

Since I did my research for *Out* during 1995 and '96, it's fair to say that the Japan depicted in the book is a Japan of a decade ago. Back then, Japan was a lot more prosperous. But on the flipside of the prosperity were the housewives who worked part-time jobs and the foreigners who worked the low-end jobs. Even around me, there were women whose husbands had white-collar jobs, yet still insisted that their wives work for their own spending money, additional household income, or to help pay for a child's education. These women left in droves to work part-time at menial jobs. When I heard about how much these women made, I was shocked; not only were they making less than the student workers, but also they received no insurance, no social-security benefits. In addition, they had to work knowing that they could be laid off at a moment's notice when profits slumped the least bit.

This type of circumstance was all too common in Japan. And this was how I came to write *Out*. Represented in the background of *Out* are elements of significant Japanese societal problems and issues of gender inequality, family problems, foreign workers, and the political constitution. A novelist takes the elements of life experienced unconsciously by those who live it and tells a very sad story out of it, though exaggerated if you write a novel that has impact. If there are people who felt liberated by my novel, then the novel served one of its purposes, and when those outside of Japan read it, they will see something they were not able to see before: the underbelly of prosperity. They will also see that when it comes to human sadness and hardship, ethnicity and gender make no difference. This is the power of the novel. I research, then write my novels according to what I am interested in at the moment. In other words, it's my way of contemplating the time we live in.

One of my novels currently being translated, *Grotesque*, depicts the story of a woman who has a career at a large corporation by day, but who works as a streetwalker at night. It's the story of how she ultimately meets with unnatural death. The main theme of the book is beauty and its ugly stepsister, and the story is finally a study of female sexuality. The other novel being translated, *What Remains*, is the story of a young girl who was kidnapped and grows up to become a novelist. The story travels back to address what actually happened and explores what kind of man the kidnapper was. It addresses the difficult theme of how words and the imagination bloom in a person who is robbed of her freedom.

As I depict shocking and disturbing crimes in many of my novels, I have been known as either a noir or crime-fiction writer. Since I also take up women's issues in my novels, I have also been called a feminist novelist. I must say that I very much dislike being defined by the boundaries of a genre or, for that matter, being defined, period, because I only write about the truths I see using my own imagination. As I mentioned earlier, I take from people's unconscious and think about the times we live in. I do not know where the novel will take me. When I am defined by a genre, I am defined from one particular angle. I worry that my work will not reach readers beyond those boundaries. That makes me extremely anxious. I write believing that the power of the imagination can change the world.

LUC SANTE: The legend of Georges Simenon expresses itself in statistics: four hundred books, ten thousand women, half a million pencils, some exalted quantity of pipes. The books have gone through staggering numbers of editions, have been translated into every possible language, made into some sixty movies and innumerable items for television. The Simenon legend is industrial, like one of those nineteenth-century literary factories, of which Balzac and Dumas come most readily to mind. Unlike Dumas, however, Simenon could never be accused of running an atelier in which underlings came up with plots and undertook the less glamorous portions of the labor. He may have relied upon typists and secretaries, some of them cleverly disguised as wives, but every word he wrote originated in the fevered recesses of his own mind.

The first thing I ever knew about Simenon was that he'd written an entire novel while enclosed in a glass booth in full view of the public. I heard this from my father, and for some reason I was persuaded that he himself had witnessed the stunt, which did not seem implausible since our town was only ten or fifteen miles from Simenon's native city of Liège in southern Belgium. The feat never actually occurred, although a Parisian publicist nearly talked Simenon into pulling it off in the mid 1930s. My father was not the only person who believed it had really happened. By that point, Simenon was publishing three to twelve books a year, which must have seemed leisurely to him after the frantic pace of his first professional decade. In 1929, he had achieved his peak of annual production: forty books under an assortment of pseudonyms.

Perhaps because he wished to dispel the notion that he employed subcontractors, Simenon allowed his method to be known. On the other hand, maybe he told interviewers about it just because the method itself was so prodigious. On a large yellow envelope, he would, over the course of a week or two, write the names of his characters and whatever else he knew about their lives or backgrounds, their ages, where they'd gone to school, their parents' professions. The envelope might additionally contain street maps of the novel's setting, although it would never say a word about the book's eventual plot. Once he was satisfied with these notes, he would enter the hermitage of his study and knock off the book at the rate of a chapter every morning, optimally in a week or ten days. After finishing, he would be drained, battered by violent psychological storms and concurrent physical symptoms. It was a bit as if he'd given birth. It should be noted though that he could write books this way even when he was ostensibly on vacation.

Not all his books were written so quickly, although the majority of them were. In this and many other countries, Simenon is best known for his detective novels featuring the agreeable and placable, slow-moving, intuitive, preternaturally observant Inspector Maigret. But among the novels he published under his own name, the Maigret books are outnumbered nearly two to one by the titles he called *romans durs*, hard novels—hard in the sense that they are uncomfortable. In nearly all these books, a character, generally someone who's been leading a humdrum, predictable existence, is confronted by an unexpected occurrence, setting in motion a series of events that will test his limits, an experience he may not survive. These books feature a broad range of characters who are subjected to an apparently unlimited inventory of psychological torments. You imagine Simenon selecting a pedestrian seen in passing somewhere near one of his homes or on one of his many travels, speculating as to what that person's internal and external life must be like, and then devising a suitable chamber of horrors in which to release his captive specimen. Because Simenon was so prolific and so various, it is difficult to render a concise account of his work and impossible to cite any one book as typical of him. His early, pseud-onymous output is pretty crude; and several of the earliest Maigrets feature plot turns that would not seem out of place in a Philo Vance mystery. But even then, in the early 1930s, he was capable of writing emotionally demanding novels that drive the knife deep into the reader's heart.

Simenon, the son of first-generation petit-bourgeois parents who took in lodgers to supplement the family income and whose idea of higher education was limited to secondary school with the Christian Brothers, entered his liter-ary career with a distinctly working-class idea of the trade. It was a means of living by one's wits, related to showbiz and not too far from simple hustling, and it required a constant output with no pretensions and no looking back. Somewhere along the line, though, he made a signal discovery: Much of what passes for literature merely consists of studies of people in their clothing—that is, people operating within the rigid confines of social codes. He, on the other hand, wanted to write about the naked human, who is forced by circumstances to confront life without the usual protections. Those same social codes made him an outsider and kept him one, even at the height of his fame. He had served his apprenticeship writing pulp fiction and had cemented his reputation with detective novels. Furthermore, he was Belgian. He also lacked a writing style detectable by the belletristic apparatus of the prewar era. Therefore, he was forever barred from being accepted as a man of letters by the people in Paris who decided such things. André Gide was his great admirer and sponsor. At first Simenon chafed at this restriction, the first symptom of his discon-tent being that he packed Inspector Maigret off to rural retirement in 1934. Although he bowed to popular demand and brought him back eight years later and spent the last quarter century of his career alternating metronomically between the Maigret and the hard novels, which he also called *romans-romans*, novel-novels.

The latter are so numerous—there are 117 of them—that I confess to not having read even half, but they include many that should be better known. *Dirty Snow* is a supremely bleak evocation of the horrors of the Second World War and the chaos of its aftermath and an existential endgame that can be usefully compared with the works that Sartre and Camus were issuing at the same time. Almost immediately after the publication of *Dirty Snow*, he came out with *Pedigree*, an autobiographical novel of his youth before and during the First World War, a massive book three or four times the size of most of his others, which achieves an epic grandeur of thought and a beaverish accumula-tion of mundane details. It may be his masterpiece, or one of them, although it's never been published in the United States. And those two books merely represent his output for the fourth quarter of the year 1948.

Simenon's work, when you begin to delve into it, is unlike that of any other author except perhaps Balzac. It seems less like the labor of one person than the entire hitherto unsuspected national literature, not just in its size, but in the range of its approaches and preoccupations. He may be the most famous unknown writer of the twentieth century.

from **LEONARDO'S BICYCLE** by Paco Ignacio Taibo
(translated by Martin Michael Roberts)

He deceived the concierge by telling her he was fifty-two on the day he turned fifty-three. A pickup truck with loudspeakers passed by below his apartment window, beginning the election campaign. He left the faucets open so that the water would run for some time while he was shaving himself, as if the year he had pilfered would go down the drain along with the dirty shaving foam. Throughout the morning he had listened to dire old and scratched records by the Glenn Miller Orchestra, pretending to work on a new novel. He ate canned tuna fish with mayonnaise, and some whole wheat bread that was slightly moldy.

It was only when, alone, he switched on the TV to see a ladies' basketball game from the U.S. college league that José Daniel Fierro found the peace he had lost and felt he had discovered a worthwhile way to celebrate the ominous birthday that was bringing him closer to old age.

His liking for American lady basketball players was the result of a succession of accidents, all with marked soap-opera-like overtones, admissible in the case of people unlike him, those who always emerged unscathed from harsh reality. If he had not broken his ankle while walking down the steps in the National Film Theater one night after a film lecture. . . If he had not installed cable television in his apartment in order to keep his plaster cast company. . . If he had not spent three months struggling with the writing of a novel that, frankly, did not exist. If it were not for these twists of fate, he would never have discovered his latest sexual perversion. Because faithfully following women's basketball games from the American college league—or the ladies, as the commentators preferred to call them—was not a sporting passion, much as José Daniel tried to fool his puritan subconscious, saying that if some liked boxing, horse racing, or sumo wrestling, then he. . . .

It was sex pure and simple and, moreover, it was sporting sex, platonic, long-distance, and minority sex. In a country where there are so many majority sports obsessions, being in love with a lady American basketball player was a minority sporting passion, a tacky one really, without any allies to call on the phone to comment on the games, and that seemed to reduce everything to a masturbation substitute. . . .

"And you can see Jackie O'Brien's D-cup when she reaches out to catch the rebound . . . And you can even see her pubic hairs when she makes that tremeeeeendous leap in the air."

It was sex-at-a-distance. Three weeks previously, the commentators in Houston, who José Daniel admired at a distance, had picked the Texas Longhorns as their favorite team, and he had followed them intently from that moment on.

"And slipping as she loses her balance, we see twenty-year-old Ludmilla Washington landing with her ass against the basket uprights. . . And she likes it! Ladies and gentlemen, she likes it!"

Thanks to the discovery of the Texas Longhorns, José Daniel began to write down the times of all the games on TV and, faithful as could be, while buses went by on the street with their exhaust pipes open and the sweet-potato sellers' carts whistled past, he would drag his broken leg over to the brown chair his ex-wife left behind, put a six pack of Tecate to one side, and begin to watch the American college girls.

"And just as Eloisa Waterfront throws the ball while she closes in on the enemy's turf, she sets up a terrible wobbling in her crotch, with her vaginal fluids lubricating the fabulous pace that brings her up to the basket, alternately lifting her buns up, one-two, one-two, bringing her to the edge of orgasm, and making her give the ball away, while she concentrates on coming, ladies and gentlemen, but she takes no notice, she does not care . . . That's how you *get to heaven*, baby. Thirty-six to twenty-nine, you stupid bitch."

The Texas Longhorns were a marvel of extramural and (José Daniel added in his spoken journal) uterine fury. Passion, pure and simple. They fought for each ball as if their lives depended on it, they argued with referees as if they were permanently suffering from premenstrual tension, they celebrated each basket with howls of enthusiasm, made fun of their opponents, blew kisses to their acne-faced adolescent fans in the front rows, missed easy shots, and scored impossible ones.

He adored them.

But that day, his damned birthday, with fifty-three years weighing him down, he was about to see a sight that would change the next few months of his life and, to a certain extent, his whole life (as José Daniel would like to have said in a novel, writing like Victoria Holt). First, the phone rang. Then Karen Turner entered the fray, and the cameras gave the writer, who rose hobbling from his chair, a big close-up of her freckled face.

And then, as Jose Daniel Fierro hesitated between answering the phone and sitting down again, drawn by the electromagnetic pull of the new player's face, the writer, condemned to the loneliness of his room by a broken foot, watched the girl smiling at him, and went completely crazy. As an old soap opera had once said: "He lost his powers of reason over an illusion."

PACO IGNACIO TAIBO: Maybe that book explains why I'm writing what you can call mysterious or crime fiction or something like that. I started with that love relation between a writer with a broken leg and a female basketball player from the ladies—they called them the ladies, I liked that—the ladies. But then I decided, this is too easy, this old-man passion, sex—sex, which is, by the way, very common these days.

So I decided to put together another story in that same book, which is the story of why Leonardo da Vinci, in the fifteenth century, invented the bicycle. But nobody believed that, so I had to do research for months trying to show how he invented the bicycle. I started writing, writing, writing, and then I discovered what Freud said about Leonardo, so the Leonardo story about how he invented the bicycle went into the book. Then I decided that this is too easy—basketball, mystery writer, in love, Leonardo da Vinci's bicycle. . . So I went to a story I had in my closet about the dark moments of Barcelona in 1920, at the end of the war. There was a huge street fight between the owners of the factories and their gunmen and the police against the anarchist unions. It was some kind of OK Corral version that lasted three years, and two thousand people were killed in the streets.

But I thought, that was too easy for a novel. So I picked up in the closet a beautiful story about the last American who abandoned the Saigon embassy in Vietnam, after the war. The last one—he wanted to take the last helicopter. So I started studying all of what I could find about Saigon in the 1970s and I discovered the last one was a guy who had a drug organization, very, very strong in Saigon, and he was afraid to lose it so that's why he was the last one. So I said, "Well, let's put these things together, then we really will have a novel." But, but—I felt that was too easy.

So I decided to put together a huge story. And I remember that somebody told me—and I think it's not true, but I like it—that he was in Rio de Janeiro once with a friend of his when one night they kidnapped his friend, and after two days of being disappeared, they put in the street the guy they kidnapped without a kidney. They had operated on him illegally and stolen his kidney and well, he was there without a kidney. So I said, "Well, I like this story—you know, stealing kidneys—I like it very much. Let's put it in the novel. Why should we take out this beautiful story about stealing kidneys?"

I had all those things, but I think I needed extra ingredients for the novel. So I remembered that once in Mexico I arrived and they tried to sell me boots, but only for the left foot. This is a Mexican story, don't worry. So I said, "You have to put this story in." So we need two guys, one that doesn't have a right leg so he can buy the left foot, and we need somebody else without the other leg, and I was involved in that kind of interesting metaphysical reflection about which leg, and how can you buy boots, et cetera. This has to go into the novel.

If you think this is complexity—no, this is Mexican realism. This is a game; this is Walt Disney for Mexicans. Mexican reality is more horrible—they take our kidneys every day, in a metaphorical sense of course, and they eat them, and they spit them in our face. I went into crime fiction because that's the only way to do realism with this kind of material.

When I was very, very young lots of years ago, I thought that mystery was the back entrance into the real thing. The real thing was explaining a country and explaining myself—I didn't know what I wanted to explain about myself, but I saw that the best way of explaining things is writing them. Writing is the only way to explain reality, to reorganize reality. It was not very clear what I wanted to explain about myself, but it was very clear what I wanted to explain about my country. I wanted to explain that crime is the basement of the building known as Mexico. And crime in every sense—crime in the sense of abuse of power, crime in the sense of corruption, crime in the sense of innocent people inside jails, crime in the sense of guilty people in the top of the social structure of the country—this is in all of the stories. So I said, "Mystery, crime fiction, is the way to do it." You go through the back door, and then you get the story, and then you can tell everything, and then at the same time you can explain yourself and you can understand something because you don't understand anything, which is also a Mexican tradition.

And in those days, I believed in the theory of the iceberg—you know, 90 percent under water, 10 percent outside—and I said, "Well, mystery is the way to talk about the 90 percent." What's happening? Why are things reconnected in this or this way? But I was wrong. I was extremely wrong—mystery is not the back door; mystery is the front door. Through mystery, you go *into*. That's the way social literature comes into the twentieth century and now into the twenty-first.

Sometimes your writing is smarter than you. There are things that you cannot recognize in a rational way, but they are there. When I was young, my writing was smarter than me—much smarter than me. Now, I'm smarter than my writing, which is a nightmare. Mystery is a closed genre. I think after many years of writing mysteries, there's a jail in mystery, a structural jail. There's a structure of mystery—crime, investigation, resolution—that is very narrow. A writer will start repeating himself, doing the same book over and over with the blessing of his publishers, who love the same book if you write it three or four times. It can kill you.

So I start thinking that I need, as a writer, to keep breaking the structure of mystery and move to something that can be called, say, like "The Complete and Absolute Adventure Novel." That sounds good, no? Yeah, you put names to things and then try to write them—that's a good exercise. I'm crossing the structures of mystery, which I like very much, I'm crossing the structures of noir, and I'm crossing the structures of the social and political novel. But notice that I'm also crossing the structures of the French *feuilleton*, the serial novel of the nineteenth century by Victor Hugo and company, and I'm also trying to put in non-realism, which is the Mexican version of Kafka, which is Mexican realism, by the way. This is not a closed space; mystery is not a closed space. Good mystery stories are the front door.

NATSUO KIRINO

LITERATURE AND POWER
Writing About Politics

JOHN RALSTON SAUL: The question we'll consider today has three parts. Does the history of the last century offer much support for the view that the literary imagination has any special purchase on political wisdom? Can literature mitigate the pressures of ideology and nationalism, or is it destined to be their servant? Do writers have any special responsibilities beyond those of other citizens? Since it's my job to set the tone, my answer would be that there are no answers to these questions. That's particularly apparent to those of us who come from the twenty-odd supposed Western democracies, because we have by far, I think, the largest literary class in the history of the West. It has more freedom, even though we are unhappy, to express itself. And yet it seems that we have no effect, almost no influence, on the broad reality out there. Why is this the case?

Actually, it seems to me that there are three possibilities for writers. You can throw yourself in at a key moment and give language to people when they need it. Or you can be stubborn: Even though you know language won't change anything, you just want to be counted on for having assumed the obligation and occupied the public space. In a sense, what we're doing is providing signposts on the "darkling plain," if I'm allowed to quote a very romantic poem. And the third possibility is to attack the language in place, whether it's through fiction, or poetry, or essays: to say that the language in place is in effect an ideology, and we have to find some new form of language that can break down the language in place and make it possible for people to feel that they can change things.

We have with us today Tomás Eloy Martínez, who felt the obligation to go into exile, to stay in exile from Argentina, and to create a literature that would allow people in Argentina—and then around the world—to understand better what had gone wrong. We have Oksana Zabuzhko, who has just lived through a remarkable opportunity in Ukraine to be part of the Orange Revolution, in which language and stubbornness combined played a major role. Shashi Tharoor is a writer, biographer, and Under-Secretary-General of the United

Nations, and therefore lives on that undefinable line, or tension, that joins literature to power. Francine Prose, who of course is American and writes from within the American experience about much more than the American experience, writes to change the understanding of this civilization, to understand not just what's happening but what it actually means. And Bernard-Henri Lévy set about breaking up the patterns of thought and language in France. He was pretty successful—which is why people were enraged. And then he felt the obligation to go outside his own society and speak out about Bosnia, Sarajevo, Iraq, Pakistan.

OKSANA ZABUZHKO: When I first read the title of our panel, what immediately came to mind was an episode from the last day of the Ukrainian Orange Revolution. Those of you who watched TV reports during those days might try to picture this scene: late night, in the city's downtown, on the seventeenth day of the uprising, some two million people around, exhausted yet intoxicated with a sense of victory, with the results of the fraudulent election. And on the stage in the middle of the square, Yulia Tymoshenko, now the country's prime minister, addressing the crowd with tears in her eyes: "The days of the revolution will forever stay in our history, we will cherish them in our hearts," and this striking phrase: "We'll do a book about it!" A strange statement for a politician, and sort of naïve: What kind of a book? Who was going to write it? The days of the uprising are shortly going to produce tens if not hundreds of books of different genres, so why single out a particular one?

The message was clear. Ms. Tymoshenko was promising to turn the seventeen-day personal experience of love and faith into a story, a narrative to be memorized and told possibly for generations. A good politician never fails to tell people exactly what they want to hear. True. What bigger prize can you offer those who have been challenged by the severest of threats and have overcome them than to make a story out of his or her experience? People want their lives to make a story. Every human being has this need, if only to make sure that his or her life makes sense. Long before the appearance of writing, a story told then disseminated has been taken as indisputable proof that the events in the narrative were worth living through. "I'll make out of your life a narrative which gives you meaning." This sentence has an allure which, for the nonreligious mind, verges on the promise of salvation.

This thought occurred to me some nine years ago when I published my first novel—a confessional story about a broken relationship, about a woman intellectual with an identity crisis—which turned into the biggest literary scandal of the '90s in Ukraine. My greatest shock came not from critics proclaiming me a witch who deserved to be burned were it not for our civilized times, but from crowds of enthusiastic female readers, ranging in age from their early twenties to their early sixties. They responded with the same exclamations: "This is my story. I feel as though I wrote it."

Their response was something I would never have predicted, if only because the narrator's story was anything but typical. What made it so intimately recognizable for so many were the feelings. That's where the true power of literature lies. That's what makes literature irreplaceable by any other human activity, even in our visual age. Once you buy feelings depicted in a book as yours, you are trapped. You trust the author, as he or she has provided you with invaluable testimony that you are not alone in this world. You let the author into your inner life. You accept his or her way of seeing things as yours, and without noticing, you get a ready-made mold for your feelings—words, ideas, dramatic collisions, language, which you appropriated on some subliminal level to shape your own life so that it too would be worth telling.

This is where the power of literature collides with that of politicians: Ms. Tymoshenko assumed that one book documenting the events would do as a narrative for hundreds of thousands of individuals. Authors are interested, or at least are supposed to be interested, in individuals. No political power in its extreme absolutistic version ever extends further than making people believe they feel what they really don't. The target is attainable, as we all know only too well, both from the twentieth-century history and from the present. By spending billions on the media, you can instill fear and anxiety. You can make people believe their lives are not full until they buy a Ferrari, or will be all messed up until they vote for Mr. So-and-So, to skip more gruesome examples. What you can never do, though, is endow a person with a sense that he or she authors his or her life as the protagonist of a story worth being shared with other people.

In a Persian fairy tale, a king addresses a foreigner with a remarkable demand: "I give you a year to tell me a story, but you should only tell what happened to you, and if you tell me what you heard from someone else, I'll cut your head off." I find this a fascinating requirement—a dream of a privilege never granted to a living human being. None of us has a year to turn our whole life into a narrated story, and no devoted listener, not even our dearest ones, would agree to spend that much time to help us make sense of our lives. This fairy tale presents the most perfect image of the benevolent, ideal power, as perceived from the standpoint of an individual. Power as it should be: a ruler who not just allows but orders you on pain of capital punishment to be your own author.

In real life kings act exactly the opposite. It's in literature alone that we can still find the remote reverberation of ideal power cherishing and celebrating an individual self. Literature tells us what happened to someone else so that we are able to understand what's happening to us. The trouble starts when writers try to play earthly kings and talk to the masses. The tempting advantage of such a politically powerful position is that it always implies immediate gratification, while the power of literature has a long-term effect and may not become visible until after the writer's death. Writers and politicians live in different time modes—an extra reason not to confuse the two parallel circuits, which by definition should stay apart. If Ms. Tymoshenko asks me to write the book that she has so precariously promised to the crowd, my obligation would be to say "No, thank you."

SHASHI THAROOR: Oksana reminds me that the relationship of literature to power was brought to light most famously in the election of that longtime dissident Václav Havel to the presidency of Czechoslovakia. Words, he said at the time, can prove mightier than ten military divisions. The word "solidarity," Havel said, was capable of shaking an entire power bloc. Words have the power to change history. That was an interesting thought, and he certainly was an extraordinary example of it, but it didn't work like that half a world away in Peru where Mario Vargas Llosa, the eminent novelist, believed that as an author, he had a "unique understanding of the people, their needs, their concerns, their spirit." So he ran for president, and lost. Though other writers have assumed positions of power in their countries, and many have demonstrated the power of words to shake governments, serious novelists and poets have generally been unsuccessful in determining their readers' political destinies. After all, the only president who can lay claim to a best-selling novel is Saddam Hussein.

As an Indian novelist, I find that literature's relationship to power is particularly complex in countries like mine. Most developing countries are also formerly colonized countries, and one of the realities of colonialism is that it appropriated the cultural definition of its subject peoples. Writing about India in English, I could not but be aware of those who have done the same before me, others with a greater claim to the language but a lesser claim to the land. To think of India in the English-speaking world even today—and despite the exception of Salman Rushdie and others who followed him—is to still think in images conditioned by Rudyard Kipling and E. M. Forster. But their stories are not my stories. Their heroes are not mine. And my fiction, rather consciously— perhaps self-consciously—seeks to reclaim an aspect of my country's heritage for itself, to tell in an Indian voice a story of India. And let me stress: a story of India, for there are always other stories and other Indians to tell them.

How important is such a literary reassertion in the face of the enormous challenges confronting a developing country? What does it have to do with power? Can literature matter in a land of poverty and suffering? I believe it does. We're all familiar with the notion that man does not live by bread alone.

In India and elsewhere, I'd argue that literature and the telling of stories are indispensable to our ability to cope with that mighty construct we call the human condition. After all, why does man need bread? To survive, but why survive if it's only to eat more bread? To live is more than just a sustained life; it is to enrich and be enriched by life. Our poorest men and women in the developing world feel the throb of literature in their pulse. They tell stories to their children under the starlit skies, stories of their land and its heroes, stories of the earth and its mysteries, stories that have gone into making them into what they are. One responsibility of literature in a developing country must be to contribute toward, to help articulate, and to give expression to the cultural identity of the postcolonial society. Both colonialism then, and arguably globalization today, have fractured and distorted cultural self-perceptions. Development will not occur without a reassertion of identity: This is who we are; this is what we are proud of; this is what we want to be.

But those who have taken political roles in many developing societies also seek to seize this process by controlling the form, the shape, and the content of that identity. They seek to use their power to define the identity of their society or their culture in terms acceptable to the state. Now the task of the writer is to find new ways and provide old ones of expressing his culture, just as his society strives in the process of development to find new ways of being and becoming. This involves, in India's case, resisting the notion that Indian identity can be narrowly defined in any one set of terms. My own novels speak of an India of multiple realities, and of multiple interpretations of reality. I once said that if we had to do an Indian version of the American slogan *E pluribus unum*, it would have to be *E pluribus pluribum*. Throughout my fiction runs an acknowledgment of the multiplicity of truth and a consciousness of the many truths that have helped give shape and substance to the idea of India. So in speaking of a cultural reassertion of identity, I do not want to defend a closed construct. I believe Indians would not become any less Indian if, in Mahatma Gandhi's metaphor, we opened the doors and windows of our country and let foreign winds blow through our house.

My compatriots in India and I have been fortunate in having been free to express ourselves, but we cannot forget that the developing world is full of writers who have to function in societies that do not grant them this freedom. Writers in some developing countries have to cope with the perception that development and creative freedom are incompatible—that literature, for instance, must serve only the ends of a society as defined by the government, or operate only within the boundaries of the permissible as defined by the social or religious authorities. For such writers, the function of literature becomes much more than the creative rendering of social observations. In societies where truth is what the government or religious establishment says is true, literature must depict alternative truths that the culture needs to accommodate in order to survive. The paradox of the power of literature is that only when it is persecuted does it show its true colors. So it's probably no accident that some of the world's most remarkable literature in recent years has been introduced by writers who are either in exile from oppressive political systems—Gabriel García Márquez, Milan Kundera, Breyten Breytenbach—or struggling to hold up a mirror to the oppressive societies within which they live—Nadine Gordimer in South Africa, Neruda in Chile, Havel himself. Literature has always had the potential to raise the awkward question, to awaken the dormant consciousness, and therefore to subvert the established order, which may explain, despite the quote from Havel with which I began, why good writers rarely have the opportunity to make effective presidents. They are better at revealing than at ruling.

TOMÁS ELOY MARTÍNEZ: Michel Foucault says that power is a relationship of forces, or, more precisely, that all relationships of forces are relationships of power. He makes it quite clear that "force" here is plural. Foucault says that the set of factions permits the construction of a list in which there is neither oppression nor possession, but rather modifications in values. Everything acts upon everything, everything shifts. Literature is particularly unstable. It is that which is unstable, uncertain, which we don't know how to label. Literary criticism can classify certain texts, but what the work of the imagination is for one reader today will not be the same in two hours or tomorrow. Neither is a text the same for one who reads it in Tokyo, Buenos Aires, or New York at this very moment. It is possible to classify a literary work, stratify it, reduce it to a mere story. But any such operation will always be provisional because the work is a relationship in itself. It is an occurrence and constant mutation. It is transfigured every time it is seen, and it affects us in a different way every time we look at it. William Faulkner said that he used to read Cervantes's *Don Quixote de la Mancha* once every two years because he always encountered a different book.

In the last quarter century, much has changed: the failure of the Sandinistas in Nicaragua, the fall of the Berlin Wall, the atomization of the Soviet Union, the destruction of the Twin Towers, and such lamentable consequences as the invasion of privacy under the pretext of terrorism and the abominable torture at Abu Ghraib and Guantánamo. From the sexual liberation of the '60s, we have entered into an era of repression, control of action with actions upon actions. These are times in which reality is read as it is not. Saddam Hussein appears in the place where Osama bin Laden should be. And the empty arsenals of Iraq appear where it was said there were arms of mass destruction. Reality is slippery, mercurial. It is no longer possible to speak of fighting political power because power also moves from the army to corporations to drug dealers to money-lenders to weapons traffickers to politicians who build fortunes at an impressive speed in order to eventually return them to the army, to weapons traffickers, and so forth.

Today, perhaps, we must go in the direction of reconstruction, and by this I mean the attempt to recover the imaginary and the cultural traditions of a community. Once appropriated by the novel, it is given a different context, a new life. One of the secret forces of culture is its capacity to strengthen itself with adversity, to elude censorship, to tell its truths and continue incorruptible and disobedient when all those around remain silent or submit. The diverse strategies have attempted to silence culture's uncomfortable voice. Makers of culture have been repressed by imprisonment, the stocks, by burnings at the stake, with false confessions like those of Galileo before the inquisition and those of Sergei Eisenstein or Isaac Babel before Stalin.

One of the latest strategies of political power has been to simulate indifference. Each time culture raised its voice, power did not hear it. When power declares itself illiterate, when power does not read, writing does not harm it. Some neo-liberal democracies have assimilated that lesson. The philosopher Baruch Spinoza was asked, "How much can a body do?" Now we ask, "How much can a text do?" Novels do not change the world overnight, but they can recover the needs of the community, not to invalidate them or to idealize them, but to recognize them as a tradition, as a force leaving its sediment on the collective imagination.

FRANCINE PROSE: I think the question of what the writer can and should do about politics and power and the power of the state has entirely to do with what kind of writer one is. The essayist or polemicist has one kind of responsibility, and when I write essays now, as an American I feel that my responsibility is to say I live in a house in which a crime has been committed, and further crimes are being planned. I don't for one moment imagine that I can stop these further crimes from happening by saying it, but I do so partly to preserve my own sanity, to preserve the sanity of others who are noticing what's going on, and also to try and keep what tiny shreds of credibility our culture and our country have in the rest of the world.

I write for papers in this country and abroad. Earlier in the Iraq war, I was living in Italy, and a newspaper in the United States in New York asked me to write an essay about what it was like to be an American in Europe during the war. And I said, among other things, that I felt that the Italians treated us the way you would treat someone you basically liked, but who you knew had a serial killer in the family. And I didn't mean just George Bush, I should point out. The newspaper said, "We can't run that line." And I said, "Yeah, I knew that was going to happen." And then later they said, "Actually, we can't run the essay." And I kind of knew that was going to happen too. I feel that I have a responsibility to let people here and abroad know and to get things right.

When I'm writing novels, I feel a different kind of responsibility. As we all know, polemic is the enemy of literature because the polemicist feels the need to distort language and character for a particular agenda instead of writing the most beautiful language or the character that's most true to human nature, regardless of whether this truth goes against that particular agenda. Consequently, people say there's no such thing as great political art. But of course that's not true. Recently I saw the new production, the new translation, of *The Threepenny Opera* on Broadway, and I was shocked and terrified. What made the play so exhilarating and so terrifying was how modern it seemed, how topical it seemed; it could have been written yesterday. As most of you know, Hitler shut down production on *The Threepenny Opera*, and everyone connected with the new one has been joking that if it gets shut down, we might choose to leave the country the way Brecht and his associates did.

The novelist, the realistic novelist, wants to write about what we call human nature and society, and I think it's impossible to write realistic fiction without talking about those two things. I also think that literature of the past says as much about politics as the most polemic fiction. I think that if you read enough Balzac you can pretty much figure out how Dick Cheney's mind works. I think if you read *Moby-Dick* and think for a moment of Captain Ahab as our current administration, you can kind of tell where the ship of state is headed. And if you read something like Thomas Pynchon's *Gravity's Rainbow*, you begin to realize that your most paranoid fantasy will turn out to be the truth.

Lately, when I read literary journals or magazines, or even live in this culture, I feel as if we're involved in a plane crash—a big plane crash—and all the other passengers are aeronautics engineers. They're saying, "You know, I don't really like that little whistle I'm hearing," or "The engine sounds funny to me." But still, we don't have any choice. We can't actually get off the plane; we can only stay on the plane. The hope is that what we write during this particular journey, if that's what it happens to be, will survive the crash, will outlive us, and will be useful to future generations and to people in other countries.

I've been reading more history than I have fiction, and I've been reading in particular books about Hitler, books about Stalin, and books about the dirty war in Argentina. I've been reading them the way a hypochondriac reads health newsletters, looking for the warning signs of what could go wrong. One of the books about Argentina describes the way in which the generals perverted the language, and that it's extremely important to listen to the language we're hearing and to listen to the way our government is using the language, and to pay attention. At the same time, what I want my own children to read, what I want all young people to read, is great literature—and also, for example, books about Vietnam, because those are books about ways in which writers in particular and a population in general did alter government policy and did make a difference.

BERNARD-HENRI LÉVY: I know that French writers are supposed to speak too long, so I will try to be short. I don't think that the power of literature has to do, first of all, in any sense with identity, and with national identity. We know, from the origins of literature, that literature, when it is *good* literature, has nothing to do with identity. The great writer Joyce said that he wrote in Unglish, not in English. Dante said that he did not write in Italian, did not write in French; he invented it. I don't think that the responsibility of literature has anything to do with national belonging. Milan Kundera makes a distinction for every writer between the little context and the grand context: the little context of the national environment, which does not say anything, which is the worst advisor of the writer, and the grand context, which has nothing to do with national identity.

I don't think that literature and its power have anything to do with humanism or even with good feelings. I know that we are in a country where there is sometimes a tendency to drive the writer into political correctness, to practice a sort of ethical cleansing, to oblige the writers to be good guys. The best American writers—Norman Mailer, Truman Capote, Flannery O'Connor—are not good guys.

I don't think that literature has anything to do with positive thinking. As everybody knows, Céline, one of the greatest writers of the last century, was an infamous Nazi collaborationist. How did the first Céline become the second one? He became the second one at the very moment when he became a positive thinker. The first Céline that there is no solution, that the human being was a failed species, condemned to radical evil, that there was no exit, and that role of the writer was to explore this no-exit road. Then came another Céline who remembered that in a former life he was a doctor, and that the job of the doctor is to cure the illnesses of his brothers in life. He said, "Let's be positive. Humanity is ill. I'm going to identify the illness. I'm going to find the good medicine and I'm going to impose the good medicine on the ill patient." And the way to do that was to exterminate. The bad virus was the Jews.

This does not mean of course that literature has no responsibility and no power. There is an important distinction between the power of literature and the power of writers, which are two very different things.

MARTÍNEZ: I have a comment and a question. We, most of us, talk about power as a political problem, power as a political force. But power is a relationship. We can find power in love, power between father and son, power between boss and employees. We can see sexual abuses as a derivation of the problem. Literature may have nothing to do with power, as Bernard-Henri said, but power has a lot to do with literature. Power silences it, and censors it. At the same time, Borges supposed that censorship is good for literature, because literature is like water that finds a way to escape the power and, finding a way, comes to the real literature—not the photography of reality, but a different kind of reality.

And the question is for Francine: How does power use the language? A teacher of Simón Bolívar discovered that the use of some words in the wrong way perverts the words: Using "democracy" is different if Nelson Mandela uses it than if a person in the Bush Administration uses that same word. "Freedom" was different when Reagan used it than when someone else uses it. Power moves the meanings of the words.

PROSE: One of the ways that happens, as you said, is distortion and euphemism. I've been reading Nadezhda Mandelstam's great memoir of the Stalin years, and one of the things she says that seems so modern and up to the moment is that people stopped using the word "conscience" and only used the word "patriotism." Now we're hearing "patriotic" and this hideous misuse of "freedom." But the word "conscience" is almost never used in political discourse; it just doesn't seem to be relevant.

CONTRIBUTORS

Chimamanda Ngozi Adichie was born in Nigeria in 1977. Her short stories have appeared in journals including *Granta*, *Zoetrope*, and *The Iowa Review*. Her first novel, *Purple Hibiscus*, was published in 2003. She is a Hodder Fellow at Princeton University.

Elizabeth Alexander is the author of four books of poetry—*The Venus Hottentot*, *Body of Life*, *Antebellum Dream Book*, and *American Sublime*—and an essay collection, *The Black Interior*. She is a professor of African American Studies at Yale University.

Svetlana Alexievich's narratives are constructed from interviews with witnesses to shattering events in the Ukraine, and twenty-one documentary films have been based on her screenplays. Her latest work is *Voices from Chernobyl*, a book of essays.

Jakob Arjouni was born in Frankfurt in 1964. He has written novels, plays, screenplays, and the mystery series *Happy Birthday, Turk!*, *One Man, One Murder*, and *Kismet*. His other publications include his urban novel *Magic Hoffmann* and the short-story collections *Ein Freund* and *Idiots: Five Fairy Tales and Other Stories*. He divides his time between Germany and France.

Margaret Atwood is the author of more than forty books of fiction, poetry, and critical essays. Her books include *The Tent*, *Oryx and Crake*, *The Blind Assassin*, *Alias Grace*, *The Robber Bride*, *Cat's Eye*, and *The Handmaid's Tale*.

Antoine Audouard, who was born in Paris, was the publishing director of Laffont-Fixot for six years. His novel *Farewell, My Only One* has been translated into fourteen languages. His most recent work of fiction is *A Bridge of Birds*.

Paul Auster is the author of numerous novels, screenplays, essays, and books of poetry. His most recent novel is *Brooklyn Follies*; his other books include *Oracle Night*, *Timbuktu*, *The New York Trilogy*, *The Music of Chance*, and *The Book of Illusions*. He lives in Brooklyn, New York.

Fadhil al-Azzawi was born in 1940 in Kirkuk, Iraq, and spent three years in jail under the Ba'athist regime. He founded the magazine *Shi'r* (*Poetry*), and has edited many newspapers and magazines. He has published ten volumes of poetry in Arabic and one in German, novels, short-story collections, criticism, and translations from English and German. His most recent work is *Miracle Maker: Selected Poems*. He lives in Berlin.

François Bizot is the author of many works, including the novel *Les déclassés* and the art book *Underground, l'histoire*. His memoir, *The Gate*, chronicles his long experience as an ethnologist in Cambodia. He is the co-founder of Radio Nova, *Nova* magazine, and TSF, a jazz radio station.

Breyten Breytenbach is the Executive Director of the Gorée Institute, a Pan-African Center for Democracy, Development and Culture in Africa, and a member of the faculty of New York University's Creative Writing Program. His most recent publications are *Dog Heart*, a travel memoir, and *Lady One*, a volume of poems.

Yvette Christiansë was born in South Africa under apartheid and emigrated with her parents via Swaziland to Australia at the age of eighteen. She is the author of *Castaway*. In addition to writing poetry, Christiansë teaches English and postcolonial studies at Fordham University.

Tsitsi Dangarembga was born in Zimbabwe, where she lives now. She graduated from the German Film and Television Academy in Berlin and owns a film production company. Her 1996 film, *Everyone's Child*, was the first feature film directed by a black Zimbabwean woman. *Nervous Conditions* was her first novel, and she is currently at work on a second book.

Achmat Dangor was born in Johannesburg in 1948. He was one of the co-founders of the Congress of South African Writers and has published stories, poetry, and novels, including *Bitter Fruit* and *Kafka's Curse*. He also was the director of the Nelson Mandela Children's Fund until 2001. He lives in Johannesburg and New York.

Assia Djebar was born near Algiers in 1936. She published her first novel, *La soif*, at age twenty. Several of her novels are available in English, including *Women of Algiers in Their Apartments*, *Fantasia: An Algerian Cavalcade*, and *A Sister to Scheherazade*. Her most recent book is *The Tongue's Blood Does Not Run Dry*, a collection of stories. She lives in New York and Paris.

Carolin Emcke has been a staff writer at the German newsmagazine *Der Spiegel* since 1998, covering human rights violations and war crimes in Lebanon, Colombia, Nicaragua, Kashmir, Pakistan, Afghanistan, and Iraq. Her publications include *Kollektive identitäten, sozialphilosophische grundlagen* and *Von den kriegen: briefe an freunde*.

Nuruddin Farah was born in Somalia in 1945 and has lived in exile for more than twenty-five years. His work includes two trilogies, the second of which comprises *Maps*, *Gifts*, and *Secrets*. His other novels include *From a Crooked Rib* and *Links*.

Jonathan Franzen is the author of the novels *The Twenty-Seventh City*, *Strong Motion*, and *The Corrections*, and a collection of essays, *How to Be Alone*. He lives in New York.

Cornelia Funke was born in Westphalia. After studying education theory, she worked with children while completing a course in book illustration at the Hamburg State College of Design. She has written more than forty works for children, including the novels *Dragonrider*, *The Thief Lord*, and, most recently *The Wildest Brother*.

Philip Gourevitch, editor of *The Paris Review* and staff writer at *The New Yorker*, is the author of *We Wish to Inform You That Tomorrow We Will Be Killed With Our Families: Stories From Rwanda* and *A Cold Case*.

Ha Jin was born in China in 1956. He has published several volumes of poetry—including *Between Silences: A Voice From China* and *Facing Shadows*—and short fiction in addition to his two novels, *Waiting* and *War Trash*. He is a professor of English at Boston University.

Ryszard Kapuściński spent four decades reporting on Asia, Latin America, and Africa, in the process befriending Che Guevara, Salvador Allende, and Patrice Lumumba. He has witnessed twenty-seven coups and revolutions and has been sentenced to death four times. His books include *The Shadow of the Sun*, *The Emperor*, *Another Day of Life*, *Imperium*, *The Shah of Shahs*, and *The Soccer War*.

Natsuo Kirino was born in Japan in 1951. *Out*, a novel, was the first of Kirino's books to be published in English. She is also the author of *Soft Cheeks* and *Disparitions*, and several of her novels have been made into feature films.

Wayne Koestenbaum's publications include works of nonfiction such as *Andy Warhol* and *Cleavage: Essays on Sex, Stars and Aesthetics*, the novel *Moira Orfei in Aigues-Mortes*, and five books of poetry: *Best-Selling Jewish Porn Films*, *Model Homes*, *The Milk of Inquiry*, *Rhapsodies of a Repeat Offender*, and *Ode to Anna Moffo and Other Poems*. He is a professor of English at the CUNY Graduate Center and a visiting professor in the painting department of the Yale School of Art.

Hanif Kureishi is the author of numerous books, including *My Ear at His Heart*, *Gabriel's Gift*, *Intimacy*, *The Black Album*, and *The Buddha of Suburbia*. His screenplays include *My Beautiful Laundrette* and *Sammy and Rosie Get Laid*. He lives in London.

Katja Lange-Müller, who studied biology and worked as a nursing aide in psychiatric hospitals, spent a year in Mongolia and left the GDR in the early 1980s. Her publications include *Kasper Mauser—die Feigheit vorm Freund* and *Die Letzten—Aufzeichnungen aus Udo Posbichs Druckerei*; her most recent work of prose is *Die Enten, die Frauen und die Wahrheit Erzählungen und Miniaturen*. She lives in Berlin.

Joseph Lemasolai Lekuton, who grew up in northern Kenya, came to the United States in his late teens. He is the author of *Facing the Lion: Growing Up Maasai on the African Savanna* and *Naiwoto: A Warrior in Two Worlds*. He has also provided more than a hundred nomadic children with education scholarships, established the Karare Boarding School, and constructed a water system for a dozen villages in northern Kenya. He divides his time between Kenya and Washington, D.C.

Bernard-Henri Lévy, a war reporter, philosopher, and writer, began his career writing for the French journal *Combat*. He has held several diplomatic positions with the French government, and written numerous books, including *Barbarism with a Human Face*, *Who Killed Daniel Pearl?*, and *War, Evil and the End of History*. His most recent book is *American Vertigo: Traveling America in the Footsteps of Tocqueville*.

Claudio Magris was born in Trieste in 1939. He is the author of numerous essays and critical studies; his works include *L'anneau de Clarisse*, *Itaca e oltre*, *Illazioni su una sciabola*, *Stadelmann*, *Danube*, *Microcosms*, and the play *La Mostra*.

Norman Manea is a writer-in-residence and the Francis Flournoy Professor of European Culture at Bard College. His works include *The Black Envelope* and, most recently, *A Hooligan's Return*, a memoir.

Tomás Eloy Martínez was born in Argentina in 1934. During the military dictatorship, he lived in exile in Venezuela, where he wrote his first three books. As a fellow at the Woodrow Wilson International Center for Scholars, Martínez wrote *The Perón Novel*. He is a professor and director of the Latin American Program at Rutgers.

Khaled Mattawa was born in Libya and came to the United States in his teens. He is the author of *Zodiac of Echoes* and *Ismailia Eclipse*, and the translator of three volumes of contemporary Arabic poetry. His poems have appeared in *Best American Poetry*, *Pushcart Prize Anthology*, and numerous magazines.

Zakes Mda is a writer, painter, composer, and film producer. His novels include *The Whale Caller*, *The Heart of Redness*, *The Madonna of Excelsior*, and *Ways of Dying*. He divides his time between South Africa and the United Sates, working as a professor of creative writing at Ohio University, a beekeeper in the Eastern Cape, a dramaturge at the Market Theatre, Johannesburg, and a director of the Southern African Multimedia AIDS Trust in Sophiatown, Johannesburg.

Minae Mizumura attended high school and college in the United States before returning to Japan to begin writing in Japanese. Among her works are *Light and Darkness Continued*, *Shishosetsu: From Left to Right*, and *A Real Novel*, which retells *Wuthering Heights* in postwar Japan. She has taught at Princeton University, the University of Michigan, and Stanford University.

Antonio Muñoz Molina is the author of numerous novels, including *Sepharad*, *Prince of Shadows*, and *Winter in Lisbon*. His most recent book is *Ventanas de Manhattan*, an evocation of New York City.

Rick Moody is the author of *The Diviners*, *Garden State*, *The Ice Storm*, *Purple America*, *The Ring of Brightest Angels Around Heaven*, and *Demonology*. He is the co-editor (with Darcey Steinke) of an anthology of essays, *Joyful Noise: The New Testament Revisited*. His short work has appeared in *The New York Times*, *The New Yorker*, *Harper's*, *Esquire*, *The Atlantic*, and *The Village Voice*.

Michael Ondaatje was born in Sri Lanka. His most recent work is *The Story*, a book of poetry featuring David Bolduc's watercolor illustrations. He is the author of many works of fiction, poetry, and memoir, including *The English Patient*, *Running in the Family*, and *There's a Trick With a Knife I'm Learning to Do*. He lives in Toronto.

Robert Polito is the author of *Savage Art: A Biography of Jim Thompson*, *Doubles*, and *A Reader's Guide to James Merrill's* The Changing Light at Sandover. He edited two Library of America volumes, *Crime Novels: American Noir of the 1930s and 1940s* and *Crime Novels: American Noir of the 1950s*. He directs the Graduate Writing Program at New School University in New York.

Elena Poniatowska has written more than fifty books, including *Dear Diego*, *Massacre in Mexico*, *The Skin of the Sky*, *Tinisima*, *Nothing, Nobody: The Voices of the Earthquake*, and *Lilus Kikus and Other Stories*.

Francine Prose is the author of numerous books of fiction, including *A Changed Man* and *Blue Angel*. Her recent books include *The Last Flight of Jose Luis Balboa*, *War Souvenir*, and *Caravaggio*. She lives in New York City.

Laura Restrepo's novels have been published in over a dozen languages, and include *Leopard in the Sun*, *The Angel of Galilea*, *The Dark Bride*, *A Tale of the Dispossessed* and *Delirio*. Her latest work is *Dulce Compania*, a novella. She lives in Bogotá.

Patrick Roth was born in Germany in 1953. His publications include *Johnny Shines oder Die Wiedererweckung der Toten*, *Riverside*, *Corpus Christi*, *Riding with Mary*, and the trilogy *Resurrection*.

Salman Rushdie, who is concluding his term as president of PEN American Center, has also served as honorary Vice President and Member Trustee-at-Large. His many books include *Midnight's Children*, *Haroun and the Sea of Stories*, *The Satanic Verses*, *The Ground Beneath Her Feet*, *Fury*, and *Step Across This Line: Collected Nonfiction 1992–2002*.

Shan Sa left China for France in 1990, studied in Paris, and worked for two years with the painter Balthus. Her books include *Empress*, *Porte de la paix celeste*, *Les quatres vies du saule*, and *La Joueuse de Go* (published in English as *The Girl Who Played Go*). Her novel *Imperatrice* was published as *The Red Empress*. She lives in Paris.

Luc Sante teaches writing and the history of photography at Bard College. His books include *Low Life*, *Evidence*, and *The Factory of Facts*.

John Ralston Saul is the former president and is now honorary patron of Canadian PEN. His latest work is *The Company of Others*. His books include *Voltaire's Bastards*, *The Collapse of Globalism*, *The Doubter's Companion*, *The Unconscious Civilization* and *On Equilibrium*. He lives in Toronto.

Elif Shafak grew up in Spain before returning to Turkey, where she lives at present. She has published five novels, including *The Saint of Incipient Insanities*. Shafak has taught at the Istanbul Bilgi University and at the University of Michigan at Ann Arbor, and writes for a range of journals in Turkey.

Meir Shalev grew up in Nahalal, an agricultural cooperative, and then moved to Jerusalem, where he lives today. He has produced and hosted several radio and television programs and is a regular columnist in the Israeli press. Shalev writes essays and fiction for children and adults, including the novels *Four Meals* and *The Blue Mountain*.

Hanan al-Shaykh was born in Lebanon and grew up in Beirut. Her publications include the novels *Suicide of a Dead Man*, *The Praying Mantis*, *The Story of Zahra*, and *Beirut Blues*; the short-story collection *I Sweep the Sun Off Rooftops*; and two plays, *Dark Afternoon Tea* and *Paper Husband*. She has lived in London since 1984.

Peter Stamm has worked as a freelance writer and journalist for *Neue Zürcher Zeitung*, *Tages-Anzeiger*, *Weltwoche*, and the satirical magazine *Nebelspalter*. Since 1997, he has edited the literary journal *Entwürfe für Literatur*. He published his first novel, *Agnes*, in

1999, and has continued to write fiction as well as several radio and stage plays. His most recent novel is *Unformed Landscape*.

Paco Ignacio Taibo was born in Spain, and has lived in Mexico City since 1958. He has written more than fifty books, including novels, short stories, and essays. He is particularly known for his detective novels, the most recent of which is *Muertos incómodos*.

Yoko Tawada was born in Tokyo in 1960. Her books include her debut, *Missing Heels*, and the short-story collection *The Bridegroom Was a Dog*. She writes in Japanese and German; her most recent book is *Where Europe Begins*, a collection of stories.

Shashi Tharoor is the United Nations Under-Secretary-General for Communications and Public Information and the author of eight books of fiction and nonfiction. His books include *Nehru: The Invention of India*, a biography of India's first Prime Minister, *The Great Indian Novel*, and the essay collection *Bookless in Baghdad: Reflections on Writing and Writers*.

Lyonel Trouillot, a poet, novelist, and essayist, writes in Haitian Kreyòl and French. Trouillot is a founding member of the Haitian Writers Association. His books include *Street of Lost Footsteps*.

Eliot Weinberger's publications include *What Happened Here: Bush Chronicles*, *Works on Paper*, *Outside Stories*, and a recent collection of political articles, *9/12*. He is the author of a study of Chinese poetry in translation, *Nineteen Ways of Looking at Wang Wei*, and the translator of *Unlock* by the exiled poet Bei Dao. He has also translated Octavio Paz and Jorge Luis Borges. He lives in New York City.

Oksana Zabuzhko's works include the short-story collection *Oh Sister, My Sister* and *Field Work in Ukrainian Sex*, as well as four collections of poetry, including one translated into English as *A Kingdom of Fallen Statues*, two volumes of literary criticism, and two collections of essays.

Beowulf Sheehan (photography) is a graduate of New York University and The Eddie Adams Photojournalism Workshop. The son of a linguist and a mariner, he is well traveled and multilingual. Sheehan's work has appeared in *The New York Times*, *The Village Voice*, and many international publications.

Yukinori Yamamura (cover) is a native of Kobe, Japan. His sculpture has been exhibited internationally, and he has been an artist-in-residence in Germany, Kenya, Norway, Iran, the United States, and elsewhere. In each host country, he studies history and customs to synthesize work that articulates a sense of the locale and its people.

ACKNOWLEDGMENTS

Excerpt from *Purple Hibiscus* by Chimamanda Ngozi Adichie, copyright © 2003 by Chimamanda Ngozi Adichie. Anchor Books, a division of Random House, Inc.

Excerpt from *Idiots* by Jakob Arjouni, translated by Anthea Bell, translation copyright © 2005 by Anthea Bell. Other Press, LLC.

"A Poor Woman Learns to Write" by Margaret Atwood, copyright © 2006 by Margaret Atwood. Reprinted with permission of the author.

Excerpt from *The Tent* by Margaret Atwood, copyright © 2006 by Margaret Atwood. Nan A. Talese / Doubleday.

"Almost No Memory" by Lydia Davis, from *Almost No Memory*, copyright © 1997 by Lydia Davis. Farrar, Straus and Giroux.

"Happiest Moment" by Lydia Davis, from *Samuel Johnson Is Indignant*, copyright © 2001 by Lydia Davis. Hardcover © 2001 McSweeney's Books. Paperback © 2002 Picador.

"You Are Gorgeous and I'm Coming" by Frank O'Hara, from *The Collected Poems of Frank O'Hara*, copyright © 1995 by the estate of Frank O'Hara. University of California Press.

Excerpt from *Out* by Natsuo Kirino, translated by Stephen Snyder; English translation copyright © 2003 by Kodansha International Ltd.

Excerpt from *Anil's Ghost* by Michael Ondaatje, copyright © 2000 by Michael Ondaatje. Alfred A. Knopf, a division of Random House, Inc.

"Poem XIX," by Adrienne Rich, from "Twenty-One Love Poems," from *The Dream of a Common Language*, copyright © 1978 by Adrienne Rich. W.W. Norton and Company.

Excerpt from *The Loves of Judith* by Meir Shalev, translated by Barbara Harshav, copyright © 1999 by Meir Shalev. Ecco Press.

Excerpt from *Unformed Landscape* by Peter Stamm, translated by Michael Hoffman, copyright © 2005 by Peter Stamm. Other Press.

Excerpt from *Leonardo's Bicycle* by Paco Ignacio Taibo, translated by Martin Michael Roberts, copyright © 1996 by Paco Ignacio Taibo. Warner Books.

NOTES

In "Pablo Neruda: *¡Presente!*", John Felstiner's translation of Federico García Lorca's description of Pablo Neruda should have read as follows:

> I say you are about to hear an authentic poet, one who has forged himself in a world that's not ours, that few people perceive. A poet closer to death than philosophy, to pain than intellect, to blood than ink. A poet filled with mysterious voices that luckily he himself doesn't know the meaning of. A true man who does know that the reed and the swallow are more permanent than the hard cheek on a statue. . . .
>
> He stands up to the world, full of honest terror, and lacks two things so many false poets have lived with—hate and irony. When he's about to condemn and raises his sword, suddenly he finds himself with a wounded dove between his fingers.

We thank Joonseong Park for his permission to reprint an excerpt from his translation of Song Yong's *Diary of a Vagabond* (© 2004), for which he won a PEN Translation Fund Award.

The editors would also like to thank proofreaders Rebecca Bengal and Emily Schlesinger for their quick and careful work on this issue, and, especially, outgoing managing editor Bridget Cross for her invaluable contributions to *PEN America*, past and present.

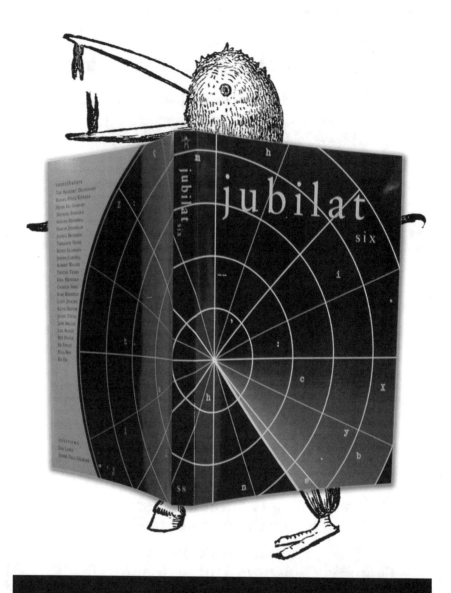

poetry art interviews prose

www.jubilat.org

Department of English, Bartlett hall
University of Massachusetts, Amherst MA 01003

great fiction

www.orchidlit.org

Yuri Andrukhovych Ukraine · Daniel Oliver Bachmann Germany · Tomas Mikael Bäck Finland · Rafael Ballesteros Spain · Ilhan Berk Turkey · Natalka Bilotserkivets Ukraine · Andrej Blatnik Slovenia · Pablo García Casado Spain · Cristina Cîrstea Romania · Flavia Cosma **New European Writing** l Pino Spain · Roger Derham Ireland · Lidija Dimkovska Macedonia · Martin Enckell Finland · Michel Faïs Greece · Zoran Feric Croatia · Florin Ion Firimita Romania · Stephan Furnadzhiev Bulgaria · Emilian Galaicu-Păun Moldova · Bettina Galvagni Austria · Sergey Gandlevsky Russia · Matthiàs Göritz Germany · Georgi Gospodinov Bulgaria · Dieter M. Gräf Germany · Gintaras Grajauskas Lithuania · Mehis Heinsaar Estonia · Herberto Helder Portugal · Kristien Hemmerechts Belgium · Stefan Hertmans Belgium · Mehmet Murat ildan Turkey · Marcin Jagodziński Poland · Sándor Kányádi Hungary · Kostas Karyotakis Greece · Laurynas Katkus Lithuania · Saulius T. Kondrotas Lithuania · Ryszard Krynicki Poland · Mara Malanova Russia · Juan José Millás Spain · Sophia Nikolaidou Greece · Jaromir Nohavica Czech · Niklas Rådström Sweden · Noberto Luis Romero Spain · Hélène Sanguinetti France · Monica Sarsini Italy · Sakis Serefas Greece · Sasha Skenderija Bosnia · Boris Slutsky Russia · Jean Tardieu France · Olga Tokarczuk Poland · Penelope Toomey Slovakia · Christa Wolf Germany · Pèter Zilahy Hungary

BSINTHE

5

SUBSCRIPTIONS

Individuals
1 year/2 issues $12
2 years/4 issues $20

Institutions/International
1 year/2 issues $25

Send to

Absinthe Arts 21
P.O. Box 11445
Detroit, MI 48211-1445
USA

www.absintheNEW.com

archipelago books

Elias Khoury
Gate of the Sun

Translated from the Arabic by Humphrey Davies

"Because the world is the way it is, because whole groups of people can be maligned, neglected, ignored, for too many years, we need the voice of Elias Khoury—detailed, exquisite, humane—more than ever. Read him. Without fail, read him."

—Naomi Shihab Nye

"A book of nostalgia and love ... The book tugs at the reader's heart page after page, poem after poem, line after line, you cannot remain apathetic for a moment..."

—*Haaretz*

Mahmoud Darwish
Why Did You Leave the Horse Alone?

Translated from the Arabic by Jeffrey Sacks

on sale now:

www.archipelagobooks.org

VISIT
The Paris Review online

SEARCH
the archive

READ
the interviews

LISTEN
to poems

BROWSE
the calendar

BUY
prints & back issues

SUBSCRIBE
now

PEN **WORLD VOICES**

The New York
Festival of International Literature

April 25–30, 2006

Faith and Reason: Five days of readings,
discussions, and celebrations with writers
from around the world.

Chris Ab   har Abidi Adonis Boris Akunin   Magdi Allam Sherman Alexi

Homero   A a Al Aswany Bernardo Atxaga Nadezhda Azhgikhina Robert

Calasso   et e Moor Hans Magnus Enzensberger Baltasar Garzon Nadin

Gordimer   lica Gorodischer Philip Gourevitch David Grossman Milton Hatou

Moses Is   Hanna Jansen Necla Kelek Etgar Keret Elias Khoury Venu

Khoury-G   László Krasznahorkai Jhumpa Lahiri   Jonathan Lethem Lyubom

Levchev   i Henning Mankell Melania Mazzucco Suketu Mehta Ritu Mena

Adam M   Naomi Shihab Nye Helen Oyeyemi Orhan Pamuk Ann

Politkovskaya ne Provoost Salman Rushdie Gustav Seibt Åsne Seiersta

Hwang So   g Colm Tóibín Dubravka Ugresic Eloy Urroz Ayu Utan

PEN American Center

For more information, visit www.pen.org